THE KANSAS CITY A'S
&
THE WRONG HALF
OF THE YANKEES

D1715033

THE KANSAS CITY A'S
&
THE WRONG HALF
OF THE YANKEES

Jeff Katz

MAPLE STREET PRESS
Hingham, Massachusetts

Maple Street Press LLC is in no way affiliated with Major League Baseball, or any minor league affiliates. The opinions expressed in this book are those of the author and not necessarily those of Maple Street Press.

Left front jacket photo of Roger Maris: National Baseball Hall of Fame Library/MLB Photos via Getty Images

Right front jacket photo of Roger Maris: Louis Requena/MLB Photos via Getty Images

Jacket design: Garrett Cullen

Interior design: Bryan Davidson / Jennie Sparrow

Jeff Katz. *The Kansas City A's & the Wrong Half of the Yankees*

ISBN 978-0-9777-436-5-0

Library of Congress Control Number: 2007923765

Maple Street Press LLC
11 Leavitt Street
Hingham, MA 02043
www.maplestreetpress.com

Printed in the United States of America
07 7 6 5 4 3 2 First Edition

To my family

Table of Contents

Acknowledgments

A major reason for relocating to Cooperstown in June of 2003 was to be near the National Baseball Hall of Fame and Museum. It had always been an annual highlight to visit the Hall and, now that I get to see its wonders daily, I am an even greater fan.

Thanks to Jeff Idelson, VP of Communications and Education, for his constant friendship and support. There's no better person. The A. Bartlett Giamatti Research Center in the Hall of Fame Library is a treasure trove of information and Claudette Burke and Freddie Berowski were of great assistance. They were always quick to get answers. Gabe Schecter and Bill Francis, better researchers than I, were consistently interested and excited about this project. I can't say enough about Tim Wiles, Director of Research, over-30 baseball teammate, fellow Codirector of the Cooperstown Concert Series and friend. Tim's advice and input were invaluable and I wouldn't be writing this without his help. Thanks also to Melissa Kean at Rice University.

Jeff Horigan of *The Boston Herald* wrote a wonderful Foreword during an extremely busy summer. He covered the Red Sox daily *and* moved. Still, he found time for my request. Thanks Jeff!

Constructive criticism and words of encouragement were thankfully frequent—Rick Angell, Rich Campbell, Alan Cantor, Mike Clabby, Elliot Katz, Marty Lackner, Jimmy Seidita and Bill Ulivieri deserve thanks for their time and advice.

My family has shared my enthusiasm for Cooperstown and humored my dreams of becoming an author. Nate, Rob and Joey are the best friends a father could have. Whatever I have set my sights on Karen has always been supportive. That kind of support is impossible to appreciate enough. She is a great editor, a greater mom, and an even better wife.

FOREWORD

For nearly 85 years, only one business enterprise in the United States has been exempt from federal antitrust regulations: Major League Baseball.

Unlike every other institution throughout the land, big league baseball was granted immunity by the Supreme Court from the Sherman and Clayton antitrust acts, which had been instituted to ensure that monopolies didn't develop in interstate trade and commerce.

Justice Oliver Wendell Holmes basically declared baseball to be a single entity that was free to operate as it wished, even though the vast majority of games and transactions involved franchises located in different states. Threats to remove the exemption pop up in Congress from time to time, particularly when a legislator's hometown team has been wronged by the system, but each time the efforts fade away because of the whining and warnings of sure collapse—always from baseball's rulers.

Given the authority to govern as they deem fit, Major League Baseball's commissioners have clung to their right to make any decision based on the "best interest of baseball" and wielded it like a scepter, prepared to invoke it—without being required to offer an explanation—whenever the "integrity" of the game is threatened.

Bowie Kuhn flexed his muscles and prevented Charlie Finley from selling off Vida Blue, Joe Rudi, and Rollie Fingers in 1976. Bart Giamatti used this right to orchestrate Pete Rose's banishment in 1989. Bud Selig invoked it to muzzle Marge Schott and remove her from power in Cincinnati in the 1990s, and several stood behind it to impose—or threaten to impose—lockouts that wouldn't stand a chance of being deemed legal by the courts in any other industry.

Of course, commissioners can be just as easily convinced to look the other way on crucial matters. The most egregious modern example is Selig sticking his head in the sand as baseball, with the help of anabolic steroids and banned performance enhancers, bulked up to comical proportions in the late 1990s and early 2000s. With the public reluctant to forgive baseball following the unpopular 1994–1995 work stoppage, Major League Baseball turned a blind eye when it became clear that the pursuit of the sacred home run records would draw back the fans, unable to envision the vicious backlash that would be incurred a few years later.

A scenario just as incredible took place in the 1950s, when commissioner Ford C. Frick permitted the New York Yankees to annex the Kansas City Athletics as a de facto farm team. American League opponents (such as the Tigers, Senators, and White Sox) launched protests that either went unheard or were squashed. By doing nothing, Major League Baseball was in cahoots.

It's difficult to fathom something similar taking place today. While covering the Boston Red Sox for the *Boston Herald* since 2000, I've witnessed first-hand the close scrutiny that the Sox now keep on their archrivals, and vice-versa. It was typified by embittered team president Larry Lucchino dubbing the Yankees the "Evil Empire" after his team lost out on the signing of Cuban ace Jose Contreras in December 2002 to New York's deep pockets. Lucchino had simply reached his breaking point after seeing the Yankees experience success after success in their bids to restrict players from heading to the Sox via free agency or trade. One can only imagine how he might have reacted had he been leading the Boston franchise in the 1950s!

As Jeff Katz details in the pages that follow, Yankees owners Del Webb and Dan Topping played an instrumental role in setting up their business partner, Arnold Johnson, as owner of the ballpark in Kansas City, which paved the way for him to acquire the team in an incredible tale of deceit. With the apparent aid of American League president Will Harridge, Johnson acquired the Philadelphia A's, despite equal and superior hometown bids. Everyone's worst fears took place.

Just as suspected, Johnson began funneling his top players to the Yankees, as the small-market A's became the subservient, Steinbeckian "Lennie" to the controlling, large-market "George" in the Bronx. The

Yankees, for all intents and purposes, controlled two of the eight teams in the league. Some would argue that things have hardly changed, although they are not carried out in such an obvious and blatant fashion.

Imagine how poorly the Yankees would have done had the likes of Clete Boyer, Bobby Shantz, Ralph Terry, Art Ditmar, Enos Slaughter, Ryne Duren, and, of course, Roger Maris not made the well-worn trek from Kansas City to New York, all in exchange for has-beens and non-prospects. It is unlikely that the Yankees dynasty would have been sustained through the 1964 World Series without the duplicity orchestrated between the two teams.

It's hilarious to think how the likes of Messrs. Lucchino, Henry, Werner, and Epstein would react if the Yankees set up such an arrangement these days with, say, the Kansas City Royals. You can bet that the Red Sox would take their fight all the way to Congress and the Supreme Court. While 29 other teams bemoan the bottomless pockets of the Yankees today, they should be thankful that they don't have to deal with the scenario that their ownership forefathers faced a half-century ago.

The Kansas City A's & the Wrong Half of the Yankees will show you that long before "Star Wars" and before Lucchino's generation was old enough to realize it, a propeller-driven "Evil Empire" was already controlling the baseball universe. Dig in and let Jeff Katz be your guide.

Jeff Horrigan
Boston, August 2006

PREFACE

Imagine the joy of being a kid in Kansas City, Missouri, late in 1954 when Major League Baseball was on its way to your town. Perhaps you had had some satisfaction in watching the Triple A K.C. Blues play at Blues Stadium. After all, they were the main farm team of the World Champion Yankees. Gosh, even Mickey Mantle had spent time with the Blues in 1951! That *was* pretty exciting, but you knew it would be so much better to have the big leaguers here all the time.

All through 1953 and 1954, the *Kansas City Star's* Ernie Mehl, the best sportswriter in town, would write about getting a team in Kansas City, and the thought of it being even slightly possible was making you feel like you did the day before your birthday—the anticipation making you feel like you would explode.

What a life-changing day November 8 was. Some businessman you'd never heard of—Arnold Johnson—bought the Philadelphia A's and was bringing them to Kaycee. Sure, the A's weren't very good—last place, in fact—but they were Major League. And they were Connie Mack's team, one of the most storied franchises in the history of the game.

It seemed like everyone in the city went to the ballpark to see the new A's. Almost 1,400,000 people attended and watched the A's get a little better, sixth place rather than eighth. It gave you hope that maybe, just maybe, your team could be a pennant winner some day if they could only improve each year.

1956 brought disappointment as the team sunk back into the cellar. This time it was for real. The next three years saw next-to-last-place finishes, and 1960 found the team back on the bottom.

Then there were all those trades with the Yankees, and it hardly ever seemed that your team got the best of it. Sure, the Blues were a farm team for the Bronx Bombers, but the A's were different. They were one of eight teams in the American League; they had to be independent with no ties to New York, right? Yet there was an uncomfortable closeness between the two and it made you wonder and become a little uneasy. Your pals shared the same feelings. Later on as adults you would think, "Even as kids we snickered about the A's being a farm club for the Yankees."[1]

How did it go so wrong? By 1960 you and the community had had it. Attendance was a little more than half what it had been in the thrilling inaugural year. The joy you had felt just a few years before was gone.

To understand how the A's became a farm team on a Major League level, it's important to know that the Yankees owners, Dan Topping and Del Webb, and the Kansas City A's owner, Arnold Johnson, had business dealings that began in January 1952 with their formation of a syndicate to purchase stock in Automatic Canteen, a firm selling food and cigarettes via vending machines. In addition, Johnson and Webb were partners in a construction project. In December of 1953 Arnold Johnson bought Yankee Stadium and the minor league Kansas City Blues Stadium, from his business cohorts Topping and Webb.

During the summer of 1953 Kansas City was desperate for a Major League ball club, and when the St. Louis Browns were transferred to Baltimore to become the Orioles, Kansas City saw that they needed a Major League–ready ballpark to boost their chances of garnering a franchise. City officials desperately tried to wring a price for Blues Stadium from Del Webb during the summer and fall, and Webb repaid their earnestness with lip service and duplicity. While Kansas City thought it was in the running as a prospective buyer, unbeknownst to them, Webb was negotiating with Johnson, who visited the Blues park with *Kansas City Star* sportswriter Ernie Mehl in tow. Mehl, instrumental in Kansas City's attempts to get a team, put the bug in Johnson's ear to go after a big league team. The city of Kansas City never had a chance to control their Major League destiny.

The following year, Arnold Johnson bid on the struggling Philadelphia A's and was immediately welcomed to the select group of Major League owners by American League president Will Harridge. Harridge jumped the gun, as several owners who smelled a Yankee plot objected to Johnson. When equal or better bids than Johnson's came forward, with the added benefit of keeping the team in Philadelphia, these potential buyers were put through rigorous questioning, whereas Johnson was greeted without inquiry, his Yankee connections seemingly enough to hold sway over Harridge and most of the American League. The Yankees had their way and Arnold Johnson, their business partner and landlord, was approved as the A's owner in November of 1954.

The worst fears of a Yankees and A's conflict of interest were realized as, from 1955 to 1959, the A's shipped to New York any player the Yankees felt they needed to help their cause. The A's would receive a slew of nonprospects, over-the-hill players, and, even worse, players who would find their Major League footing in A's uniforms, only to be quickly sent on a return trip to Yankee Stadium once their talents were evident. During this period, Yankees–A's trades soared, as Yankee call-ups from their own minor league teams declined. This was all to end upon the death of Arnold Johnson in March of 1960.

The disenchanted kids who gleefully welcomed the A's to Kansas City for the 1955 season had reason to be suspicious.

---

1. Rucker, Leland. "Inept A's Showed Kansas City a Good Time," *USA Today Baseball Weekly*, June 17,1992 (Vol. 2, Issue 12), p. 35.

I

STADIUM SALES

Part I Timeline

January 1945: Dan Topping and Del Webb (along with Larry MacPhail) purchase the New York Yankees for $2.8 million from Jacob Ruppert estate.

October 1947: After post–World Series tirade, Larry MacPhail is bought out by his partners, leaving Topping and Webb as sole shareholders in the Yankees.

March 17, 1953: Approval is given for Boston Braves to relocate to Milwaukee. This begins era of franchise relocation.

July 22, 1953: Del Webb touts Kansas City as a Major League city at American League owners meeting in Cincinnati.

Early August 1953: Mayor William E. Kemp of Kansas City, Missouri, is authorized by the city council to meet with Del Webb to negotiate a purchase price for Blues Stadium. A letter is sent to Webb requesting a price.

June 1953: A series of columns by *Kansas City Star* sportswriter Ernie Mehl pushes for a Major League team for Kansas City, citing the need for a ballpark and pointing to the Philadelphia A's as a possible candidate for relocation. Del Webb had told Mehl that the A's were in trouble.

September 1, 1953: Del Webb is expected to give a price for Blues Stadium. Nothing was delivered.

September 11, 1953: The Kansas City city council resolves to purchase Blues Stadium. A meeting is set with Del Webb for the following week but never transpires. Webb claims a World Series appearance by the Yankees made such a gathering impossible.

September 19, 1953: Representatives from the Kansas City city council meet with Webb in Chicago, the home base of Arnold Johnson. Webb pledges cooperation.

September 29, 1953: Approval is given to the St. Louis Browns to relocate to Baltimore. Kansas City is felt to be in the running to gain the Browns franchise, but the lack of stadium ownership is a major roadblock.

October 13, 1953: New ballpark construction proposed for Kansas City. Mehl protests, citing necessity of working with the Yankees.

Early November 1953: Negotiations begin between Arnold Johnson and Yankee owners Topping and Webb for Johnson purchase of Yankee and Blues Stadiums. Around this time, Johnson and Mehl visit Blues Stadium together, and Mehl suggests that Johnson buy a Major League team. Johnson likes the idea.

December 13, 1953: Mehl column divulges possible sale of Yankee Stadium.

December 14, 1953: A meeting is planned between Mayor Kemp, Ernie Mehl, and others with Yankees in New York. It is postponed until January 1954.

December 17, 1953: Arnold Johnson purchases Yankee and Blues Stadium from Dan Topping and Del Webb for $6.5 million. Johnson resells the land under Yankee Stadium to the Knights of Columbus for $2.5 million and incurs $3.5 million in mortgages (including $2.9 million from Topping and Webb), leaving his net cash outlay at $500,000.

Dramatis Personae

Arnold Johnson: Chicago financier, director of Automatic Canteen after syndicate purchased bulk of stock, Phoenix Towers construction partner of Del Webb, purchaser of Yankee and Blues Stadiums.

Del Webb: Co-owner of the New York Yankees since January 1945, construction magnate, Las Vegas developer, part of Automatic Canteen syndicate (with Arnold Johnson), Phoenix Towers construction partner of Arnold Johnson.

Dan Topping: Co-owner of the New York Yankees since 1945, multimillionaire at age 21, socialite, part of Automatic Canteen syndicate (with Arnold Johnson).

J. Arthur Friedlund: Attorney, leader of syndicate to purchase Automatic Canteen stock, secretary and general counsel to the New York Yankees.

Ernie Mehl: sportswriter for the *Kansas City Star*, chief rooter for Major League Baseball in Kansas City.

George Weiss: General manager of the New York Yankees.

Parke Carroll: General manager of Yankees minor league farm team, the Kansas City Blues. Later, business manager, vice president, and key participant in player deals for the Kansas City A's.

William E. Kemp: Mayor of Kansas City.

Chapter 1

THE DEAL

"We're better off."

—*Del Webb, Yankees co-owner*

hree distinguished-looking men, dressed in dark business suits, stood before reporters and a mural of Yankee Stadium at the Fifth Avenue offices of the New York Yankees, the preeminent Major League Baseball team, to announce a major real estate deal. Yankee Stadium, the Mount Olympus of sport, was to be sold for $6.5 million.

Dan Topping and Del Webb, owners of the Yankees and the only two shareholders in N.Y. Yankees, Inc., explained the terms of this intricate deal. The sale, finalized on December 17, 1953, included Yankee Stadium and its four acres of land. Also included in the sale was the ballpark of the Triple A Yankee farm club in Kansas City, Blues Stadium. The Yankees would now be renters, rather than owners, of their hallowed home.

Six weeks in the making, the transaction at its core was a way for the Yankee ownership to get out of the real estate business. "We're better off renting than owning," said the grinning Webb.[1] And why wouldn't he grin? He and Topping had cleared $2.7 million in profit from the sale of the stadium. "We're better off," said Webb, stating the obvious.[2]

In January of 1945, Webb, Topping, and the tempestuous Larry MacPhail, the future Hall of Fame executive late of the Cincinnati Reds, Brooklyn Dodgers, and U.S. Army, joined forces to pay the heirs of Jacob Ruppert's estate $2.8 million dollars for the Yankees, Yankee Stadium, and the whole Yankee farm system. "Dirt cheap" was how Dan Topping, grandson of the former president of Republic Iron and Steel and of turn-of-the-century tin plate kingpin Daniel Reid, described the price exacted from the Ruppert family, desperate for cash to pay off their inheritance tax.[3] Topping, a multimillionaire at age 21, was born, according to Larry MacPhail, not with a silver spoon in his mouth, but "with a gold one."[4] Living the role of the rich, young socialite, Topping had been married to a beautiful starlet named Arlene Judge and, after their divorce resulting from Topping's "cruel and inhuman" treatment, was soon to wed skating star Sonja Heine. His playboy ways were widely known, and by the end of his life he had married five times.

The idea of purchasing the Yankees had come to him while golfing with Del Webb in 1944; Topping was known worldwide as a top amateur golfer, having made the quarter-finals of the 1935 British Amateur and three times qualifying for the U.S. Amateur. His interest in sports owner-ship pre-dated the Yankees. He became involved in 1934 as part-owner of the Brooklyn Dodgers of the National Football League and Topping clearly was a Yankee owner in training. In 1939 he presented to George Halas, owner of the Chicago Bears, the "highest price ever offered for a professional athlete" for the services of quarterback Sid Luckman.[5] Later, Topping owned the New York Yankees of the All-American Conference, a football league formed to rival the NFL.

While Topping was, according to Webb, the "first among equals,"[6] Webb had risen to the level of equal from a background that was noth-ing like that of the fortunate Topping. Born in Fresno, California, in 1899, Webb was a high school dropout who began work as a carpenter at the rate of 50 cents an hour. When the contractor he was employed by skipped town, Webb took over his business and, in five years' time, had built the firm up to a worth of $5 million. World War II put Webb's construction business in high gear, turning out hospitals, military bases, and internment camps. He was soon receiving $100 million in govern-ment work and was turning to the growing building needs of the newly created mecca of Las Vegas.

Webb's firm was involved in the construction of the Flamingo Hotel, but Webb insisted that his involvement preceded the entry of renowned mobster Bugsy Seigel. After Seigel was shot in June of 1947, Webb became part owner of the hotel and casino in lieu of money still owed his concern. His partners included organized crime figures Meyer Lansky and Gus Greenbaum. Further down the road, the Del Webb Company would construct the Sahara and Mint Hotels, and, while organized baseball prohibited ownership of gambling establishments, the baseball owners took Webb at his word that his points in the hotels were merely payment for construction projects, rather than ownership.

The Yankee ownership trio became a duo after the 1947 Yankee victory over the Dodgers in the World Series. Before the first pitch of Game 7, MacPhail announced at the press box snack bar that if the Yankees won, he would retire. After relief ace Joe Page shut down Brooklyn for the win, MacPhail loudly declared in the celebratory clubhouse that he was through. That was the beginning of a wild night.

A more detailed report cites that MacPhail, insulted by Branch Rickey during an attempt to console the Dodgers architect, entered the Yankee clubhouse and began an alcohol-induced scene that would last through the night. Assuaging his hurt feelings by causing a ruckus, the thunderous redhead delivered a punch to the eye of former Dodger road secretary John McDonald, loudly threw insults around the champion's clubhouse, and fired Yankee Farm Director George Weiss. MacPhail continued at the Biltmore Hotel, where he again tearfully pronounced that he was leaving baseball. Topping and Webb were more than happy to facilitate MacPhail's drunken exit. They bought out his share of the organization for $2 million and, not surprisingly, brought back the briefly removed Weiss and made him general manager.

The third man in the triumvirate, and new owner of Yankee Stadium, was much less known. He was Arnold M. Johnson, a 46-year-old industrialist from Chicago who resided with his wife, the former Carmen Burr, and two young children in their North Lake Shore Drive penthouse overlooking Belmont Harbor. Born on the South Side of Chicago in 1907, young Arnold was a wheeler-dealer at an early age. As a way to acquire some pocket money, Johnson organized a group of kids to pass out handbills, circulars, and newspapers, thereby becoming a juvenile general contractor. His love of reading, apparent during his time at Hyde Park High School, would remain with him as an adult; his penthouse was lined with over 1,000 books.

Johnson continued his education locally and graduated from the University of Chicago in 1928 with a major in business administration.

He was student council president, and, after turning down multiple job offers upon graduation, entered the business world with a $75 a month position at Lamson Brothers, a grain and stock brokerage house in Chicago. A year later he had switched to Merrill and Lynch, before Pierce, Fenner, & Smith joined the firm. Having saved $1,000, Johnson bought his first stock. Ernest Mehl's account of the birth of the Kansas City Athletics spins a tale of Johnson that is a work of myth making and cliché, but it reveals how the Chicago financial whiz kid approached his business deals. Johnson's first financial deals set the tone for his future transactions. After an initial share purchase in an unnamed "manufacturing company,"[7] Johnson bought more stock on margin. Later on, he saw quite a bit of selling, an abnormal amount of selling, that made him unload his stock. When "news" came out, although Mehl does not provide one whit of detail regarding this news, the company's share price fell by 80 percent. "Never again, Johnson decided, would he buy stock on margin."[8] Apocryphal though this story might seem, it illustrates how Johnson would always, in future business dealings, strive to take as little risk as possible. "All those reorganizations taught me at least one thing; I decided I would never stick my neck out," he confessed.[9]

In 1932 Johnson joined City National Bank and Trust, newly formed out of Central Republic Bank and Trust Company. As a 25-year-old banker, Johnson was in charge of prospecting for opportunities in the salvage of distressed companies. Mehl notes that Johnson's specialty was to bring "order and success to a wrecked business."[10] When he rescued Northwestern Terra Cotta Company from a $1.5 million debt, he was named to its board of directors. As watchdog for the bank, Johnson made sure to invest his own money in Northwestern, displaying confidence in his own talents.

World War II interrupted Johnson's march to the top of the financial pyramid. (Replacing him at Northwestern Terra Cotta was J. Patrick Lannan, who would partner with Johnson in future investments.) His four-year stint in the Navy as a lieutenant, second grade, began with training as a gunnery officer, but he quickly became a navigator and boat group commander. As a beachmaster in amphibious landings, Johnson was involved in seven D-Day landings. He was Chief of Staff on the *USS Calloway* during the Battle of Luzon in January 1945, and, as luck would have it, he was relieved of duty just before 42 shipmates were killed, his replacement included. He won a Bronze Star and Legion of Merit for his Pacific service and, soon after his return in 1945, became a vice president in the banking department at City National Bank.

As a member of the Fin 'n Feather Club and the exclusive Saddle and Cycle Club in Chicago, Johnson had more than a passing interest in sports. He became involved in a private venture, the reorganization of the National Hockey League's Chicago Black Hawks. In association with Black Hawk general manager Bill Tobin, a syndicate had been created to buy the Hawks from the late Maj. Frederic McLaughlin, a group that included Arthur Wirtz (with whom Johnson had a joint venture from 1941 to1943 to purchase real estate securities from the Reconstruction Finance Corporation), Jim Norris of the International Boxing Club, and Bruce Norris. Johnson had been a vice president and treasurer of the franchise, but at the time of the Yankee Stadium purchase he was listed only as a corporate director.

Though Johnson would acquire interest in other companies with which City National had dealings, he soon turned his eyes toward the Automatic Canteen Company of America, an operation that sold food and cigarettes through vending machines to the tune of $100 million per year. Automatic Canteen, formed by Nathaniel Leverone and his brother Louis, became a target for Johnson, who realized his path to the top of the bank would be a long time coming. At Automatic Canteen he could slip into the number two slot as chief lieutenant to Nathaniel Leverone.

A syndicate was formed to purchase all of Louis Leverone's 40,000 shares of common stock, as well as 10,000 shares of preferred stock. Toward the end of 1951, Louis decided to sell his stake in the firm, and an investment group led by J. Arthur Friedlund, a Chicago attorney and secretary and general counsel to the New York Yankees, paid $1.5 million for the elder Leverone's holdings. The sale was completed in January of 1952, and one month later Johnson was named director; a year later he was vice chairman. Members of the purchasing group included Johnson; J. Patrick Lannan, director of International Telephone and Telegraph; Harold S. Darr, principal shareholder of Frontier Airlines; Friedlund; and Yankee owners Dan Topping (who became a director in March 1953) and Del Webb. Johnson was in for 2.5 percent and the role of vice chairman, while the Yankee owners were in for 1.3 percent each. Later, Johnson would join Webb as a partner in the construction of Phoenix apartments, Phoenix Towers. These deep business relationships between Johnson, Topping, and Webb, which were the bedrock of the Yankee and Blues Stadium sales, as well as the key to Johnson's successful purchase of the Philadelphia A's in 1954, would be glossed over in all accounts.

Johnson's thoughts on buying Yankee Stadium came to him "one night when he was in bed," according to Ernie Mehl.[11] "Inheritance taxes, he [Johnson] reasoned, were a source of worry to those with large holdings."[12] But Johnson did not need to think of random owners of such "large holdings." Wide awake to the fact that their syndicate partners, Topping and Webb, had this dilemma, Johnson and Friedlund had been talking to the Yankee co-owners for months about such a deal. Friedlund was coincidentally both director and general counsel to Automatic Canteen as well as to the Yankees and could certainly handle the complicated and intricate negotiations. Friedlund had some experience, as he had negotiated the January 1945 purchase of the Yankees by Topping, Webb, and MacPhail from the Ruppert estate.

Topping and Webb explained the terms of the deal to the press, although they would not reveal all of the details.[13] Johnson, along with his Automatic Canteen syndicate cohort Lannan, purchased, in the name of Arnold Johnson Corporation, Yankee Stadium, the four acres of land it sat on, and Blues Stadium in Kansas City for $6.5 million. Of this price, $3.6 million was paid in cash, with the remaining $2.9 million being the assumption of a mortgage. The Yankees, now tenants with a tax-deductible operating expense, would rent from their new landlords at $600,000 for the first year of the lease, followed by descending amounts down to $350,000. The 28-year lease, if held to the end, would bring $11.5 million to the Johnson Corp.

While there had been a report by William J. Mulligan, deputy supreme knight from Hartford, Connecticut, that the Knights of Columbus, a Catholic laymen's fraternal organization, were going to buy the stadium, it was also announced that the Knights of Columbus would pay the new stadium owners $2.5 million for only the land beneath the stadium and adjacent parking properties (the *Chicago Daily Tribune* reported a $2 million price). The Arnold Johnson Corp. would then pay an annual rental to the Knights for the land of $125,000 for the first four years and $181,250 a year for the next 24 years, for a grand total of $4.85 million. Subtracting this from the income received from the Yankee lease, Johnson stood to make a profit of $6.65 million over the course of the leases. The papers, signed at Bankers Trust offices in Rockefeller Center, were for a 28-year lease with the Knights, with a renewal option of 42 more years. The Johnson Corp. retained an option to buy back the land for $3 million at the end of 15 years. The Knights would receive automatic possession of all stadium buildings whenever the lease ended. Johnson, in turn, would sublet the land to the Yankees.

Luke Hart, executive head of the Knights, and a key petitioner in 1954 to add the phrase "under God" to the Pledge of Allegiance, was pleased. The Knights of Columbus was looking to move 25 percent of their $16 million in government bonds into higher income generators, and if Johnson Corp.'s purchase option was eventually exercised, it, along with an annual 4 percent return, would provide $1 million in profit. The Yankees also were happy because they no longer maintained their largest capital investment, and Topping and Webb made a nice capital gain. Topping and Webb showed a profit of $3.65 million over their original purchase price of the franchise. After paying their 26 percent capital gains tax of $900,000, the two men were left with nearly $1.35 million each. Plus, they still owned the team.

What did Johnson get? Johnson, in the form of his Arnold Johnson Corp., ended up with two properties of value, one obvious (Yankee Stadium) and one less clear (Blues Stadium). On the surface, the deal was confusing enough, but Johnson's financial wrangling did not end there. Recalling his aversion to risk resulting from his long-ago near loss in buying stock on margin, Johnson had a plan to minimize his exposure.

As announced, of the $6.5 million purchase price, $2.5 was immediately recouped in the sale of the land to the Knights, leaving a new net payment of $4 million. In addition, Johnson received $2.9 million in a deal with Topping and Webb in return for a 20-year second mortgage on the stadium, as well as lease rights to the land. This brought the price down further to a mere $1.1 million.

More money was to come Johnson's way. The Atwell Corporation, a company that served as a trading tool for private funds and estates, had a first mortgage on Yankee Stadium, a 10-year contract that was reassigned to Salkeld & Co. seven weeks later in a transaction that garnered another $500,000 to Johnson. This brought the total cost down from $1.1 million to $600,000. The Kansas City property that was part of the deal allowed another $100,000 to be raised through mortgage. Yankee Stadium, the land it sat on, and a ballpark in Kansas City had all been purchased by the Arnold Johnson Corp. for a net cash outlay of $500,000. The properties had recently been appraised at $8 million dollars.

Figure 1.1

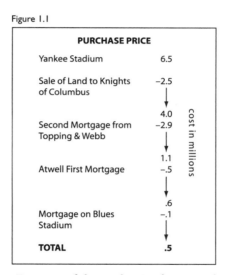

Finances of the Yankee Stadium Deal.

Johnson was "emphatic in saying he does not intend to get into the operating end of baseball," reported the *Los Angeles Times*.[14] Mehl went even further. Johnson, he recounts, "demurred when the Yankees owners insisted upon including the stadium in Kansas City. He had *no possible use* [author's emphasis] for this stadium. He could not picture it as a sound investment."[15] This is hardly credible. Johnson only had to open the *Kansas City Star* on any given day during the summer and fall of 1953 and he would have known that the city was determined to acquire Major League Baseball for its town. Baseball teams need a place to play, and Blues Stadium was the best one in town.

1. *Chicago Daily Tribune.* "Yankees Net $2,700,00 in Park Deals: Sale Dissolves Corporation," December 18, 1953, p. C1.
2. Ibid.
3. Ibid.
4. *Newsday.* Obituary, June 1, 1974. Topping, Dan, biographical file, National Baseball Hall of Fame Library.
5. *Chicago Daily Tribune.* "Halas Spurns Brooklyn Bid for Luckman," October 14, 1939, p. 20.
6. Sullivan, Neil J. *The Diamond in the Bronx: Yankee Stadium and the Politics of New York.* New York: Oxford University Press, 2002, p. 77.
7. Mehl, Ernest. *The Kansas City Athletics.* New York: Holt, 1956, p. 39.
8. Ibid.
9. Smith, William. "Chicago's New Millionaires." *Chicago Daily Tribune,* December 12, 1954, p. Q21.
10. Mehl, p. 39.
11. Ibid., p. 34
12. Ibid.
13. *Chicago Daily Tribune.* "Yankees Net $2,700,00 in Park Deals: Sale Dissolves Corporation," December 18, 1953 p. C1.
14. *Los Angeles Times.* "Yankees Sell Baseball Park," December 18, 1953, p. C1.
15. Mehl, p. 34.

Chapter 2

THE CITY

The map of Major League Baseball had been static for a half century. Not since the American League Baltimore Orioles moved to become the New York Highlanders (later Yankees) for the 1903 season had a franchise changed cities. The announcement on March 17, 1953, that the Boston Braves would be relocated to Milwaukee changed the future of baseball; the reverberations of this revolution are still felt today (witness the recent fortunes of the Montreal Expos and their move to Washington, D.C.). From this date forward, teams would shift to cities offering more lucrative opportunities, providing stadiums at little or no cost to the incoming ball club. The relocation of the Braves and the immense financial boon that redounded to the Braves ownership, Major League baseball, and the city of Milwaukee stirred cities similar to Milwaukee to seek out a Major League franchise. In the next few years cities such as Baltimore, Minneapolis–St. Paul, and Houston joined the ranks of big league towns. In the summer of 1953 Kansas City was pushing hard to be the next city to snag a Major League team. The details of the Braves' move is crucial to the story of Kansas City's desire for a stadium and ball club.

Braves owner Louis Perini had watched attendance for his Braves plummet dramatically. The Boston Braves won the National League pennant in 1948 and drew 1,455,439 fans. Even in a flag-winning year, the Braves drew 100,000 fewer customers than the Red Sox, demonstrating the difficulties of playing and competing in a two-team city. A World Series loss to the Cleveland Indians, four games to two, coupled with a subsequent fourth-place finish in 1949, saw attendance drop precipitously to a little over 1 million patrons. This decline continued each year, and by 1952 total attendance was only 19 percent of the 1948 high, a paltry 281,278. These were dire circumstances by any standard.

National League owners unanimously approved the transfer of one of their charter members to the thirteenth-largest American city at a three-and-a-half-hour March meeting in St. Petersburg, Florida. A major factor in the approval was that Milwaukee had built a stadium with seating for nearly 36,000 spectators. Arrangements for a 12,000-seat expansion had already been made in anticipation of the arrival of the Major Leagues. Another spur for the move was the enthusiastic demand from Milwaukee and its citizens. Perini cited this pressure coming from Milwaukee as causing him to move his schedule up by a year. The American Association gladly accepted $50,000 from the owner of the now Milwaukee Braves for the Milwaukee territory that the association possessed. "Other cities can take a page from Milwaukee's book," chimed Perini. "The trend is here"[1] for franchise moves, he continued, and Greater Kansas City, with its nearly one million residents to draw on, was watching intently.

• • •

The relationship between Kansas City and New York was a troubled one. As a minor league club owned by the Yankees, the Blues' role was to create future Yankees. The more success these players had on the field, the sooner they would be called up to New York. The Yankees were little concerned about the pennant hopes of their minor league enterprises. Although the Blues were obviously under the control of New York, the lack of concern for the fortunes of Kansas City caused bitter feelings. Being a minor league town resulted in something of an inferiority complex for the Midwest metropolis. "I am quite sure that there are thousands of people in and around Kansas City that wouldn't spend a dime to see anything connected with the New York outfit," a local resident wrote to the *Kansas City Star*.[2] Hall of Fame scribe Joe McGuff wrote that the Yankees had repeatedly hampered the fortunes of the local Blues, flouting the July 31 call-up rule by bringing valuable players to the majors while giving Kansas City nothing in return. A letter to McGuff by a reader cited "the general contempt of the minor league Kansas City club" showed by the parent Yankees.[3] The desire for a big league team of its own was on Kansas City's front burner.

"Webb Sees KC as Major League Entry," screamed the headline of the July 22, 1953, issue of the baseball bible, *The Sporting News*. Del

Webb, according to *The Sporting News* publisher J. G. Taylor Spink, was reported to be working on a deal in which he would sell his Yankee holdings and then buy the St. Louis Browns, bringing them across the state of Missouri. Webb was outspoken at the American League meetings held in Cincinnati that baseball should be looking west in relocating teams. Webb's frequent visits to Kansas City led to speculation that he would be an ideal figure to begin baseball's trek westward by purchasing Bill Veeck's Browns. Whether Webb was already in negotiations with Arnold Johnson, his fellow Automatic Canteen syndicate member, to sell Blues Stadium and therefore give Johnson a leg up in pursuing a Major League team, is unknown. However, negotiations were either soon to begin or already in the works.

Spink noted that a major league move to Kansas City would pave the way for a shift of Triple A baseball to Denver, a rabid baseball city, which would result in a monetary windfall for the American Association. Spink disclosed that Ernie Mehl had spoken to the city council in mid-June and pushed for the purchase and expansion of Blues Stadium by the city. Mehl's deep involvement was further delved into with Spink's revelation that Mehl had been working for months on a Browns relocation and that he was adamant that group of franchise buyers was present, although who these people were remained a mystery.

In an editorial, the *Star*, while surprised by this report of Webb's torch carrying for Kansas City, seized upon it and urged the city to not let this opportunity pass. The boon of a Major League presence in the city would go beyond the financial. Citing the benefit to Milwaukee of "many millions of dollars," the editorial goes further in stating that the benefits are more than mere commerce.[4] As the only western team, and with a larger surrounding population, a Kansas City franchise would be better situated than Milwaukee in drawing fans from a wide geographic area. The conclusion was that "we must not slip on this chance."[5]

In early August of 1953, almost immediately after Webb's pronouncement at the American League meeting, the Kansas City city council authorized Mayor William E. Kemp to meet with Yankee owner Del Webb to discover whether the Yankees would be willing to sell Blues Stadium and at what price. Some years before, Del Webb told Ernie Mehl that the city should consider purchasing the ballpark. More recently, Webb had restated this over dinner with the Kansas City sportswriter. With the Braves' success apparent, the city council had become very serious about acquiring a Major League franchise and a place for it to play. Blues Stadium was, in the summer of 1953, becoming a hot commodity.

On August 8 the general committee of the city council was presented with a report from the planning commission. Commission member Art Merkle had sent a letter to Del Webb requesting a price for Blues Stadium. The commission felt that a little more than $4 million would be required to buy Blues Stadium, as well as to provide for additional parking and expansion of capacity. The growing intensity on the city's part to buy the ballpark showed that Arnold Johnson's view that Blues Stadium was not a "sound investment" was patently false. Just months before his December real estate purchase, it was impossible for him, a proven shrewd businessman, to be unaware of the goings-on in Kansas City. Since he was either involved in, or on the verge of, negotiations to purchase Blues Stadium at this time, it strains credulity to think he did not know that he was on to something very valuable. In addition, he had another link to the current events in Kansas City, with his partner Del Webb intimately involved in the fortunes of Kansas City baseball. The city still had money remaining from a bond floated in 1947 that could be used for a stadium purchase and increase in capacity. In Spink's article he noted that plans had already been in the works to enlarge the stadium and were now being stepped up.[6]

Many voices were speaking up for Kansas City that summer. In addition to Webb's loud and clear message at the Cincinnati meeting, there was vocal support coming from Cal Hubbard, the Missouri-born dean of American League umpires. Hubbard presented a Sunday edition of the *Kansas City Star* to League president Will Harridge to demonstrate the growth in development in the city. "I told him to look that over and see whether Kansas City isn't the logical spot for a major-league club. I keep touting Kansas City," he said.[7] But it was the daily rallying by sportswriter, editor, and ordained minister Ernest Mehl that was at the forefront of the charge.

Mehl's "Sporting Comment" columns in June of 1953 were consistently written with an eye toward the big leagues. His June 24 piece recalled the days when Kansas City acquired its Federal League franchise. The Kansas City Packers were big league from 1914 to 1915. Another June column had Mehl quoting Baseball Commissioner Ford Frick as claiming there may be a need for a third Major League, a Western League, in which Kansas City would have its own club.[8] Joe McGuff referred to Mehl's desire for a club in his town as a "personal campaign" by a man who most locals took as a "dreamer."[9] During this period, Mehl had turned to his friend, Yankee and Blues owner Del Webb, for advice on how to get a club. While it's unclear whether this conversation took place before Webb spoke out on behalf of Kansas City at the American League meeting, Mehl and Webb were working together in at least an informal way to get a team established in Kansas City. In the end of June, Mehl began specifically pointing to the financially staggered Philadelphia A's. Del Webb had already told Mehl that the Mack family might have to sell their troubled franchise, and Mehl served as Webb's mouthpiece.

Mehl realized that a city with a stadium had a leg up on the competition. "First there must be stadiums," he wrote on June 16, and "only a few of the present larger minor league cities can be considered in the running."[10] A page-one story on August 13 verified the exploding enthusiasm for Major League baseball. Writers sent 500 letters and petitions expressing their desire for top tier baseball in "The Heart of the Nation." Sedalia, Missouri, sent a list of 86 citizens who would support a team, and a letter from 117 Kansas Citians also pledged their fealty to any new team. A large segment of writers expressed their disgust at the way the Yankees had treated their minor league subordinates. A woman wrote that she "and thousands like me, will be out there supporting any major league team we might draw." But, she went on, "there is no future in mustering enthusiasm for a minor league team, the farm system being the way it is."[11] An 11-year-old child, perhaps the one quoted in the preface, shared his sad feeling about the Kansas City baseball situation. "Although I enjoy baseball very much, what is there to cheer about? The Blues have the blues."[12] A. E. McNulty of North Lawn Avenue believed that if a Major League team was brought in, Kansas City could "quit taking the back seat."[13] Various other correspondents wrote that buying Blues Stadium would be an act of civic duty and would help business in the growing burg.

The Star was pushing for a stadium purchase as well. Citing the city council's recent actions in pursuing a meeting with Del Webb to inquire on the selling price of Blues Stadium, the editorial stated that it seemed like a deal could be consummated in a short time. The gamble, of course, was that if no team relocated, the city would then be burdened with the ownership of a ballpark that was only used for AAA play. This risk could be diminished by filling dates with football games and various other events that local high schools might want to schedule. Bonds already passed could be used to purchase the arena from the Yankees and expand seating. Citing Milwaukee's infusion of over $8 million in out-of-town business resulting from the presence of the Braves, "supreme effort" was called for to make a reality of a "splendid dream."[14] The potent magnet of Major League baseball was pulling hard in The City of Fountains.

The Yankees, in the form of Parke Carroll, general manager of the Blues, spoke on the issue on August 17. Representing the views of Dan Topping, Del Webb, and George Weiss, Carroll promised that the New York outfit would not stand in the way of Kansas City acquiring a Major League ball club and would make Blues Stadium available to the city. "A sacrifice on the part of the organization would be required," said Carroll, and he further stated that the Yankees were available to do business with the city for the sale of the ballpark.[15] "The sooner the better," Carroll proclaimed.[16] Despite the Yankee abuse of the Blues' roster for the team's needs, Carroll, citing that the Yankees "cherish its relationship with Kansas City,"[17] expressed concern over the fate and interest of the minor league franchise. Yet, for the next few months, the Yankee brass toyed with Kansas City, countering the city's serious attempts with delays and excuses.

The summer of 1953 saw several visits to Blues Stadium by Yankee brass. On June 25 Del Webb attended a Blues contest, en route to Chicago. Dan Topping, Roy Hamey (assistant to general manager George Weiss), Pat Patterson (scout), and Lee MacPhail (farm director) attended a game together in mid-July, as did Weiss himself just two days later. Mehl, who was usually so attentive to Yankee matters, didn't see these visits as worthy of coverage.

While the sale of the stadium would happily be considered, Carroll had no sense of what the appropriate price should be until a meeting took place between a committee sanctioned by the city council and the

Yankees. That committee, made up of Kansas City Mayor William E. Kemp, city manager L. P. Cookingham, and R. J. Benson, chairman of the general committee of the city council, was hoping to meet with Webb. The mayor had conversed with the Yankee co-owner in early August and was waiting to make an appointment to speak with Webb later in the week of August 24. How much of the planning commission's estimate of $4 million for Blues Stadium and its expansion was for the stadium alone would have to be discovered.

A stadium by itself would not guarantee a Major League franchise, and Mayor Kemp declared his opposition to pursuing such a deal. Although he was confident of acquiring a team, Kemp felt the city council were in agreement that, while enthusiastic about the prospect of a team's relocation to Kansas City, it was pointless to get Blues Stadium, enlarge it, and then have no team to play there. Parke Carroll had said that the Yankees could not make any guarantees to the city, perhaps being coy about Yankee power within the American League, as events will show. Mayor Kemp was expecting a phone call from Del Webb the morning of August 18 and hoped, during this chat, to arrange an official meeting to discuss the price of the stadium. "If we can get together on a price," said the mayor, "the next step will be . . . an effort to obtain assurance of a major league team here."[18]

Again the *Star*'s editorial page warned against letting this opportunity slip away. The mayor was chastised for his "gingerly approach."[19] A pivotal moment had arrived for Kansas City—go for broke and invest in a ballpark with no guarantee of obtaining a team or resign themselves to being a backwater town. Playing it safe by requiring a guarantee of Major League status first, would, the *Star* said snidely, "leave Kansas City with a safe minor league team."[20] Milwaukee had expanded their stadium with the hope of luring a team down the line, yet the Brew City had no assurances. They had taken the risk, and the *Star* advocated that Kansas City do likewise. "Chances appear to be excellent. It would be tragic to fritter them away."[21]

Commissioner Ford Frick chimed in with a warning that cities hoping to acquire a Major League team needed to satisfy any present holder of territorial rights in their area. "I'm getting sick and tired of reading in the papers about somebody talking of building a ball park to get a big league club when, to the best of my knowledge, they haven't talked with the fellow who owns the minor league club in town."[22] This seemed to work to Kansas City's advantage, as the Yankees had already announced their willingness to cooperate.

While Frick cautioned local chambers of commerce and civic groups to tone down their pushing, momentum was on the increase. The Katz Drug Company placed a full-page ad in the *Star* titled "What Major League Baseball Would Mean to Kansas City!" Citing the benefits to business and the youth of Kansas City, the Katz ad invited the citizenry to "join the crusade" by clipping and returning a coupon for all to vote in favor of bringing Major League baseball to town and pledging their support. The drugstore even hoped the World Series would be brought to town—a wish that was extremely optimistic and would prove to be wishful thinking.[23]

The far-reaching demand for baseball was noted in yet another editorial. The "uprising" of support was occurring not only in Kansas City but spreading to the whole region. Citing the huge response to the Katz ad and nearly 9,000 letters and petitions sent to the mayor's office, the *Star* believed that a team for Kansas City was less a dream than a concrete proposal in need of a course of action. The team of the West that would be the new Kansas City club would have the potential of drawing huge crowds. "The city can't afford to hold anything back."[24]

During the summer of 1953 there was much debate as to the fate of the Bill Veeck–owned St. Louis Browns. Veeck bandied about various cities as the destination for his forlorn club, including San Francisco, Los Angeles, Baltimore, and Kansas City. When Veeck returned to St. Louis from a West Coast jaunt in which he failed to rouse interest in the Browns but may have stirred up more interest in the other municipalities, he spoke to Mayor Kemp. Veeck told the mayor that he had bypassed visiting Kansas City because he didn't want to raise the city's hopes, although he had put them on his list of possibilities. Veeck was focused on Baltimore because of its nearly one million population (it was the sixth-largest city in the country) and the presence of a newly expanded 60,000-seat Municipal Stadium (according to the ever hyperbolic Veeck, seating was closer to 50,000). While Veeck was turning toward Baltimore, some Kansas Citians were talking to his Brownie partners.

Veeck had, he told the mayor, heard that his associates were approached about an interest toward changing the team's ownership. Seemingly excluded, Veeck had not spoken to them about it.

Kansas City held on to its hope for a Major League team—if not the Browns, then perhaps another club. Mehl received a letter from Philadelphia, home to, as Webb had already told him, the struggling A's. C. William Duncan of *The Philadelphia Inquirer*, then in the news department but formerly president of the Philadelphia Sportswriters' Association, wrote to Mehl that Kansas City is "by far the better choice." Duncan continued that it "depends a lot on the Yanks and the stadium angle."[25] According to Duncan, Blues Stadium was "a beaut" and Kansas City a splendid city that would be extremely successful should baseball arrive.

Back on the stadium front, on August 26 Mayor Kemp missed a phone call from Del Webb, who one week before had gone on record that he would meet with his associates and they would be willing to sell Blues Stadium to the city. This was the first of many failed attempts to get in touch with Webb, who, though initiating this call, would from here on toy with the hopes of the Kansas City politicos to wrench a price for Blues Stadium from the Yankees co-owner. In light of Webb's future evasions and pretense of good faith to Kansas City while negotiating behind the scenes with his associate Arnold Johnson, it is unlikely that he called to deliver the goods. When the phone rang, the mayor had unfortunately just stepped out for lunch. Mayor Kemp was going to pursue an independent appraisal of the property, and, by September 1 Webb was expected to convey a price.

What had been happening on the Yankee end of the deal? Negotiations for the eventual Yankee Stadium and Blues Stadium sale would, if the December 17 announcement was to be believed, begin in very early November, yet it's unlikely that Johnson's middle of the night inspiration to buy Yankee Stadium started at that exact moment. Johnson had talked for months with Topping and Webb about the financial possibilities of a Yankee Stadium sale. Is it conceivable that Webb would not, even in casual conversation, recount to his Automatic Canteen—and sometimes construction—partner Arnold Johnson the news from Missouri? The Braves' success, which spurred Kansas City's interest, was happening in the Wisconsin backyard of Chicago, Johnson's hometown. Could he have been unaware of it?

Great anticipation awaited September 1, which would result in the first concrete proposal on a prospective sale of Blues Stadium to the city. The *Star*'s editorial page cited that the council's action on Blues Stadium as a precursor to bringing a Major League team to town would be "one of the greatest single achievements" in recent memory.[26] Some critics felt that buying the stadium was just helping the Yankees, but the *Star* again pointed out that there was little risk, as the stadium could bring a good deal of rental income. Any quibbling had to take a backseat to the big issue, which was getting a team to Kansas City.

Despite Mayor Kemp's requirement that a team come before Blues Stadium be purchased, it's clear that there was a serious movement on behalf of city government to obtain a Major League franchise. In the previous six weeks, the planning commission had come with its report on the worth of Blues Stadium, and the city council had sought a meeting with the Yankees and Del Webb. The mayor himself had talked to Bill Veeck regarding the Browns and was waiting for Del Webb's call on the first of September.

Considering all of this, Ernie Mehl took a surprising turn in his column on that much-anticipated September day. He wrote in his "Sporting Comment" that the city was "not very interested" and viewed the purchase of Blues Stadium as "ridiculous" without a guarantee of a ball club. Mehl saw the city as making only a "token effort" because of the influx of supporting letters from residents. Mehl went further in believing that city officials would love to see an end to these entreaties and an end to this whole "silly business."[27] The city had never given the impression that it was willing to buy Blues Stadium, said Mehl, flying in the face of the concentrated efforts of Kansas City to arrive at an agreement. Mehl went on to claim that the Yankees didn't even want to sell the ballpark. He made this claim even though Webb had, a few years back, himself suggested that Kansas City look into buying Blues Stadium from the Yankees. So why hadn't Webb yet delivered a price to the city?

Mehl's negativity toward the city in this strong column certainly could lead one to speculate on his motives. Why would he disparage the city's efforts and, in the same piece, defend the Yankees and Del Webb? Webb had already been on record in support of a sale of the ballpark. Parke Carroll had already said that the Yankees would like to work out an agreement with the city. Again, one wonders where Arnold Johnson was during all this. Were the Yankees already working on negotiations behind the scenes with Johnson?

Johnson himself shed some light on this. As part of the due diligence he performed before concluding the Yankee Stadium deal, Johnson went to investigate the Kansas City ballpark that was to be included in the transaction. "When I was looking over the property, Ernest Mehl suggested that while I was at it why didn't I get a major-league franchise and move it to Kansas City. Sounded good to me."[28] Had Johnson already visited Kansas City? While negotiations wouldn't begin until early November, it's not a stretch to think that Johnson would look over his prospective properties in advance of trying to hammer out a price for them. Ernie Mehl, as always, was on the scene. For a sportswriter, Mehl was a key player, first, as confidant of Del Webb in regard to the status of Blues Stadium and the Philadelphia A's and second, as company to Johnson as he toured the Kansas City ballpark.

Whatever the reasons, September 1 came and went without a price for Blues Stadium being delivered by Mr. Webb. No word had come to the mayor's office from Webb, and a decision was made to hire Osborne Engineering of Cleveland, Ohio. Osborne was being brought on to appraise Blues Stadium and the potential cost of a second deck. It was hoped that their conclusions would determine that the ballpark and construction could be accomplished at a reasonable cost. Osborne expected to be finished by the end of September. The impression was that the city was willing to forge out on its own to determine fair value as it waited for the procrastinating Yankee co-owner.

Despite Bill Veeck's stated preference for a Browns transfer to Baltimore, the prospect of Kansas City as the frontrunner arose again around this time. Mehl wrote the city was "probably number one on the list of acceptable cities"[29] and that the American League club owners would agree. Behind the scenes the American League was playing hardball with the flamboyant Browns owner. Although Veeck owned a controlling interest in 80 percent of the club's stock, he was heavily in debt to the League and, to a large degree, at the mercy of a group of owners who despised him. Veeck's promotional history, such as his sending the midget Eddie Gaedel to the plate in a game against the Detroit Tigers in 1951, led the owners to conclude that Veeck had lowered the dignity of the game. Mehl had "just a hunch" that if the right person came along to buy the Brownies, they could be moved to Kansas City in a "profitable transaction."[30] Was Arnold Johnson the "right person" who Ernie Mehl had in mind? While we don't know if Johnson's visit to Kansas City to size up his eventual acquisition had occurred by this time, again it seems logical that Johnson visited Kansas City sometime before his early November negotiations began.

Despite Mehl's insistence that the city was not serious about its attempts to buy Blues Stadium, on September 11 the city council adopted a resolution to make every effort to acquire an option to buy the ballpark at a fair price. Again an effort was made to get details from New York, and a conference was scheduled between Mayor Kemp, Councilman Robert J. Benson, and Yankee co-owners Topping and Webb for the following week. The approved declaration would, it was hoped, give the city a solid position on which to approach negotiations.

Earlier in the week Mayor Kemp had sent a letter to Topping requesting a meeting to discuss the possibility of New York selling the stadium. A copy of the letter was sent to Webb, perhaps not the first choice recipient after he disregarded the scheduled September 1 conference. It was hoped that the chances of bringing a team to the Midwest would also be discussed. Mehl's assertion that American League owners were more in favor of Kansas City than Baltimore emboldened the city council to make its position known on record. While the mayor again stated his unease with the idea of buying the stadium before a team was secured, the indications that Kansas City was in a favored position gave some comfort. The council understood that Major League baseball would bring great advantages to the city. However, a sensible price would have to be arrived at, and the city would not commit itself unless that happened. The resolution passed by a 5–1 vote.

What were the results of the meeting? The same as the September 1 get together—nothing. Again Del Webb had an excuse as to why it was inconvenient to meet with Mayor Kemp. This time it was that "it would be impossible to reach definite terms on the sale of the Blues stadium until after the World Series."[31] A meeting planned for the weekend of September 18 was cancelled upon the receipt of Webb's comments. Webb, having just returned from a trip to the West Coast, spoke with Kemp and, according to the *Star*, "was unable to give reasons for this decision."[32] Mayor Kemp expressed his anxiousness to get concrete information from the Yankees, as it was impossible to continue with plans to obtain a Major League team without the stadium situation lined up.

Webb told the mayor that he would call later in the week in regard to a possible meeting to be held in Chicago, as Webb was scheduling a trip there. Chicago, of course, was the home of soon-to-be Blues Stadium owner Arnold Johnson. Webb's stonewalling of Kansas City was certainly curious, although received without comment by the local press. Not knowing the behind-the-scenes story that would soon unfold in the shape of the blockbuster December sale, there was no reason for government officials or unsuspecting residents to be concerned.

The Chicago meeting did take place on September 19. Councilmen Benson and Ilus W. Davis, future two-term mayor (1965–1969), met Webb and American League attorney Art Freedlund at The Drake Hotel off Michigan Avenue. Despite all evidence to the contrary, Webb told the city officials that he "would co-operate in every way possible" with Kansas City's attempts to purchase an option on Blues Stadium.[33] Then Webb contradicted this statement by tacking on a series of hurdles that he felt were needed. Prefacing his demands with a statement that this was "an inopportune time to concentrate on acquiring the option,"[34] he thought that first Kansas City needed to obtain a detailed analysis about whether the city had what it took to sustain a Major League franchise, such as population figures and other relevant data. Once this was compiled, the final report was to be submitted to American League president Will Harridge, who would submit it to the American League owners when they were scheduled to meet to discuss the fate of the Browns on September 27 in New York.

There were reports that Webb was attempting to orchestrate a plan. This scheme would entail a purchaser who would buy the beleaguered St. Louis American League franchise and focus on a move. Baltimore would not be the only possible locale; Kansas City, Houston, Minneapolis, Montreal, and Toronto were also possible locations. Webb noted and commended the enthusiasm prevalent in Kansas City and reiterated his words of cooperation, as opposed to his actions of delaying that had already been witnessed.

From Chicago, Benson and Davis accompanied Webb to the season finale at Milwaukee's County Stadium. Part of the crowd that helped set the all-time National League single season attendance record of 1,826,397, the councilmen once again had to bear Webb's spurious claims of helpfulness. First, Webb pointed out that an option to purchase Blues Stadium was not necessary at all. The Yankees had promised to sell, and Webb was personally standing behind that vow. These protestations of honor and integrity would prove to be nothing but deceptive tactics used by the New Yorkers to forestall Kansas City.

Also among this group was President Harridge, who turned and asked Councilman Benson, "Do you think Kansas City will do as well with Major League Baseball as Milwaukee has?"[35] Benson emphatically said yes. Mehl gave a nod to Benson that he had always understood the importance of the acquisition and expansion of Blues Stadium to show by action that Kansas City was ready to go when a franchise could be found.

While backing up Benson's efforts, Mehl parroted Webb's stalling tactics used at the Chicago meeting. In words that evoked Webb's demands from that meeting, the *Star* columnist said that it was of crucial importance that the city find out if the population is large enough and whether it has the drive to support a team. Praising the city officials' work while not commenting at all on his friend Webb's consistently inadequate responses seems disingenuous on the part of Mehl.

True to their word, Osborne Engineering delivered their appraisal to acting city manager Reed McKinley. The final report included an appraisal of the stadium and an estimate on doubling its capacity to 35,000 spectators. The stadium was in very sound condition, and a second deck could be added quite easily, concluded Osborne. A second deck had originally been planned for the ballpark but was scrapped for financial reasons. Blues Stadium was in fine shape and could be counted on for many more years of service. The final dollar figures? Not to be revealed just yet, announced McKinley. Still to be determined was the Real Estate Board's appraisal of the value of the land at the site *and* a sale price from the Yankees. Webb's refusal to deliver on his word would cause further delays.

On the afternoon of September 24, Ernie Mehl told the Junior Chamber of Commerce that getting the Browns was very possible, if a Kansas

City committee could convince the American League owners at their meeting three days later to delay for a month the impending relocation to Baltimore. The committee, composed of Mayor Kemp, Councilmen Don Jackson and, again, Benson, as well as John McDermott, former president of the Junior Chamber of Commerce, would need the deferment to find backers to buy the Browns as well as buy Blues Stadium and enlarge it.

At the Hotel President, Mehl claimed that reports of a definite shift of the Browns to Baltimore "were without foundation."[36] There were behind-the-scenes machinations to send the Philadelphia A's to Baltimore (ironically) and the Browns to Kansas City. "Success has been so close in the last six weeks that we could almost taste the breaks in the situation," said Mehl.[37] The Yankees (along with the A's and Senators) were pushing for the Browns to head to Kansas City if the stadium situation could be resolved, yet, while the Yanks may have been seeming to support Kansas City, it did not jibe with their pushing Kansas City off in their quest for a price on Blues Stadium.

The "Sporting Comment" column on the Sunday morning of the American League meeting gave a preview of the upcoming presentation. John McDermott had come to a startling realization. He found that the population within a 150-mile radius of Kansas City was over 3 million people. While Greater Kansas City had 875,000 residents, the pool of possible supporters within a three-hour drive was impressive. Citing Milwaukee's ability to draw from a 400-mile sector, Mehl felt that American League owners would be moved by Kansas City's large number of possible ticket buyers.

Hearkening back to an anti-East Coast sentiment, Mehl posited that New Yorkers and other easterners were in general ill informed about the rest of the country and that Kansas City, at first blush, might not seem like a suitable Major League site. However, the roar of success resounding from Milwaukee had caused some formerly closed eyes to open. An interesting thought was that the triumph of the Braves' experience was of greater value than even East Coast baseball, because the "novelty" of baseball on the Atlantic had worn off.[38] Sports do not have to be in the east only, Mehl continued, and then brought up an interesting point, as well as foreshadowing the much later Kansas City baseball experience.

Quoting those who doubted that Kansas City would support a losing ball team, Mehl questioned whether any city in the nation would cast their undying fealty to a cellar-dwelling club. Kansas City would probably not consistently attend a failing team's games, but what city would, asked Mehl. Interesting in light of what would indeed happen once the bloom was off the Kansas City Athletics' rose, Mehl perhaps could not anticipate how quickly Kansas City fans would abandon a cellar dweller.

Good news for Kansas City did emerge from the September meeting. The American League owners shot down Veeck's desire to move to Baltimore. More a rejection of The Sportshirt (Veeck's moniker) than the city itself, the decision provided Kansas City with real hope. Mehl, most recently critical of his perception of the city's lack of seriousness, now highly praised the presentation of the Mayor and the other representatives. Mayor Kemp cited the increasing population, as well as the passion for a team exhibited through the summer. He also pointed to the huge success of the Starlight Theater, an outdoor venue, which, after years of planning, opened in 1951 and was enthusiastically supported. Benson reaffirmed the Mayor's claim of tremendous support, while McDermott brought out his figures on inhabitants within 150 miles of Kansas City.

The geographic balance of the American League (AL) would remain undisturbed with a move west across Missouri. The Browns were seen as a western team for scheduling purposes and, by staying in Missouri, would so remain. Interestingly, Mehl said that the Browns would draw far more in at least the next two years if they moved. "It would take that long at least for the novelty to wear thin."[39] Mehl showed a fascinating lack of certitude in regard to long-term appeal of Major League baseball in Kansas City. On another note, Del Webb helped Kansas City's cause as he led the fight against Baltimore at the owners meeting and requested a 30-day delay to hear from other municipalities. This delay would give Kansas City more time to make their case as to why the Browns should head across the state.

"Kansas City's time of decision is at hand" was the call of the *Star*'s editorial of September 29.[40] Commending the mayor's forceful leadership and those civic-minded leaders who had been known to come through in a pinch, the *Star* felt that Kansas City's position was extremely strong. To the *Star*, the 150-mile population figure was very conservative, and the paper recognized that baseball would draw well into the Great Plains area. Milwaukee's Braves added $8 million to the city's economy, even with Chicago only 90 miles away; Kansas City's territory would be much larger. Years before teams such as the Minnesota Twins, California Angels, and Colorado Rockies were created and named with an eye on a regional audience, Kansas City civic leaders already saw the potential. While the focus here was on getting a team, the editorial assumes that a stadium deal could be worked out. As of yet, there was no sign of true Yankee sympathy with the city's repeated requests to settle the situation.

On the day this editorial was written, Kansas City's hopes crashed to earth. Once Bill Veeck sold his interest in the Browns to Clarence Miles for nearly $2.5 million, the way was cleared for a Baltimore approval. While a unanimous 8 to 0 vote allowed the move to Maryland, Del Webb was spreading a report in favor of Los Angeles or Kansas City. Webb's push for these two sites was motivated by his construction interests rather than his baseball concerns.[41] Baltimore, with a finished stadium, seemingly had nothing to offer Webb's building concerns, while the other two locales needed some work to get up to Major League standards. Mehl claimed that the lack of readiness of a stadium in Kansas City was a major cause of Kansas City's loss. He did not, however, explain why this occurred. For over a month Kansas City officials had been pressing the Yankees for details for just this reason—to be prepared with a ballpark whenever a team became available. It was through Webb's delays that the city had been put in a position of unpreparedness. Mehl mentioned the approval of Baltimore even "after the proposal made by Webb himself," a usage that seemed to impute higher status to Webb and the Yankees within the league, as if refusing Webb in person was somewhat heretical.

Although Webb made the motion to accept Baltimore and voted in the affirmative, reportedly to preserve unanimity within the League, he did wrest a provision that expansion would take place in the future, preferably out west. Two other teams, the Senators and Athletics, had to be swayed to vote for the transfer. With each of those two franchises' attendance possibly injured by their nearness to Baltimore, it took much persuasion to pass the vote that would result in an out-of-kilter setup with five teams on the East Coast.

Mehl felt that Kansas City had the inside track even on the morning of the vote and noted that, since it was Veeck's personality that was at issue, had Kansas City found money to buy him out, the decision in favor of Baltimore would have never come about. Yankee involvement in a pro–Kansas City plan caused alarms to go off for the other clubs. The proposal "suggested by the Yankees was refused largely because there are several clubs in the American League actuated in their dealings by a strong resentment against the Yankees organization."[42] The Yankees willingness to sacrifice the Blues franchise worked against Kansas City, according to Mehl, always supportive of the Yankee line. Yet Webb, in his summary of the meeting, said that the Yankees as owners of the property in Kansas City "*might* [author's emphasis] have been open to further negotiations to surrender the territory."[43]

Now, with the Browns out of the picture, Mehl began to set his sights on the floundering Philadelphia A's. Webb had already mentioned the A's as a prospective target for Kansas City, and now they were the only team left. The A's couldn't financially last more than one season, but out of respect for Connie Mack and all he had done for baseball, there was no pressure to force relocation. Mehl cited the power of Prudential Life Insurance Company (actually Connecticut General Life Insurance Company), which exerted power over the franchise because of a large mortgage but was not interested in the competitive well-being of the club and, in fact, might have wanted to get out of baseball all together.

Mehl refuted the legitimacy of Los Angeles as a site. While the Western outpost demonstrated an enthusiasm for a big league squad, the expense was prohibitive, in part because of indemnification that would have to be paid to the Pacific Coast League. PCL President Clarence "Pants" Rowland was on record as opposing such a move with threats of legal action. The presentation of the Kansas City committee at the September 27 meeting impressed American League owners and brought the city into a favored position. In the opinion of Dan Topping and George Weiss, Kansas City's prospects were alive and well and the way was opened to start working for the Philadelphia A's to move to Kansas City.[44]

While a good showing was made during the last-minute scramble for the Browns, Kansas City still needed better preparation. According to an October 1 editorial, the formation of a local purchasing group would have immediately been attempted had there been more time. The stadium, though, was still a problem. The Yankees, for all their protestations of assistance and repeated claims of not standing in Kansas City's way, had offered no "more than a promise of an adequate stadium."[45] Now that big league baseball had seen the striking benefits of a midwestern region with no competition, as opposed to an East Coast saturated with baseball, the way seemed clear for the acquisition of, most likely, the A's. Now Kansas City would start to act on their own in trying to solve the stadium dilemma.

On the night of October 13, city councilman Thomas J. Gavin proposed the construction of an all-purpose stadium near the Missouri River on a 130-plus acre parcel purchased by the city in 1952. Speaking at the Advertising and Sales Executive Club before 20 directors of the Business District League, Gavin noted that he was in favor of getting a team for the city but not of purchasing Blues Stadium. The $400,000 used to purchase the river site would come from a bond fund whose purpose was to build a stadium. Therefore, the land had no other legal use, said Gavin.[46]

Having seen Milwaukee's County Stadium and come away impressed, Gavin saw no reason why a stadium with no obstructed views could not be built, replacing the "obsolete and outmoded" Blues Stadium.[47] Presaging the movement of the 1960s and 1970s to build new stadiums outside of downtown city locations, a river ballpark would have none of the parking problems that would occur at the Blues Stadium location at Twenty-Second and Brooklyn and could be the home to events like the American Royal livestock show and rodeo. The American Royal was such a huge event that the 1969 American League expansion team granted to Kansas City would bear its name.

A strong rebuttal came from Orville W. Anderson, vice president of the Business District League. Anderson claimed that a five-year delay would ensue with the construction of a new ballpark, a "monstrosity" in his view. This holdup would ruin any chances of big league baseball landing in Kansas City. The American League is looking for "fertile baseball territory," Anderson went on, and "the time is near." While nothing regarding a sale of Blues Stadium had as of yet been divulged by the Yankees, Anderson strongly believed that the ballpark could be bought for "less than $500,000 and that it could be put in shape for a third less than the cost of building a new one."[48] How Anderson came to such a figure was uncertain. He also made it apparent that the existence of an American Association franchise would need to be cleared up before a Major League franchise could take over the territory.

Gavin's push for a completely new edifice may have been a result of frustration with the Yankee talks that were not only going nowhere, but hadn't even begun. Favoring a ballpark by the river may have been the councilman's attempt to have Kansas City begin to act alone or force the Yankees to come to the table. In an aside, former Junior Chamber of Commerce president John McDermott stated that the A's were a possible candidate for relocation in the very near future but they would need to decide by December.

A few days later, Gavin announced that he would introduce a resolution to permit the city manager to seek architects and engineers to arrange details for a riverside ballpark east of the A.S.B. Bridge (Armour-Swift-Burlington). His hope was to get a bond proposal on the ballot for the spring 1954 election to add on to the existing bond funds. Gavin felt that enough money was available to start construction and that the sooner a stadium could be built, the better the city's chances would be.

The resolution, introduced on the night of October 16, was referred to the general committee for a public hearing to be held on the 29th of the month. The city manager was delegated to engage those professionals who could prepare specifications and cost estimates. As an all-purpose stadium, the new arena would be the showcase not only for big league baseball, but also for the American Royal, football, boxing, wrestling, and other sporting events. In addition, entertainment such as concerts, dances, county fairs, and conventions could be scheduled. The city manager, while in charge of retaining qualified services, would need to report and gain approval from the council.

"There is only one possible solution to a realization of the goal here and that is to work with the New York Yankees."[49] Ernie Mehl was not going to take the council's strides toward independent action lying down. Far from his cry that the city was not serious about getting a team, Mehl now opposed strong city action. As we get close to the beginning of the Johnson-Topping-Webb negotiations for Yankee and Blues Stadiums in early November, and more than likely well into Johnson's investigating the Kansas City property, Mehl began to toe the Yankee-Johnson line. That argument accepted the Yankees as the preeminent power in league matters, and nothing could occur without their full consent.

Mehl derisively commented that it was ridiculous that the Yankee organization should be asked to give up their ballpark and franchise in Kansas City for free. Despite Mehl's vigorous defense of Yankee interests, no one had ever asked for that consideration from the New York club, and everything Kansas City had attempted through the second half of 1953 was to get Del Webb to the table to come up with a fair price for purchase, not a giveaway.

With the Philadelphia A's on the horizon, Mehl legitimately claimed that a new stadium would take time to build and that conditions in the Major Leagues could change by the time it was finished. Kansas City needed to be completely prepared for the moment when the Mackmen (a nickname in honor of legendary A's owner-manager Connie Mack) possibly came up for sale. The Yankees, while showing that they were in no way truly willing to "play ball" with Kansas City, did need to be dealt with in some way. Mehl's kowtowing to them, in his passionate desire to see the majors in his town, made him a tool of Yankee propaganda. Also, as Arnold Johnson had been quoted, Mehl had most likely met the Chicagoan and knew that in the coming 6 to 8 weeks, the stadium deal would be done. It behooved him to slam any city attempts to work independently of the Bronx Bombers.

In an inadvertent shot at the Yankees and their delays, Mehl claimed that had Blues Stadium been available, the Browns would have been delivered to Kansas City. Inside sources had told Mehl that a solid offer from Kansas City at the American League meeting would have resulted in the granting of the franchise. How that would have occurred without a purchaser of the Browns themselves was not discussed. Mehl angrily impugned Gavin, "Anyone who advocates the building of a new stadium now doesn't know the picture, doesn't care or has a motive entirely beside the public interest."[50] In Mehl's estimation, taking care of the Yankees had now become a matter of civic importance.

Granted, a Kansas City franchise on a Major League level would result in some compensation to the Yankees for losing their American

Association territory (as Milwaukee was paid $50,000 when the Braves were looming), but buying the stadium did not necessarily have to follow. As evidenced by the future Dodgers move to the Los Angeles Coliseum in 1958, baseball could easily, albeit oddly, be played in a football stadium until a new stadium was ready. Although no stadium alternatives were discussed at the time, the University of Kansas' Memorial Stadium in Lawrence, just 36 miles to the west of Kansas City, was a little over 30 years old and had seating for 35,000, the goal of a double-deck Blues Stadium. How Missouri-Kansas rivalries and the scheduling conflict between a full baseball and a college football season would have been hammered out is unknown. It is surprising that the debate focused on how to deal with Blues Stadium and not on finding any suitable stopgaps. One underestimates Yankee influence at their own peril. As Joe King of the *New York World Telegram* noted, Del Webb had "a strange stranglehold on the league." That strong grip seemingly applied to Ernie Mehl as well.[51]

Mehl again dismissed the new ballpark idea a few days later, but in an odd way. He cited that a few years back, some businessmen wanted to build a new indoor arena to replace the Municipal Auditorium. They felt that a pro hockey team from the American Hockey League could be lured to Kansas City and that the ever-popular touring ice shows would make a stop there once or twice a year. Also, college basketball championships, which had more followers than could fit in the 1930's era building, could be kept with a bigger hall. Wrestling and boxing could be accommodated as well in a grand new palace.

Alas, no sizable area could be found downtown for such construction, and it was never pursued. The lack of such an arena was a great loss to the city, as residents could not now enjoy ice shows, championship bouts, or top-notch hockey. Where should a great new indoor arena be built? The optimum solution would be on the property by the river that Councilmen Gavin was proposing for a baseball facility. Ernie Mehl, champion of Major League baseball in all its importance to the status and well-being of Kansas City, felt an arena for ice shows was a more pressing need than a new ballpark for baseball.

Why? Mehl clearly believed the Yankees "must be dealt with and that means the purchase of Blues Stadium."[52] He continued that, while the riverfront seemed ideally suited for an indoor sports venue, it would not be well utilized as a baseball site. Since only baseball, and, he grudgingly admits, football, could be played at any new stadium, it would not be optimally used. For some reason building a new baseball stadium while Blues Stadium was standing made no sense, but an updated indoor arena was a perfect idea while the Municipal Auditorium still remained.

An editorial ran backing a compromise suggested by Herbert M. Woolf of the Downtown Committee. Woolf posed an obvious two-pronged solution. Blues Stadium should be bought now to solve the pressing immediate need, and a new ballpark should be built by the river in time to provide Kansas City with a top-of-the-line modern ballpark. Support for this resolution was growing, but some issues regarding the purchase of Blues Stadium needed to be resolved. There were risks associated with buying the ballpark, in the event that a Major League team was acquired. Those risks were delineated in a well-thought-out analysis. If the city left Blues Stadium in a matter of years, the possible monetary losses would be ameliorated by the 18 acres of land that could be used for future development or housing. The only cause for deserting Blues Stadium would be the arrival of a Major League team. If Kansas City remained home to only a minor league club, the financial risks of owning the field could be offset by a reasonable lease agreement with the Blues and the scheduling of other events.

The important thing is to act, claimed the *Star*. They saw a true coming together of various civic and business leaders in an effort to become big league. As to guidelines for proceeding, *The Star* saw no recourse but to rely on insiders in the baseball community who insisted that the only true chance was in having a stadium first, before a team was ensured. The opportunity to acquire a Major League franchise might arise before a new stadium was built, and Blues Stadium would be necessary in the short term. The bottom line was, according to the *Star*, that Blues Stadium *must* be purchased under any circumstances. The only reason for this was not that it was a prerequisite to getting the territory for Major League use from the minor league holder of said territory, but to appease the Yankees, and "the support of the Yankees is essential to winning an American League franchise."[53] Ideally, the Yankees would be counted as one of eight votes. In practice, they wielded power proportional to their on-field success.

This editorial was dated November 16, and while the *Star* and Ernie Mehl ran circles around themselves trying to figure out a way to best serve Yankee interests, the Yankees themselves were already deep in the midst of negotiating a price for the sale of Blues Stadium with Arnold Johnson. That sale, to be announced in less than a month, would show that all of Kansas City's honest efforts to meet with Dan Topping and Del Webb were never truly taken seriously. Webb's claim that he needed to wait until the World Series was over to address Kansas City's request for a sale price seemed all but forgotten by both sides (the Yankees had defeated the Brooklyn Dodgers four games to two on October 5). There was a certain pitiable quality to the sincere endeavors of the Kansas City contingent, working at an increasing intensity, while behind the scenes everything was being sorted out by a different set of power brokers.

The pointless exertion continued. On November 23 Mayor Kemp appointed a general committee to further the efforts to get a Major League team. A subcommittee was also created, which included Ernie Mehl. This group's purpose was to seek out satisfactory facilities, as well as directly negotiate with Major League owners. The new committee was formed when a group of representatives from business and labor were called to gather all interested parties into one united front.

The Yankees' power over the American League, and baseball matters in general, would show itself at the yearly meeting of minor leagues soon to be held in Atlanta. Up for consideration would be an amendment about drafting minor league territory. With a sharp eye to what might eventually occur in Kansas City, the proposal read that the minor league club was entitled to "just and reasonable compensation." While a lump sum payment alone was enough for Milwaukee, from now on, "such compensation shall include the value of the baseball facilities owned by the minor league club (that is, the baseball park and its appurtenances, the real estate occupied by the park and adjacent estate used for parking facilities)."[54]

The possibility now arose that there would be no way around buying Blues Stadium from the Yankees. As Mehl said, this is "the first order of business."[55] It would be impossible to proceed unless Blues Stadium was paid for. While this had been seemingly accepted by all participants, if the amendment was passed, it would be ironclad. Kansas City was in a unique situation because a big league team owned its minor league park. Other municipalities such as St. Paul, which was also interested in a franchise, did not have to deal with this issue. The Brooklyn Dodgers did have a team playing in St. Paul's Lexington Park, but they did not own the facility.

The stadium was only one issue; another was which team to focus on. At this point the Philadelphia Athletics were the target, and, with their financial ruin seemingly unavoidable, a city must be ready when the time arrived. A move west to regain American League balance, distorted by the Browns' move to Baltimore, was necessary, and it looked like the Twin Cities were the only legitimate contender other than Kansas City.

Mehl trotted out the old, tired story of Yankee assistance again. The personal guarantee (another promise unfulfilled) of Dan Topping that an equitable price would be put on the stadium was mentioned yet again, as was the Yankee offer to help in any and all ways to get a franchise relocated to Kansas City. The Yanks wanted to help for two reasons. One was to get out of their minor league real estate and, as Mehl cited, have working agreements with their minor league clubs. They could then place their young prospects without dealing with the property and franchise management. This is interesting, since the Yankees' sale of the park would be a precursor to getting a *Major League team* placed there, not a minor league team for the Yankees' benefit. There was also the hope that a fresh start for the A's in Kansas City would result in larger road attendance for visiting teams. Mehl affirmed that if the Yankees "are selfish in their wants it so happens these wants coincide with what Kansas City wants."[56]

The announcement of the sale of Yankee and Blues Stadiums was just three weeks away. Mehl's insistence that Topping and Webb were still there to bargain with Kansas City over Blues Stadium would soon show itself as demonstrably false, but Mehl was still the water carrier for the Yankees' lies. Did he know what was going on behind closed doors? He had met Arnold Johnson, but it could be that he was unaware of the details. If unaware, his writings were merely ill informed and journalistically shallow. If he did know, then he was hypocritical in his service on civic committees to pursue the purchase of Blues Stadium and insincere in his reporting of "the facts."

The absurdity of the situation was furthered by a planned meeting of Mayor Kemp and James Kemper, co-chairs of a committee to obtain a

Major League franchise, along with Ernie Mehl, in New York to confer with officials of the Philadelphia A's and the Yankees. There was no mention whether the Yankees, or the Athletics for that matter, were receptive to the delegation. This meeting was scheduled to occur just three days from the official announcement of the Yankee Stadium sale.

The Gavin resolution to build a new park by the river was being tweaked in a serious effort to move it along. An outdoor theater was added to the plan to augment the potential usage of the area. On December 11 the city council gave formal approval to prepare preliminary plans and cost estimates for the project. L. P. Cookingham, the city manager, cautioned that before an architect could be hired, all interested parties should gather to determine exactly what needs would have to be served and what structure would be built to meet such wants, as well as serve the community's interest on the whole. Councilman Benson set out the available money from past bond issues. From a 1931 bond there was $750,000 to be used for an outdoor arena, as well as $1.6 million as a result of a 1947 note to be used for stadium construction.

Before anyone could pack their bags for the New York trip, the "tentatively planned" meeting was postponed.[57] It was delayed until the middle of January, a date that would arrive too late in light of the December 17 transaction. Who delayed the meeting? It was likely the Yankees, as they were the ones constantly putting off the Kansas City officials. Obviously, Topping and Webb knew that their deal with Arnold Johnson was almost wrapped up, and, rather than be straight with the Kansas City brass, it was easier to put them off.

Interestingly, Mehl's column of December 13 shows that he most likely was inside the loop of Yankee information. How else, four days before Topping and Webb stood in front of reporters to announce their real estate deal, could Mehl have known some of the details? He said that while it had not been verified, the Yankees may be interested in selling Yankee Stadium. Jumping the gun on the announcement, Mehl divulged the Knights of Columbus' interest in buying and leasing to the team. Foreshadowing, in a rather coy way, the impending developments, Mehl said the Yankees were indeed willing to sell Blues Stadium, although their actions in the past and near future show they were never seriously interested in selling to the city. He said again that the Yankees were willing to do what they could to facilitate the arrival of a Major League team. What was becoming clearer was that that team would be the A's.

With all this going on, Mehl still wrote that the planned mid-January meeting might result in definitive agreement with the Yankees on the sale of Blues Stadium—very strange. Knowing that Johnson had already inspected Blues Stadium and seeming to know that a Yankee Stadium sale was brewing, could Mehl have honestly thought that the Yankees were straight shooters in regard to Blues Stadium and that it would still be available?

When the dark-suited Del Webb and Dan Topping said on December 17 that Yankee Stadium and Blues Stadium had been sold to Arnold Johnson of Chicago, their Automatic Canteen partner and, for Webb, sometimes construction partner, how did it play back in Kansas City? Buried on page 8 of the *Star* was a matter-of-fact headline: "Yank, Blues Parks Sold."[58] Mehl's column on that crucial day concerned the tale of a druggist who fronted the Oklahoma Sooners $300 for train fare, which allowed them to complete their 1903 college football season. There were no editorials following the announcement.

Four days later Mehl had collected his thoughts: the Yankees owners, always thinking of Kansas City's interest, said that a major stipulation of the sale was to make sure Kansas City was protected in case a Major League team came up for consideration. While bringing up Osborne Engineering's report that Blues Stadium could be double decked, he discounted the idea as too expensive. A cheaper alternative would be to enclose the playing field with additional stands, which could be temporary until a Major League team could be acquired. Later Mehl would relay a chat with Dan Topping, who reiterated that the sale to Johnson would in no way affect Kansas City's chances of gaining Major League status and that the Arnold Johnson Company was willing to deal with Kansas City.

Most interestingly, Mehl's lead paragraph mentioned that the sale of Blues Stadium, "coming on the heel of a player swap between the Yanks and Philadelphia Athletics has needed a bit of clarification."[59] On the day before the Yankee Stadium sale, New York sent, in the largest trade in Yankee history, infielder Jim Finigan, pitcher Johnny Gray, outfielder Bill Renna, catcher Jim Robertson, and first basemen Vic Power and Don

Bollweg in exchange for pitcher Harry Byrd, outfielder Carmen Mauro, infielder Loren Babe, and first basemen Eddie Robinson and Tom Hamilton. In a foreshadowing of future events, the Yankees sent four minor leaguers (Finigan, Gray, Robertson, and Power) and two part-timers (Renna and Bollweg) and received the 1952 Rookie of the Year Harry Byrd and a four-time American League All-Star in Robinson. The deal at the time of its making was incredibly lopsided in favor of the Yankees. While Philadelphia vice-president Earle Mack optimistically thought the deal would catapult the A's into contention, George Weiss gloated. "This will open the floodgates. The other clubs will have to scramble."[60] Arthur Daley of the *New York Times* called it "the biggest steal since the Brink's hold-up."[61]

It is always hard to know how trades will work out, and the A's ended up with a two-time All-Star (four times in his career) and perennial Gold Glover in Vic Power, while the Yankees failed to win the 1954 pennant, finishing second to the 111-win Cleveland Indians. It did seem that the Yankees were able to pick the choice players from the A's roster in their leading winner and second-best RBI man—this on the eve of transferring to their business partner the ownership of Blues Stadium. The next step was to ensure that Arnold Johnson received a team to inhabit his recent acquisition. The Philadelphia A's were now in the crosshairs.

---

1. Hand, Jack and Reichler, Joe. "Braves' Milwaukee Move Okayed," *Los Angeles Times,* March 19, 1953, p. C1.
2. Mehl, Ernest. "Sporting Comment," *Kansas City Star,* August 3, 1953, p. 12.
3. McGuff, Joe. "Blues Fans Unhappy over Two Recent Articles by Sports Writer," *Kansas City Star,* June 21, 1953.
4. *Kansas City Star.* "Major League Opportunity," July 20, 1953, p. 24.
5. Ibid.
6. *Kansas City Star.* "As a Major Site," July 17, 1953.
7. Mehl, Ernest. "Sporting Comment," *Kansas City Star,* July 14, 1953.
8. Mehl, Ernest. "Sporting Comment," *Kansas City Star,* June 16, 1953.
9. McGuff, Joe. "Sports & Culture: An Essay by Joe McGuff," September 18, 2005. Kansas City.com. *http://www.kansascity.com/mld/kansascity/news/special_packages/star_history/culture_sports/12581449.htm.*
10. Mehl, June 16, 1953.
11. *Kansas City Star.* "Push for Majors," August 13, 1953, p. 1.

12. Ibid., p. 2.

13. Ibid.

14. *Kansas City Star*. "Stadium and the Big Chance," August 14, 1953, p. 36.

15. *Kansas City Star*. "Would Sell Stadium," August 17, 1953, p. 1.

16. Ibid.

17. Ibid.

18. *Kansas City Star*. "Team, Then a Stadium," August 18, 1953, p. 1.

19. *Kansas City Star*. "How to Lose a Big League Team," August 19, 1953, p. 24.

20. Ibid.

21. Ibid.

22. *Kansas City Star*. "Warned by Frick," August 22, 1953, p. 18.

23. *Kansas City Star*. Katz ad, August 23, 1953, p. 13A.

24. *Kansas City Star*. "Big League Uprising," August 25, 1953, p. 25.

25. Mehl, Ernest. "Sporting Comment," *Kansas City Star*, August 20, 1953, p. 20.

26. Mehl, Ernest. "Sporting Comment," *Kansas City Star*, September 1, 1953, p. 14.

27. Ibid.

28. United Press International. "Arnold Johnson Dies in Florida; Head of Kansas City Athletics, 53," *New York Times*, March 10, 1960, p. 31.

29. Mehl, Ernest. "Sporting Comment," *Kansas City Star*, September 7, 1953, p. 19.

30. Mehl, Ernest. "Sporting Comment," *Kansas City Star*, September 9, 1953, p. 38.

31. *Kansas City Star*. "Wait in Stadium Talks," September 14, 1953, p. 12.

32. Ibid.

33. *Kansas City Star*. "For a Stadium Option," September 20, 1953, p. 3A.

34. Ibid.

35. Mehl, Ernest. "Sporting Comment," *Kansas City Star*, September 22, 1953, p. 18.

36. *Kansas City Star*. "May Get Browns Here," September 24, 1953, p. 1.

37. Ibid.

38. Mehl, Ernest. "Sporting Comment," *Kansas City Star*, September 27, 1953, p. 2B.

39. Mehl, Ernest. "Sporting Comment," *Kansas City Star*, September 28, 1953, p. 14.

40. *Kansas City Star*. "To a Big League Decision," September 29, 1953, p. 30.

41. Mehl, Ernest. "Go to Baltimore," *Kansas City Star*, September 30, 1953, p. 1.

42. Ibid.

43. *Kansas City Star*. "Quick Action Got Team," October 16, 1953, p. 41.

44. Mehl, Ernest. "Sporting Comment," *Kansas City Star*, September 30, 1953, p. 42.

45. *Kansas City Star*. "Big League Chances Ahead," October 1, 1953, p. 32.

46. *Kansas City Star*. "For Stadium at River," October 14, 1953, p. 3.

47. Ibid.

48. Ibid.

49. Mehl, Ernest. "Sporting Comment," *Kansas City Star*, October 25, 1953, p. 2B.

50. Ibid.

51. McBride, C. E. "Sporting Comment," *Kansas City Star*, October 27, 1953, p. 17.

52. Mehl, Ernest. "Sporting Comment," *Kansas City Star*, October 29, 1953, p. 24.

53. *Kansas City Star*. "To Get a Big League Team," November 16, 1953, p. 26.

54. Mehl, Ernest. "Sporting Comment," *Kansas City Star*, November 27, 1953, p. 38.

55. Ibid.

56. Ibid.

57. Mehl, Ernest. "Sporting Comment," *Kansas City Star*, December 13, 1953, p. 2B.

58. *Kansas City Star*. "Yank, Blues Parks Sold," December 17, 1953, p. 8.

59. Mehl, Ernest. "Sporting Comment," *Kansas City Star*, December 21, 1953, p. 20.

60. Associated Press. "A's Send Robinson, Byrd to Yanks," *New York Times*, December 17, 1953, p. D1.

61. Daley, Arthur. "Sports of the Times-Grand Larceny," *New York Times*, December 18, 1953, p. 45.

II

FINDING A TEAM

Part II Timeline

August 8, 1950: Roy and Earle Mack take out a $1,750,000 mortgage from Connecticut General Life Insurance Company to purchase stock from younger brother Connie Jr.

July 8, 1954: The "Save the A's" committee, a failed attempt to promote A's ticket sales and thereby keep the team in Philadelphia, is created.

August 3, 1954: Arnold Johnson offers $4 million to purchase the Philadelphia A's.

August 6, 1954: Harry Sylk offers $4.5 million to buy the A's and keep them in Philadelphia.

September 28, 1954: The first American League meeting is held in New York to discuss the A's situation; no vote is taken.

October 12, 1954: The second American League meeting is held in Chicago; a controversial "unanimous" vote is in favor of sale to Arnold Johnson and franchise relocation to Kansas City.

October 15, 1954: A 10-man syndicate led by Jack Rensel bids $3.75 million to buy the A's and keep them in Philadelphia.

October 20, 1954: Arnold Johnson threatens legal action against the syndicate for breach of contract.

October 28, 1954: The third American League meeting is held in New York to consider sale of A's.

November 4, 1954: Arnold Johnson gets signed commitments from Connie, Roy, and Earle Mack to sell team.

November 18, 1954: The fourth American League meeting is held in New York; sale to Arnold Johnson (8–0) and A's move to Kansas City (6–2) is approved.

Dramatis Personae

Connie Mack: The "Grand Old Man of Baseball," owner of the Philadelphia A's and manager from 1901 to 1950.

Roy and Earle Mack: Connie's sons and executives of the Philadelphia A's.

Will Harridge: American League president.

Ford Frick: Commissioner of Major League Baseball.

Walter "Spike" Briggs: Owner of the Detroit Tigers.

Clark Griffith: Owner of the Washington Senators.

Calvin Griffith: Nephew and adopted son of Clark Griffith; executive director of the Washington Senators.

Harry Sylk: Founder of the Sun Ray Drug Store chain and local bidder for Philadelphia A's.

Tommy Richardson: President of the Eastern League, member of the A's board of directors, and bidder for A's.

Jack Rensel: Advertising agency executive and spokesman for 10-man local syndicate bidding to buy the A's and keep them in Philadelphia.

Edward Vollers: Attorney for Arnold Johnson.

Chapter 3

A Brief History of the A's

Dad was in the league 54 years and only one time did he ask for a favor.
—*Earle Mack*

The wretched Philadelphia Athletics franchise that went limping into the 1954 season had seen much better days. While the A's had finished in the first division only twice in the previous two decades (fourth place finishes in 1948 and 1952), the Athletics' history could still challenge any team for pennant success and hallowed players. While an in-depth record of the team is not within the purview of this book and can be found elsewhere, a brief account is necessary.

From 1901 through 1933, Connie Mack's A's won nine American League flags, more than any other team in the loop. With five World Series championships under their belts, the A's were the premier American League franchise of the first third of the century, second only to the National League pennant winners of John McGraw and Bill Terry (in 1933) for overall top status. Even with 20 years of failure, the A's still had the second-most pennants in the junior league's history going into the 1954 campaign.

Cornelius Alexander McGillicuddy, known to all as Connie Mack, began his baseball career as a tall, gawky figure that stepped out of an El Greco painting and into catcher's gear for the Washington club of the National League. Mack had an undistinguished 11-year playing career from 1886 through 1896, his foremost achievement coming when he was the top-hit batsman of the Players League, with 20 while playing for the Buffalo Bisons in 1890.

Mack found the managerial role much more to his liking. His apprenticeship at the helm came while managing the Pittsburgh Pirates, starting at the fairly youthful age of 31 in 1894. He finished no better than sixth in his three-year stint as Pirates manager but, after managing and part-owning the Milwaukee franchise of the Western (soon to be American) League for the next four years, he was ready to rejoin the big time.

With an okay from American League president Ban Johnson, former President of the Western League, Mack launched a team in the Quaker City to challenge the National League Phillies of Nap Lajoie, Ed Delahanty, and Elmer Flick, all future Hall of Famers. In a legally contested move, Mack lured Lajoie to the newly formed American League consortium, where he led the league in his first of four straight batting titles with a .426 average. A fourth-place finish was all Connie could muster in his inaugural American League season, but the top slot was within reach.

Despite having to trade the keystone legend Lajoie to Cleveland because of legal complications that would prevent Lajoie from playing inside Pennsylvania borders until 1903, the Mackmen won the first-place banner in 1902 behind a pitching staff led by Eddie Plank and Rube Waddell. The A's first World Series appearance occurred three years later in the legendary all-shutout Series against the Giants. A five-game Series in which the A's went down to defeat, each contest resulted in a whitewashing, with New York ace Christy Mathewson hurling three of his own.

Mack's acumen for signing talent was beginning to emerge. He signed Eddie Collins off the campus of Columbia and, although he was soon dealt to Cleveland, snatched Joe Jackson from the Greenville Spinners of the South Atlantic League. The creation of the $100,000 infield of first baseman Stuffy McInnis, second baseman Collins, shortstop Jack Barry, and third baseman Frank "Home Run" Baker was a major step toward building the first Mack dynasty.

Behind a brilliant staff led by Plank, Chief Bender, and Jack Coombs, the A's had four first-place finishes and one each in second and third from 1909 to 1914. In some of the most storied moments in the annals of the national pastime, the A's defeated Frank Chance's Cub dynasty, making their fourth World Series appearance in five years in 1910. The A's exacted revenge over McGraw and Mathewson by vanquishing the

Giants in 1911, a postseason that resulted in the bestowment of Frank Baker's nickname "Home Run," as he led all sluggers with two wall-clearing clouts. Two years later the A's prevailed over the Giants again, but in 1914 the Miracle Braves of Boston stunned the baseball world by sweeping the A's in four games.

In the aftermath of the 1914 shaming at the hands of the Braves, Mack's A's encountered the first of their economic shakeups. The Federal League, which challenged the established big leagues starting with the 1914 season, attempted to enhance its chance of success with an increased raid on major league teams. Eddie Plank and Chief Bender both jumped to the Feds for better pay. Connie could not match the up-start league's offer to Eddie Collins, but Collins was kept in the American League via a trade with Charles Comiskey's White Sox. A completely different contractual mess erupted when Frank Baker wanted to renegotiate and, rather than give in to the third sacker, Mack allowed Baker to sit out the 1915 campaign.

The superstar-depleted Athletics lost with expected regularity and began a seven-year string of last-place finishes. Things began to turn upward as the A's climbed the ladder one rung at a time with a seventh-, then sixth-, then fifth-place finish from 1922 to 1924. Mack, his talent eye still sharp, had purchased outfielder Al Simmons at the end of the 1923 season from minor league Milwaukee. "Bucketfoot Al," so named for his unorthodox swing, had signed with his native Milwaukee team when no Major League club would fund his trip to tryouts. The 22-year-old Simmons was undaunted by the American League in 1924, with 102 RBIs and a .308 average in his rookie year, and so began the era of Mack's greatest team.

A rise to second place in 1925, eight and a half games behind Washington, was a positive sign for the future and saw a trio of rookies get their feet wet. Lefty Grove, the most prized minor league hurler and already a major talent with Jack Dunn's Baltimore Orioles won 10 games as a 25-year-old rookie in 1925, and a teenager, 17-year-old Jimmie Foxx, rode the pines with only 9 at-bats. "Black Mike," Mickey Cochrane, got a full season of play, starting at catcher, and hit .331 at the age of 22. Mack had bought control of Portland in the Pacific Coast League to gain the rights to Cochrane, a Boston University alumnus who cost the sexagenarian Mack $50,000.

The year 1926 saw a backslide to third place, but 1927, with the addition of ancient, but still effective, legends Ty Cobb, Zack Wheat, and Eddie Collins, saw the team's first 90-win campaign since the 1914 World Series year. Cobb, at 40, played a full year in the outfield, finishing tenth in RBIs and fifth in average, and at his advanced age still stole 22 bases for third best in the American League. An additional 7 victories gave the A's 98 for 1928, but they were still runners up to the Murderers' Row Yankees of Ruth and Gehrig. The next three years would find everyone looking up at the A's, as, arguably, the greatest team in Major League history had arrived.

Jimmie Foxx, after getting some playing time in 1928 at third and first base, as well as catcher, finally found a true home at first base in 1929 and blossomed into the player who would eventually land a place in Cooperstown. "Double X" had 33 homers and drove in 118 RBIs while hitting at a .354 clip. Simmons had a mammoth year, near the top in all Triple Crown categories (third in HRs with 34, first in RBIs with 157, and second in average hitting .365). Grove won 20 games for the third straight year and led the league for the second time in ERA (2.81), this time the first of four consecutive years at the top. Cochrane had another stellar year coming on the heels of his 1928 MVP performance.

After their 104-victory season, the A's crushed the Cubs in five games, with a surprise first game starter, 35-year-old Howard Ehmke, who hurled a 13-strikeout, 3–1 victory. The same quartet of Foxx, Cochrane, Simmons, and Grove, with additional help from outfielder Bing Miller (100 RBIs) and 22-game winner George Earnshaw, charged to another 100-win assault over American League competition and a 1930 World's Championship in six games over the National League Cardinals. Mack became the first manager in history to lead his team to five World Series titles, and at 67 years old to boot. A return to the Series against the Cards in 1931 led to a defeat in seven games.

A fall to second place in 1932, albeit with 94 victories, was the swan song to the golden age of the A's. Mack, his business losing money and holding a $400,000 note, had to divest his holdings, that is, his stars. First to go were Al Simmons and outfielder Mule Haas to the White Sox. A subsequent fall to 79 wins and a third-place finish in 1933 saw a sweeping out of the A's top players. Cochrane went to the Detroit Tigers for a $100,000 payout, and Grove went northeast to the Boston Red Sox, along with second sacker Max Bishop and pitcher Rube Walberg for $125,000. It took a little longer than the post-1914 descent into the cellar, but the A's found their way to the bottom in 1935, beginning two decades of abject futility.

Weak teams lead to weak turnout, and the third-place finish in 1933 began an embarrassing streak of abysmal attendance. From 1933 to 1954, the former colossus that finished first or second in six of the previous eight years, ended up with only one year above sixth place, and that barely with a fifth place attendance finish in 1944. While the rise to fourth place in the standings that year led to an all-time record of 945,076 paying customers, it was still good for no better than fifth in the league.

1950 was a watershed year in Athletics history. After his 17th and final last-place finish, Connie Mack, the "Grand Old Man of Baseball," retired at the age of 88. He retained the role of team president, but the change in the management structure of the team did not end with the retirement of their hoary manager. It was in that year that Roy and Earle Mack, Connie's boys from his marriage to Margaret Hogan, who passed in 1892, took out a $1,750,000 mortgage from the Connecticut General Life Insurance Company to buy out the stock in the club owned by Connie Jr. Connie Jr., the much younger half-brother of the older boys, was the son from the elder Mack's second marriage, to the present Mrs. Mack, the former Katherine Hallahan. The shares of the remaining heirs of Benjamin Shibe were also acquired. Shibe, a Philadelphia sporting goods magnate, originally put up 50 percent for the team in 1901. Connie, who owned 25 percent, bought out the other two shareholders (newspapermen Sam Jones and Frank Hough) in 1910. From that point forward the team was owned in whole by the two clans. It was a 50–50 arrangement until 1936, when Mack bought 141 shares from the insolvent estate of one of Shibe's sons, John. The Mack family henceforth retained controlling interest.

While insiders in both baseball and insurance wondered why such a loan would be tendered to a seemingly floundering ball club, Gordon Burlingame, a banker in suburban Philly and representative of Connecticut General, described it as a standard mortgage deal, expressly based on the economics of the A's facility. Shibe Park, renamed Connie Mack

Stadium before the 1953 season, was, entering its sixth decade, quite a valuable property. The A's organization received a substantial sum from rentals and concessions.

As landlords to the cross-town Phillies, the A's received 10 cents per admission to their National League games. This brought into A's coffers anywhere from $75 to $120,000 per year (since 1946). Just as fall brought the usual Philadelphia baseball woes, it also brought the National Football League season and the Eagles to Connie Mack Stadium. After taxes, the Eagles were to turn over 15 percent of total receipts. That would return in the range of $50–60,000 annually and one year hit a high of $85,000. The ballpark at 21st and Lehigh also served as a venue for other events such as high school and college baseball and football games, Negro League games, boxing matches, and concerts, which provided further rental income. Concession sales added to the profitability of the location. The Phillies got only a slight portion of sales, and the Eagles got nothing for their trouble. Run by Jacobs Brothers, the founders of Sportservice, Inc., since 1951, the concession receipts contributed close to $200,000 to the Mack vault.

Team revenue was not limited to these sources. The local broadcast rights, both radio and television, were shared equally between Mack's Athletics and owner Bob Carpenter's Phillies. The two-team package deal brought in about $230,000 per franchise and an added $100,000 or so from national broadcast rights. At approximately 28 cents per ticket, the A's picked up a minimum of $200,000 as a visiting club playing in the parks of their American League rivals. Because of this varied income stream, the A's, heading into 1954, never missed a mortgage payment, set at $200,000 per year, $50,000 per quarter, for both interest and amortization of the principal.

On the expense side, the noteworthy items were player salaries, the recent mortgage burden, and farm team costs. The 1953 roster set the A's back more than $400,000. The $200,000 yearly payment on the mortgage was a hard cost that could not be reduced. While the farm system brought in close to $200,000, its expenses were of equal size. Additional costs included upkeep of Mack Stadium and management salaries, which were not stratospheric. Roy Mack as executive vice president and treasurer, Earle as vice president and secretary, and Connie Sr. as president, each made a $25,000 yearly salary. General Manager Arthur Ehlers made close to $20,000 before departing in late 1953 for the new Baltimore Orioles. As Roy said, "people think the Macks have been getting rich off the ball club for years," but all they have gotten were good salaries."[1] The team hadn't paid a dividend in years, and all profits had gone back into the team.

As long as the A's maintained a 500,000 average attendance, they could break even, as they did in 1951 and 1952. When the crowds dropped to the mid-300,000's in 1953, a loss was unavoidable, although exceedingly small and not near six figures. In preparation for 1954, the Macks cut costs. The minor league system was reduced to six teams and, in trading Harry Byrd and Eddie Robinson for unproven Yankee prospects, payroll was reduced to below $300,00. The turnstiles, however, needed to turn.

Teetering on the financial high wire was made more hazardous by discord within the Mack family. The first inevitable dissension resulted from a generational chasm between Roy and Earle and the much younger Connie Jr. Roy, who had been groomed as a front office man starting in a 1915 minor league business office and reaching the big club as an A's executive in 1935, and Earle, who had first-hand baseball training as a "cup of coffee" A's infielder from 1910 to 1914 and Major League coach and sometime manager, had been around for a long while before Connie Jr. hit the scene.

Connie Jr., who commenced his apprenticeship with the club before World War II, heeded the advice of his father by staying with the team rather than entering business in Philadelphia. The youthful Mack railed against his older, more financially rigid siblings, who shot down every suggestion he put forth. In retaliation, he allied his shares with the Shibe heirs, shifting control away from Roy and Earle. Now Connie Jr. could implement many of his ideas, which disastrously led to the onus of the 1950 mortgage.

The A's had a surprising mini-resurgence from 1947 to 1949. A jump from last in 1946 to fifth in 1947, with a 78–76 record was followed by fourth- and fifth-place performances of 84 and 81 wins. These years of limited success were accompanied by the aforementioned rise in attendance into the 800,000 to mid-900,000 range. This emboldened Connie Jr. to splurge in an effort to win "one more pennant for Connie."[2]

Hearkening back to the glory days of 20 years before, Mickey Cochrane and Bing Miller were brought in as coaches for the 1950 season, although it came at the expense of another legend, Al Simmons, who was fired. The team spent $100,000 on Bob Dillinger, the third sacker for the Browns, who was coming off an all-star year and his third consecutive stolen-base title. Capital improvements ran to $400,000, three-quarters of which went to new box seats and miscellaneous upgrades, including repainting the old ball yard. Connie Jr. had opened the floodgates in a way never before seen in team history.

Not surprisingly, catastrophe ensued. It was clear that the team's play was shabby and, when the sun rose on May 26th, the A's were in sixth place with an 11–21 record. Later that day Earle, who had been assistant skipper since 1939 and was Connie Sr.'s choice for future manager, was booted upstairs to the position of head scout. Coach Jimmie Dykes took Earle's spot, and Cochrane was moved from coach to general manager. The team continued its horrid performance, and Connie Jr. realized it was time to get out altogether and sell the team, which he valued at $3.5 million, ballpark and minor league teams included.

The hostile relations between older and younger Macks contributed greatly to the possible sale. Connie Jr. said the differences in opinion made it impossible "for us to continue operating under the present arrangement."[3] Roy was unequivocal in his disdain for Connie Jr.'s work. There was constant bickering between the two camps, but nothing that couldn't have been overcome had the team had a good year financially, Roy said. However, when Connie Jr. enacted his spending and ballpark renovations, Roy and Earle didn't think it would draw bigger crowds, but "he [Connie Jr.] had his way."[4] The blame was left on the doorstep of Roy and Earle's little half-brother.

In June rumors of a sale began to surface, with the name of Jim Clark, a local trucking entrepreneur who had been the leader of the "Happy Hundred," an assemblage of 100 city investors who each put in $3,000 to buy the Eagles in 1949. Roy responded to this development by insisting that if Connie and the Shibes wanted out, the other Macks should get first crack at their stock. It was agreed on July 31st that the older sons, with the team comfortably nestled in the basement at 34–62, 26.5 games behind the front-running Tigers, would have a 30-day option to buy the stock they did not already possess.

Unbeknownst to Connie Jr., Roy had met Burlingame, and the $1.75 million mortgage was already in place. The young Mack was shocked that Roy and Earle could raise the needed funds, but so it was, and Connie Jr. and his group sold their 872 shares for $2000 a piece. The deal was consummated at the office of a Philadelphia lawyer on August 28th. For some reason, Roy and Earle were under the impression that they needed control of the stock before the mortgage was finalized. They borrowed money from John McShain, a great friend of the family and local builder, and the 872 shares were put in the club treasury. The lone active shares were the 302 held by Connie Sr. and the 163 each held by the brothers. Burlingame noted that McShain's fronting of the money was by no means necessary.

As if the burden of the newly created debt was not enough, by the end of the 1950 campaign the team was buried in the cellar with a 52–102 record. The floor dropped out of attendance, plummeting over a half-million to 309,805. Of the profits from the trio of good years, which amounted to approximately $450,000, $315,000 had vanished. The two subsequent years saw the team breaking even, and 1953 saw a small loss. The year 1954 would be crucial for the future of the fabled franchise.

---

1. Paxton, Harry T. "The Philadelphia A's Last Stand," *The Saturday Evening Post*, June 12, 1954.
2. Ibid.
3. Associated Press. "Macks to Keep Athletics; Sons to Buy Stock," *Chicago Daily Tribune*, August 1, 1950, p. A2
4. Ibid.

Chapter 4

SAVE THE A'S

With extreme optimism, Roy Mack thought that a rebound of attendance into the 600,000–700,000 range would shore up the team's finances and provide a bit of comfort. The largest opening-day crowd in five years came out on April 13, over 16,000 to watch pocket-sized Bobby Shantz prevail over the Red Sox, 6–4. After a week on the road, the A's came back to play before wildly inconsistent numbers of spectators. Nearly 20,000 fans came through the gates to witness a doubleheader split against the defending champion Yankees, but a three-game set vs. the Indians averaged only 4,400 per game. At the end of the series against the Tribe on May 6, the A's were tied with New York for fourth with a 9–9 record.

Roy also believed that the true test for the franchise would come when they returned to Connie Mack Stadium after a nearly three-week road trip. If this was a crucial mid-term exam, the A's failed miserably. On their return to Philly, they were in the penultimate spot with an 11–22 mark. Now the turnstiles began to turn excruciatingly slowly. Barring twin bills, which always drew above the norm, single games began to average around 2,000, and a June 4 game against the Senators drew less than 1,100. July's end saw crowds stagger below 2,000, with typical turnouts hovering at the 1,700 mark.

The team's performance on the field was disastrous as well. Eddie Joost, the two-time All-Star shortstop, was named manager to replace Jimmy Dykes before the season. The A's were on their way to having the American League's worst batting average, as well as the highest ERA. The staff gave up almost a full run more per game than the next-most woeful group (5.61 vs. Boston's 4.67). Shantz, two years before, the dominant hurler with 24 victories and an MVP Award to his credit, was in the second consecutive year of doldrums caused by a sore left arm.

If 1954 was going to be the year that would determine the team's fate, then the inauspicious start to the campaign was in need of immediate corrective action. Philadelphia mayor Joseph S. Clark, Jr. implored local businessmen on July 8 to "pick up the ball" and initiate a community drive to keep the home team at home.[1] While demurring from providing direct financial assistance, Mayor Clark threw the weight of the city's public relations at the A's problem. In front of 75 business and city leaders, Phillies' owner Bob Carpenter, and Connie, Roy, and Earle Mack, Clark laid the onus of saving the club on the laps of three groups—the Macks, businessmen, and fans. The economic impact of an A's exodus on the city's economy would be harsh, the mayor went on, and, in a brainstorming session, ideas for fundraising were pondered. A primitive version of pay television was proposed, with $10 fees to be requested from viewers in return for unrestricted showings of all A's games. A request was made to lower bleacher prices to 50 cents. In addition, concrete pledges for $55,000 worth of tickets were extracted.

So began the "Save the A's" Committee. The campaign set a goal of 600,000 tickets sold for the entire year, in line with Roy Mack's preseason hopes. At the time of the group's creation the A's had played 36 games over 29 dates and had drawn a paltry 180,000 spectators, a pace that would bring them in below 400,000. It took only three weeks to announce that the committee's effort had clearly failed. A wall of apathy and hostility greeted the exhortations, and less than two-thirds of the goal had been met, with only 51,798 fans making the trek to the stadium to witness 17 games in 13 days. A report was prepared and given to Mayor Clark late on July 29, but details were not made public. The members, preferring anonymity, did say the project had unequivocally fallen short.

Of the three groups to which Joseph Clark had handed the burden of salvaging the team, two had made their feelings clear. The fans showed their displeasure by not coming to the games. Business leaders' disgust was shown in a different manner. Most simply refused to become members of the group. There was yet another rebuff. Letters were sent to 125 civic leaders, asking them to create and lead groups to sell A's tickets. Not one positive reply was received. Some responses cited the obvious futility of trying to save an organization that was utterly dysfunctional without also cleaning house. There was the added problem that the movement was more to "Save the Macks," rather than the A's. The last of the groups to be heard from were the Macks.

For the Mack family, it was getting more and more difficult to figure how to keep the team in the city it had always called home. Comments from baseball insiders revealed a complete lack of faith in the Athletics' future in Philadelphia. Former team general manager Arthur Ehlers advocated a move, as it was apparent that Philly was not a two-team city. White Sox general manager Frank "Trader" Lane also saw that the A's would "be forced to move out."[2] Rumors began to surface in mid-June about a potential sale and transfer of the team. A syndicate formed by Albert M. Greenfield, founder of one of Philadelphia's oldest real estate concerns and deeply involved in Philadelphia business and politics, including being the prime mover who brought both the Republican and Democratic National Conventions to Philadelphia in 1948, was mentioned as a prospective buyer. Although his publicist Henry Haas denied it, Greenfield did say that, while he wasn't interested in buying the club, he would be willing to help out. Even Abe Saperstein, owner of the Harlem Globetrotters, was said to be interested in purchasing and taking the team to a new city.

The gossip exasperated Roy Mack. Despite the shaky start to the season, both economically and athletically, Roy insisted that there was neither an interest in selling nor an interested buyer, and that any news to the contrary hurt the franchise's well-being. From Connecticut General's point of view, all was well. Gordon Burlingame noted, "the club is on schedule with its payments with every penny up to this very minute."[3] An anonymous representative of the company said he was personally aware that the team's finances were in good stead for the remainder of the year. Presaging by a few weeks the creation of Save the A's, reporter Art Morrow cited the obvious. "If all the Philadelphians worried about the A's financial problems would belly through the turnstiles . . . there'd be no financial problems."[4] By the end of July there clearly were few worried citizens.

When it was apparent that Save the A's would result in wrecked hopes, the simmering Mack pot boiled over. Executive vice president Roy declared that he had made an offer to buy out his brother Earle's 163 shares. Earle, however, denied this. Roy then asserted that he had been given an option on Earle's stake but that Earle subsequently backed down. Earle did not deny this and set his selling price at $300,000, less than the $2,000 per share price of 1950.

In Morrow's A's column in the August 4 *Sporting News*, none other than Arnold Johnson makes his first appearance in the circus that was the Philadelphia A's. According to a source close to the Macks and the board of directors, an offer of one million dollars was made for the franchise alone. Assumption of debt, including the mortgage, was not reported on at this time, nor was the future status of Connie Mack Stadium. At first, Roy Mack said the reports from Johnson in Chicago were categorically unfounded, but later he conceded that "we talked to the Arnold Johnson people but we made no commitment of any kind."[5] This was a response to a rumor that Johnson had already virtually completed negotiations to gain control.

According to Ernie Mehl, Johnson had offered to buy the team in late July, but Roy said the team would "positively not be sold."[6] Why would Johnson want to buy a sinking franchise in a business that he knew nothing about and seemed replete with risk? Here was a man who had always been wise and cautious in his investments, taking great care to avoid nearly all risk. His willingness to spend money and time in such a sorry undertaking as the A's seemed out of character.

When Johnson had scouted out Blues Stadium with Mehl, it had been suggested that he go after a big league club for his soon-to-be-owned minor league park. Johnson, who had once looked into acquiring either of his hometown teams, the Cubs or White Sox, said his interest in baseball was "reawakened . . . after his purchase of Yankee Stadium."[7] The *Los Angeles Times* had quoted Johnson as saying he was completely uninterested in the baseball business upon the announcement of the stadium deal. With much inconsistency on record, the fact was this: Johnson had "decided to give this thing a whirl. It may be a tough one to crack, but I'm going to try."[8]

Mehl's *The Kansas City Athletics* consistently pumps up the image of Johnson as fearless risk taker, evidence to the contrary. On August 3, the day Johnson officially announced his $4 million bid for the Athletics, the voters of Kansas City approved a $2 million bond to obtain and double the size of Blues Stadium to 34,000 seats. Clearly, having the city already willing to pay for his ballpark as well as foot the bill for expansion took a major unknown off the table. From this point forward Johnson would not have to worry about whether his Blues Stadium investment was worthwhile.

Though the declaration of his bid came on the August 3, Johnson had been in negotiations since mid-July with the Macks. Johnson's proposed $4- or 4.5-million purchase price (reports varied) was allegedly agreed to by Earle and Connie, Sr. but not by the recalcitrant Roy. The option was brought back to the table, and Roy was given an August 11 deadline to acquire the shares of his brother and father. The Macks' money problems would potentially be solved by the flush Johnson. "There's nothing wrong with them that a few million dollars can't fix,"[9] said Johnson, who added, "I have the cash to back up my offer."[10] Frank Lane agreed that a mere $3 million could cure the beleaguered A's.

The baseball fever that began in 1953 continued to run high in Kansas City, and the bond that passed was overwhelmingly supported. The $2-million plan was okayed in a landslide, with a nearly 5 to 1 margin saying yes to baseball. An election-eve push, including a two-hour television show, with a roster of local celebrities in the various realms of politics, business, press, and sportscasting, as well as former big leaguers, pled with the residents to approve the ballpark financing. As to the coincident timing of the bid and the bond, Johnson provided some color by saying, "This is no secret. *I have been working on this for a long time* [author's emphasis]."[11] How long a time is unknown, but, as Johnson had recounted, the plans for a Major League team were hatched in his first meeting with Ernie Mehl. The ink on the Yankee and Blues Stadium deal was not even put to paper, let alone dry, at that encounter.

Truths were few and speculation was rampant. One story had Johnson leading a syndicate, which included Jim Norris, president of the International Boxing Club and purchaser of the Chicago Black Hawks along with Arthur Wirtz, head of Chicago Stadium, who was also named as a syndicate member. Wirtz quickly put down this talk by declaring that he had not spoken to Johnson about, but did know that, his fellow Hawks executive had been working on this deal. There was also some buzz that nonspecific interest was expressed by parties in Minneapolis–St. Paul, Houston, Los Angeles, and San Francisco.

The intensity of Roy and Earle's sibling strife resulted in a less than clear picture of events. Roy felt that a go of it could still be attempted in Philadelphia, but Earle said the team was broke. There were no hopes of staying in Philadelphia according to Earle, but Roy felt there was a great hope that local buyers could be found. There were reports that Roy was already dickering with possible local backers. Earle made statements that were schizophrenic. While he was on record that the team was broke, he also was quoted as saying that even with a 300,000 attendance, the team's books were in good shape and that breakeven was likely. At times resigned to the team moving, Earle also noted that he would like to keep the team where it was. Earle's take on Roy Mack was that he "talks big," but can't come through with any money to either exercise his stock option or find other suitors.[12]

And here come the Yankees. Despite the lack of concrete information, they were moving in already, even though, according to American League commissioner Will Harridge, there was no deal as of yet. Making it clear that Yankee approval was paramount, Johnson reported that he had discussed his pursuit of the A's with Yankee co-owners Topping and Webb and he was assured they would not stand in his way. In addition, the Yankees had no problem relocating the AAA Blues and supporting the A's move should the Macks accept Johnson's offer. Topping and Webb felt the league would be made stronger with a shift by Kansas City.

Not so fast, declared some other American League owners. Detroit Tigers owner Walter Briggs came out against Arnold Johnson because of his Yankees connection. Clark "The Old Fox" Griffith, legendary pitcher, Hall of Famer since 1946, and owner of the Washington Senators, said that while "I don't know this man Johnson, if a real connection is determined, we certainly will object and vote against him as an American League owner. That's fundamental, you know, that no individual can have a financial interest in more than one team."[13] Few articles had mentioned Johnson's ownership of Yankee Stadium in this initial flurry of news, but "The Old Fox" sensed a problem early on. Amidst the charges of collusion in the air, Johnson claimed that he was just pals with Topping and Webb, stating, "What could be more natural than that I ask advice from my friends?"[14]

A day after Will Harridge admitted no knowledge of any offers for the A's, he quickly developed very firm opinions on the matter. He could see no way for the team to be saved, and it was apparent to him that they must be moved. Connie Sr., an old hand at baseball politics, saw this turnabout for what it was. The A's were "washed up" in Philadelphia, said "The Tall Tactician," now that the League's helmsman had "placed a stamp of approval on both the sale of the club and the Johnson group as potential buyers."[15]

Why this turnabout from Harridge? Griffith was willing to be kind, saying Harridge "probably hasn't gone into this thing about this man's [Arnold Johnson] tie-up with the Yankees."[16] Hovering around all this was what writer Joe King had previously referred to as the Yankees "strange stranglehold" on the American League's business.[17] Could that apply to determining who would be allowed to buy a rival franchise, as well as deciding where that team would play its games? Not just the fate of the Macks would be decided. The Senators would be impacted greatly by an A's move. The Orioles would subsequently become an eastern team for scheduling purposes and would now have its home games at the same time as the Senators. Preferring a city like Toronto because of its proximity to Detroit and Cleveland, Griffith predicted that the problem of one area supporting two teams would be alleviated in Philadelphia but be newly created in the Capital District.

Roy's angel came through on August 6, when 51-year-old Philadelphian Harry Sylk, founder of the Sun Ray drug store chain and vice president of WPEN radio, created a syndicate to present a formal bid. This proposition, matching Johnson's $4.5 million, was to be presented to Roy Mack the following Tuesday. Albert Greenfield had decided to join in the group. Sylk's motives were not simply civic minded. While a prime reason was the importance of keeping American League baseball in Philadelphia, Sylk saw profit in the deal. "Running a major league club is just like running a drug store"[18] and there was money to be made there. The drug store mogul felt that he could provide the right medicine for the team. Sylk suggested a complete reorganizing from top to bottom, indicating that, even if a sale was made to the neighborhood group, it could still signal the end to the baseball life of the Macks. Sylk would say a few days later that a place would be found for the Macks, but obviously the control of the team would fall to the new owners.

A meeting between the Sylk consortium (over 16 members) and Roy Mack was set for August 10. Mirroring the outpouring from Kansas City fans, Sylk, who in his younger days sold seat cushions at Shibe Park, cited support for his plans from area denizens urging him to succeed, as well as fans' offers to help buy stock. League president Harridge, in an about-face, claimed he would love to see the A's remain in Philadelphia and that the circuit would never dream of doing something "to hurt the Mack family after what Connie Mack has done for the league and baseball."[19]

While Arnold Johnson had already been on record stating that he had real money to back up his $4.5 million bid, Sylk doubted the veracity of that figure. "I can't believe Johnson offered that kind of money for this team. We're prepared to make a fair offer for the Athletics, not a fantastic one."[20] Intimations that the bid may even go higher, spread by Johnson himself, were made, although that was quite an unlikely scenario. However, Earle Mack believed the rumors and made it clear that he would be willing to sell to the highest bidder.

The A's five-man board of directors met on August 11 to discuss recent developments, with the Roy and Earle feud in full swing. They refused to sit next to each other and glowered throughout the meeting. While the board of directors made no decision on the two proposals on the table, J. Channing Ellery, the A's general counsel, strongly stated that the prime goal was to have the team stay put. Clearly, Arnold Johnson's bid had fallen to second place and, if the newest speculation was accurate, possibly third, for it was bandied about that Roy Mack might be leading a third group of local money, backed by an unknown builder. *The Sporting News* reported that this was possibly John McShain, one of the largest contractors in the country and close friend of Roy Mack. McShain's company had built more than one hundred edifices in Washington, D.C., including the Jefferson Memorial and the Pentagon, as well as performing major renovations on the White House. Fellow construction giant Matthew McCloskey was also mentioned as a potential financier, as well as Paul Harron, president of radio outlet WIBG. Upon adjournment, it was announced that the board would reconvene in two weeks to review all tenders. With Connie confirming Earle's view that the Macks were through in baseball, the meeting ended, Roy and Earle retreating to their offices in separate parts of Connie Mack Stadium.

New York Times scribe John Drebinger cast a skeptical eye on the happenings regarding the A's. Echoing Art Morrow, Drebinger noted that while most were bemoaning the potential transfer of the team and the lack of loyalty *to* the city, the future Hall of Fame writer (1973 Spink Award winner) wondered where the fans were and what loyalty had been shown to the Macks *by* the city. All of this was reminiscent of the Braves' experience before their move from Boston to Milwaukee, as well as the Browns pre-Baltimore. Both teams were now achieving great success at the gate. The only solution, according to Drebinger, was a sale to Arnold Johnson's group and then Johnson in turn selling Connie Mack Stadium to Bob Carpenter of the Phillies. A month before, Carpenter had suspected that the Yankees were deeply involved in pushing Johnson's case and sensed he would be drawn into it unwillingly. "Who is Webb to tell other teams what to do?" protested Carpenter.[21] For his part, Carpenter had already noted that his rental agreement of 10 cents a head was a "pretty good rental agreement"[22] and that he had zero interest in buying the ballpark. It would seem that the Yankees divestiture of their stadium real estate made sense to their fellow owner.

About a week after the board meeting, Roy and Earle, in a burst of amity, intimated that they had found their knight in shining armor who would buy Connie's stock for $600,000 and invest another $2 million for rebuilding. The brothers were willing to combine their majority stock and work cooperatively to run the club for the foreseeable future. Details were to follow in the next two weeks, said Roy, and, while the Mack duo would stay in the front office, a new general manager would be brought in to handle baseball affairs. Senators manager "Bucky" Harris and White Sox general manager Frank Lane were names being mentioned by the press.

Numbers were beginning to change. The Sylk group, which had said it would match Arnold Johnson's $4.5 million, was now confirmed to have offered $2 million less. The Macks, recipients of this sum, would pay off their debts, leaving them a total of $800,000 to $1,000,000. Connie would remain as honorary chairman, while Roy would stay on as executive vice president. All three Macks would be given the chance to reinvest, and $2 million would be made available for players, managers, executives, and a parking lot. Johnson's number had also been cut, now being reported at $4,250,000. Shining a small light on things to come, Sylk declared that Johnson, despite claims to the contrary, had never made a formal offer in writing to back up his multimillion dollar bid. "I asked Roy and his attorney if they had received a bona fide offer from Kansas City," continued the drug store king, "and they said they hadn't."[23] A source close to the A's confirmed this. The Sylk offer was the only legitimate offer on the table and was ready to be executed; Johnson's reported offer was not a concrete one. Always a voice of reality, Harry Sylk said the Mack sons' expressions of finding a backer was merely "wishing out loud."[24]

All this bode ill for Arnold Johnson. What was he to do with Blues Stadium if he couldn't come through with the Athletics? It was possible that he could sell it to the city for a half million dollars as part of the two million dollar bond. Would the city still be a buyer if the Major Leagues now seemed out of reach? If he were successful in buying and moving the team, what would be the status of Connie Mack Stadium? Bob Carpenter was outspoken in his unwillingness to buy. Real estate under the ballpark was worth something (as he had found out in his sale of Yankee Stadium land to the Knights of Columbus), but with a Phillies' lease running through 1957, demolition was out of the question.

Returning to Kansas City to meet with officials, Johnson was hopeful that his offer for the A's would result in success. In all photographs smiling the broad grin of a man who always gets what he wants, Johnson felt that he was the front-runner, and the Associated Press reported that his offer was still at $4.5 million. Kansas City was behind him in force and Baseball Committee Chairman Robert Benson, city manager L. P. Cookingham, and Councilman Joseph M. Nolan were planning a visit to Milwaukee to glean further details on the city's experience with the Braves. Along with across-the-board support from politicos such as Councilman Benson and Mayor Kemp, businessmen were beginning to step up as well, among them Alex G. Lewi, president of the Macy store, and Barney Helzberg, of Helzberg's Jewelers. Helzberg had placed an ad of a little boy praying, with the text "and maybe I shouldn't ask for this but please bring the A's to Kansas City."[25]

Startling new developments emerged when the A's board of directors met on August 31. A new scheme was put forth to keep the team in Philly, but with the stipulation that Roy would be in the mix. Roy's demand that he stay involved was an obstacle increasingly hard to surmount. McCloskey, the millionaire contractor, had put forward his interest in providing financing and, although it was quickly withdrawn, he was still lingering in the background because of the latest news. The plan put forth would involve a buyout of Connie and Earle's stock for $1.2 million. Another million would be put toward a partial payoff of the Connecticut General mortgage. Operating capital would come to another $500,000. For now, it was a plan without a backer.

What of the actual offers? The Sylk–Greenfield syndicate's offer of $2.5 million for control of the franchise was rejected outright as insufficient. Notwithstanding this report, Harry Sylk asserted that "as far as I know we're still in the picture."[26] In addition, Sylk told the Associated Press that, in this secret meeting of the board, he himself had rejected a Mack counteroffer for the syndicate to buy only the stock held by Connie for $600,000. The reason for not accepting this proposal was that the old man's share was only 42 percent of the total, keeping Sylk and Greenfield out of power. Roy and Earle would both remain under this plan.

Arnold Johnson's bid, whether $4.25 or $4.5 million as variously mentioned in recent articles, was now slashed dramatically to $3.1. According to *The Sporting News*, Johnson had come to the realization that Connie Mack Stadium would be harder to sell and he had reduced his offer commensurately. *The Sporting News* further reported that McShain, who had put up money (slightly more than $1.7 million) in 1950 for Roy and Earle to buy the 872 Treasury shares at the time of the Connecticut General loan, had been willing to buy Connie's 302 shares for $604,000. The Mack daughters were pressing for this to go through, and McShain had a check at the ready.

Roy and Earle's reconciliation was predictably short lived. Earle, fearful of a McShain–Roy Mack alliance, refused to give his consent. McShain then offered to buy out Earle's shares at the 1950 valuation of $2,000 per share, but Earle, who according to McShain had signed an agreement, reneged. Roy then tried to buy Earle's shares for $300,000, with payments of $50,000 per year over six years. Earle responded by saying *he* would buy out Roy for a half million dollars in cash. As if this was not enough confusion, there was now an unknown fourth bidder for the team at $3 million, although it was not seriously being considered. As for McShain, he was soured enough by the mess that he announced he would not in anyway be involved if Earle was still on the scene.

A new group of players threw their hat in the ring. Isadore (Speed) Sley made known his interest in the A's. Sley, the president of Racquet Garage Corporation, represented an unknown partnership. Speculation had it that a prime investor in this group was the son of a chain store mogul. Sley was not new to bidding on Major League teams. In 1949, he attempted to get control of a piece of the Senators and also bid on the St. Louis Browns. A rabid A's fan and apparent glutton for punishment, Sley had taken to vacationing in West Palm Beach to watch the A's during spring training.

The dollar figures were wildly inconsistent. The Johnson price, which had gone from $4.5 million to $4.25 to $3.1, had now reportedly inched up to $3.75 million. In an Associated Press report on the haggling over Connie Mack Stadium, Bob Carpenter had confirmed that on September 9 his thoughts had been sought out on a price for the ballpark. Would $2 million be reasonable, he was asked? While Carpenter would not commit to any number, he ventured that $1.7 would be more in line. As a negotiating tool, the Phillies' owner mentioned that he was looking into new construction in West Philadelphia.

The morning of September 22 saw a meeting between Johnson and the Macks in Philadelphia. It was hoped that the day would end with a sale and move to Kansas City. Johnson's hope was that after an official sale agreement was arrived at, speedy confirmation and cooperation would come from the league as a whole to facilitate the move west. Roy seemed finally willing to accept his fate and the hopelessness of saving the team for Philadelphia, as well as his position within it. His father and brother were getting increasingly anxious, as further holdups would, in their minds, further deteriorate the value of their holdings.

Johnson's offer seemingly was the original $4.5 million, but there was a new qualification. Without Connie Mack Stadium, he was willing to pay only $2.5 million for the franchise alone. Obviously, Johnson was not going to pay his fully offered price, facility included, unless he knew ahead of time what he would get. The old Johnson risk avoidance was hard to shake.

While Bob Carpenter was resisting the pressure to own Mack Stadium, or, alternatively, trying to drive the price toward his $1.7 million comfort zone, he presented another offer. Carpenter was willing to accept $100,000 in exchange for canceling the lease. Back at Blues Stadium, Johnson was reported to have already spent $30–40,000 on preliminary surveys for double decking. A push to close the deal was imperative for him to not have wasted this money. Johnson made it perfectly clear that any deal for the A's was contingent on a subsequent transfer of the team. No move, no deal.

These were two separate events that needed different approvals. The tender for the team needed to be accepted by the Macks first. However, the Macks could not guarantee that the team would be moved. As for the American League, they needed to approve the sale *and* then the transfer. It was not certain that each vote would have the same result. A further complication was that it was decided at the 1953 winter meetings that a Major League team could apply to draft a minor league territory only during the period from October 1 through December 1. The two events, sale and transfer, would have to be coordinated so they would occur simultaneously, or close to it. The announcement of Johnson's bid in August and the coincident announcement of the Kansas City bond approval was the model he was looking for.

When the doors opened at the conclusion of the three-hour meeting, Roy and Earle had nothing to announce. With delays being the normal course of action (or inaction), the risks of getting sanction from League owners during the acceptable timeframe seemed uncertain. As of yet, no meetings of American League owners had been scheduled. Even had a meeting been called, there was not unequivocal support of Johnson or a move. Griffith now went further with his opposition. The longtime friend of Connie Mack expressed his surprise at the lack of real information, as opposed to rumor. If the sale and move to Kansas City was on the brink of occurring, he didn't know about it and felt he would if the stories had any substance. Furthermore, in Griffith's opinion, "Mr. Johnson's ties with the New York Yankees are entirely too close." He went on to say that while he knew the land had been sold to the Knights of Columbus, Johnson was "still interested in the corporation that has leased the structure itself to the ball club."[27] Griffith reiterated that the league would be thrown off balance, adding a travel burden to the other teams. The Senators' leader was not alone in his antagonism to a sale and move. It was reported that Boston and Detroit were also resistant.

Finally, a summit of league owners was set to take place on September 28 in New York. President Harridge called the meeting, since the team owners would be in town for the Giants–Indians World Series, to confer with Roy Mack as to what should be decided in regard to the future of the A's. Harridge also conceded that there were offers for the club other than Johnson's. It was mentioned that Johnson's offer was only verbal, echoing Harry Sylk's claim that no concrete written offer existed. Johnson insisted that he had the cash for the team, not like the stock and loans that he claimed were proffered by other interested parties to back "a losing proposition" in Philadelphia.[28]

The next day, "The Old Fox" ramped up his hostility toward the whole proposition. He was completely opposed to Johnson and Kansas City. Confident that his colleagues would vote down a move, Griffith produced for reporters Harridge's memo announcing the meeting. While no mention of a move to Kansas City was contained in the bulletin, owners were told to send representatives who had the "power to act."[29] League rules required at least six of the eight owners to ratify a franchise shift. Griffith mentioned the Red Sox and Orioles as fellow opponents. Loyalty to his friend had its limits. Griffith proclaimed that "there isn't anything I wouldn't do for Connie Mack, but I wouldn't vote for Kansas City."[30] Griffith was not against the concept of the A's leaving Philadelphia. He said that cities such as Montreal, Toronto, or Buffalo would all meet with his approval. The real action was about to commence. Sides for and against began lining up as the first meeting was ready to begin.

1. Associated Press. "Community Drive Urged by Mayor Clark to Help Save Athletics for Philadelphia," *New York Times*, July 9, 1954, p. 11.

2. Munzel, Edgar. "Lane Predicts Two Majors of Ten Clubs," *The Sporting News,* May 5, 1954, p. 1.

3. Morrow, Art. "Philadelphia Frets over A's Future as Macks Deny 'Bids,'" *The Sporting News*, June 16, 1954, p. 15.

4. Ibid.

5. Morrow, Art. "Roy and Earle Mack Feud as 'Save the A's' Drive Fizzles," *The Sporting News*, August 4, 1954, p. 15.

6. Mehl, Ernest. *The Kansas City Athletics*. New York: Holt, 1956, p. 46.

7. Mehl, p. 41.

8. Mehl, p. 43.

9. Kelly, Ray. "A's Fans Skip Ship, but Roy Mack Sticks to 'Burning Deck' to Finish," *The Sporting News*, August 11, 1954, p. 7.

10. Mehl, Ernest. "Kansas City Backs Offer for A's with Park Bond Issue," *The Sporting News*, August 11, 1954, p. 7.

11. *Washington Post and Times Herald*. "$4 Million Bid for A's to Go to Kansas City," August 4, 1954, p. 25.

12. *Chicago Daily Tribune*. "Earle Gives Views," August 5, 1954, p. D2.

13. *Washington Post and Times Herald*. "Griffith Against A's Shift to Kansas City," August 6, 1954, p. 34.

14. Mehl, p. 56.

15. Associated Press. "'Don't Have a Dime,' Son Earle Says," *Washington Post and Times Herald*, August 5, 1954, p. 29.

16. *Washington Post and Times Herald*. "Griffith Against A's Shift to Kansas City," August 6, 1954, p. 34.

17. McBride, C. E. "Sporting Comment," *Kansas City Star*, October 27, 1953, p. 17.

18. *New York Times*. "$4,500,000 Kansas City Offer for A's Matched in Philadelphia," August 7, 1954, p. 8.

19. *Chicago Daily Tribune*. "Negotiations on Sale of A's to Open Today," August 10, 1954, p. B2.

20. Associated Press. "16 Civic Leaders Will Try Again Today to Keep the Athletics in Philadelphia," *New York Times*, August 10, 1954, p. 22.

21. Baumgartner, Stan. "'Let Webb Move,' Carpenter Retorts," *The Sporting News*, July 29, 1953, p. 6.

22. *Washington Post and Times Herald*. "$4 Million Bid for A's to Go to Kansas City," August 4, 1954, p. 25.

23. Morrow, Art. "Local Capital Seen Rallying Behind A's," *The Sporting News*, August 24, 1954.

24. *Chicago Daily Tribune*. "Macks Find Angel to Keep Athletics in Philadelphia," August 20, 1954, p. B2.

25. Mehl, p. 52.

26. *Washington Post and Times Herald*. "Newest Plan to Keep A's in Philly," September 1, 1954, p. 27.

27. Associated Press. "Macks Meet; See Trouble for Johnson," *Chicago Daily Tribune*, September 23, 1954, p. D2.

28. Associated Press. "Athletics' Sale to Be Discussed by League Owners Tuesday," *New York Times*, September 24, 1954, p. 24.

29. Associated Press. "Griffith Opposes Shift of A's to Kansas City," *Los Angeles Times*, September 25, 1954, p. B1.

30. Ibid.

Chapter 5

THE FIRST MEETING

The Commodore Hotel, on the corner of 42nd St. and 7th Avenue, was built in 1920. Named for Commodore Cornelius Vanderbilt, railroad baron and shipbuilder, the Commodore Hotel had an interesting history. In 1948 Congressman Richard Nixon, as a member of the House Un-American Activities Committee, surprised suspected spy Alger Hiss there with his accuser, Whittaker Chambers. Earlier, F. Scott and Zelda Fitzgerald were thrown out of the Commodore. Whether the A's would also be asked to move on would be the topic of this meeting, with accusations flying between the participants and doubts about the motives of the magnates of the American League, the Yankees.

Some general issues were seemingly agreed upon going into the meeting. The A's were operating on a threadbare budget and needed financial help. Possible league takeover was one option, a sale to Arnold Johnson was another, and an infusion of money to allow Roy to forge ahead was a third. The troublesome relationship between Earle and Roy Mack was consistently at its worst when a deal was near. Also, it was clear that the relationship between American League owners was not sanguine. Griffith, already vocally opposed to the sale and shift of the A's, expressed his hope that more would join his side, among them his own son-in-law, Joe Cronin, general manager of the Red Sox. Three votes could derail Johnson's bid.

League President Harridge, citing previous success within the City of Brotherly Love, expressed his dismay at the prospective loss of Philadelphia to the junior circuit. While Kansas City had a good pool of citizens to attract to Major League baseball, Philly was at that time the third-largest city in the country. With the builders McShain and McCloskey expected to be at Roy's side, and Johnson with his Kansas City congregation also in attendance, Harridge expressed his mission for the meeting as one of clarification, rather than confrontation.

Johnson, his attorney Edward L. Vollers of Millikan, Vollers, and Parsons (who left the firm to work on baseball), Councilman Benson, and others came as part of a seven-person delegation that presented Kansas City's case. With the Helzberg's praying boy advertisement on prominent display, Councilman Benson pitched Kansas City as another success story in the mold of Milwaukee or Baltimore. While the city was not an urban giant on the scale of Philadelphia and had no stadium suitably sized for Major League ball, the woeful A's would benefit from a change in scenery. Minds were beginning to be made up.

Supporting the Johnson contingent were the Yankees (Topping and Webb), the White Sox (general manager Frank Lane, and vice president Chuck Comiskey, grandson of Charles Comiskey), and, with great ambivalence, Clarence Miles, president of the Orioles. The anti-Johnson set was an embodiment of anti-Yankee sentiment and suspicion. In addition to Griffith and Briggs of Detroit, who had their negative opinions already on record, ex-slugger and present general manager of the Cleveland Indians Hank Greenberg and Cronin seemed likely to ally with the group against Johnson. "They'll never get me to vote for Kansas City," said Briggs.[1] If a vote were taken at the September 28 meeting, it was clear that, at this moment, Johnson's offer would be spurned. It was likely that if he was rejected outright, Johnson would be out of the picture for good.

No vote was taken. Instead Roy Mack was given a reprieve of two weeks to find the cash to buy out brother Earle. Earle agreed to sell his 163 shares for $450,000, whether Roy stayed on board or not. At the same time that Earle was asking for $2,760 per share, the league ordered that Roy show in two weeks' time that he could purchase his father's 48 percent of outstanding shares (302 of the 628 non-Treasury held stock). Defeat was clear to Earle. "We're licked," he said. "I can't imagine why Roy insists upon trying."[2]

As to the deals on the table, the Johnson number was officially reported as $3.375 million for the team *and* Connie Mack Stadium (*The Washington Post* reported it as $3.75 million, possibly a misprint). In light of his recent two offers of $4.5 million for team and stadium, or $2.5 million for the team alone, Johnson was now valuing the ballpark property at a mere $875,000 when Bob Carpenter had already spoken out that he might be interested at a $1.7 million price tag. To further complicate an already cluttered story, a new offer came to the fore.

Tommy Richardson, president of the Eastern League and member of the A's board of directors since 1951, made it known that he was representing a Philadelphia group ready to match any offer, as well as keep the team where it was. While Richardson had recommended that the Macks take the initial $4.5 million offer when presented, he had watched the Johnson numbers drop and then, on September 21, received the same option to buy the team given Johnson. The following day Richardson relayed that "Johnson had demanded a showdown."[3] Richardson pled his case to Harridge that, in the interest of fairness, his offer should be subject to the same rules as Johnson's. While Johnson had six weeks to get his proposal together, Richardson had only about one week. Richardson announced his offer along with a guarantee that the A's would stay in Philadelphia at least through 1955. While Arnold Johnson's offer was dependent on an immediate shift to Kansas City, to whom he had "given his word,"[4] Richardson's tender was also conditioned upon the ability to relocate, but only after a year's time. He also strongly believed that Johnson would quickly resell the team.

After seven hours of listening to the rival presentations, (including one from Thomas Gray of the San Francisco Committee for Major League Baseball, who did not have a concrete offer), followed by much discussion, the owners adjourned for a fortnight. It was enough to wipe the smile off Johnson's face. Stunned by the delay, Johnson "came out of the meeting on leaden feet."[5] Ernie Mehl reported a bystander's comment that Johnson didn't have a chance and that he had wasted his time. For his part, Johnson would not quit. Mehl's account of this and subsequent meetings always mentions the odds of getting the A's to Kansas City. On the night of September 28, those odds were 100 to 1.

The next meeting of American League owners was set for October 12 in Chicago. Johnson rode in the front car of the roller coaster ride that marked this interim. On the upward slope was an enthusiastic ticket drive started in Kansas City. While Mehl cited naysayers who doubted that the plan would work, an effort to deliver tangible proof was necessary to show those who would decide the city's fate that the desire for Major League baseball was present. Al Lewi was placed in charge of the operation, with Arnold Johnson's blessing. A flood of requests came in from the surrounding areas. Having pushed forward the notion that the future Kansas City Athletics would draw from a wide swath, it was rewarding to the local advocates to see ticket demand from Kansas, Iowa, Nebraska, Arkansas, and, of course, Missouri. The first five days brought in 10,000 letters of support, and it seemed within reason to expect a demand for more than $1 million. Of course, none of the pledges were guaranteed.

Pushing Johnson's bid downward was a growing concern over his entanglements with Yankee brass. The American League had decided to delve into the business relationship between the participants. The league could suggest several possible actions. In the case of Automatic Canteen, Johnson could be required to either buy out Topping and Webb or sell his own holdings. Johnson's ownership of Yankee Stadium, which provided a more direct conflict of interest, could also be at risk with a possible League stipulation that he divest himself of the property. Until this time, few newspaper accounts had mentioned the deeper financial interaction between the three men. If mentioned at all, Johnson's landlord status to the Yankees was glossed over.

Syndicate baseball had been a scourge of the National League during the 1890s, when intertwined ownership of franchises was allowed, to the detriment of true competition. At the turn of the century, Giants' owner Andrew Freedman, along with John Brush, owner of the Reds and shareholder in the Giants, and two other National League owners attempted to form the National League Base Ball Trust. With the support of Frank Robison of the Cardinals and Arthur Soden of the Braves, the trust, which would foster common ownership of all league clubs and assign players from one club to another, thereby influencing competition, needed one more vote for passage. It failed. Ban Johnson, founder of the American League, felt "syndicatism" was necessary for league survival. Charles Somers helped finance entries from Cleveland, Chicago, and Philadelphia before divesting these holdings and focusing his attention on the Boston Red Sox. Outlawed in 1910, fears of syndicate ball were in the air again in the fall of 1954.

Out of the blue, a roadblock was put in Johnson's way in the form of a proclamation by Dan Topping that the Yanks' would vote against the proposed A's move. In 1953 Topping had gone on record declining any damage payment, but now he had changed his mind. "We're through being gentlemen about it," he griped.[6] Loss of Kansas City territory was the sticking point for Topping. "Unless we receive substantial payment for being deprived of our territory there,"[7] the Yankees would join those in opposition to the move. For his part, Johnson was prepared to recompense the Yankees with a reasonable settlement, although he would not go on record with what he considered adequate. "I have known right along I must make restitution to the Yankees and to the American Association," said Johnson. "I intend to be fair about it."[8] AA indemnification was $50,000, most recently paid by the National League for the rights to Milwaukee.

How real was this Yankee opposition? All along the Yankees claimed that they would not stand in the way of Kansas City acquiring a Major League baseball team. As for Johnson, he was both a friend and business partner to Topping and Webb. The New York Times maintained that Topping had already made an agreement with Arnold Johnson that it would not take very much to meet the Yankees' needs. This understanding was reached when Johnson purchased Yankee and Blues Stadium, nearly one year before. Despite Topping averring that he would oppose the move if not rewarded appropriately, he went on to say that his comment "should not be interpreted as opposition to the A's transfer."[9] It all seemed like a smoke screen—the Yankees pretending they were simply another team looking at the proposal with an unbiased eye.

In light of all this, Johnson told President Harridge that he might have to take his bid off the table. Also of concern to Johnson was whether there was enough time remaining to make Blues Stadium ready for the 1955 campaign. Engineers had reported that it would take six months to complete the expansion. Withdrawal was a distinct possibility, and, if total approval were not granted at the upcoming Chicago get-together, it would be a fact, threatened Johnson, engaging in some gamesmanship.

As to Richardson's offer, Johnson was, indeed, surprised. The turmoil between the first and second meetings only made Johnson's case more difficult. Richardson claimed to have raised funds to meet Johnson's bid, incorrectly cited as $3.75 million. The Richardson group also listed the cities that his partners would consider if the team failed at the close of the 1955 season. Toronto, Montreal, Los Angeles, Houston, San Francisco, and St. Paul were on the list of possible destinations. Behind the scenes, though, there were insinuations that Johnson was the only authentic bidder. Although the tender was verbal, one highly placed American League official said, "only Johnson has the only bona fide offer."[10] Just recently Commissioner Ford Frick had a different take on verbal agreements, as stated in a June 1 memo to all the big league clubs. As far as Frick was concerned, "oral agreements are not binding" and the owners were urged to "confirm verbal agreements immediately by an exchange of telegrams or letters."[11]

On the eve of the October 12 gathering, scheduled to take place at the Blackstone Hotel on South Michigan Avenue, Shirley Povich of the *Washington Post* astutely assessed the situation. The meeting, said Povich, "will be a test of Yankee power in the American League councils." Further, Webb and Topping "are plumping hard for the shift to Kansas City" and the A's acceptance of Johnson's offer of $3.375 million.[12] Povich was already aware of the considerable pressure being placed on Phillies owner Bob Carpenter to buy Connie Mack Stadium, despite his unwillingness to do so. Detroit's "Spike" Briggs was seemingly leading the anti-Yankee forces. Clearly, the best move for the American League would be to Los Angeles, "unless the Yankees can talk them [American League owners] out of it."[13]

All hell would break loose at this meeting. Offers came out of the woodwork for the beleaguered franchise. The Macks were not the only family shown to be dysfunctional. The American League president and owners proved themselves to be contentious and conniving. The Yankees, for their part, were a specter in the background, never speaking up, but making their preferences rule the day. And when the dust settled, there was still no resolution.

President Harridge pushed for a final determination. Headed into the meeting, Harridge declared that it was not conducive to the health of the American League to keep wavering on such an important issue. Possibly heeding his advice were the expected attendees:

- Joe Cronin, Boston Red Sox
- Dan Topping, Del Webb, and George Weiss, New York Yankees
- Roy and (possibly) Earle Mack, Philadelphia Athletics
- Calvin Griffith, Washington Senators
- Hank Greenberg and Nate Dolin, Cleveland Indians
- Walter O. (Spike) Briggs, Detroit Tigers
- Clarence W. Miles and Clyde Y. Morris, Baltimore Orioles
- Charles Comiskey and Frank Lane, Chicago White Sox

This gathering would hear from at five least groups proposing to buy the A's, all with different plans in store for the team.

The first to present was Tommy Richardson, who, despite all the previous talk about matching Johnson's $3.375 million, could only produce a check in the amount of $450,000 to buy Earle Mack's share of the team. Pleading to the ownership group for more time to raise funds, Richardson was seen huddling with Charles O. Finley, a Chicago insurance man and representative of a Chicago–Gary group also interested in the team. Additionally, Jack Rensel, an advertising agency man, entered the fray at the front of a group willing to keep the team in its native home. Rensel, derogatorily described by Ernie Mehl as a man who "peddled gum contracts to major league baseball players,"[14] had no firm offer to convey. Mehl noted that Rensel was ignored during the session.

Calvin Griffith, nephew and adopted son of Clark, was instructed to vote against Kansas City in his capacity as executive director of the Senators. That was not the only thing that Calvin brought to the table to block Johnson's bid. Griffith had on hand an offer from a Washington partnership. This bid, for $2.856 million, came from Lee DeOrsey, tax attorney and business manager for entertainer Arthur Godfrey, and Joseph Tucci, a retired plumbing contractor and horse breeder. The offer, delivered in writing to Roy Mack on September 23, was another legitimate proposal to consider. DeOrsey had some sports ownership experience, having once owned 25 percent of the Washington Redskins. Godfrey was not involved. The D.C. group claimed that this was "an offer just as good as that of Arnold Johnson's," plus they would keep the team in its native home.[15] Johnson, frustrations mounting, was incredulous. "Why take $2,856,000 when you can get $3,375,000? As for Los Angeles, they can't put a club out there. I've studied that situation. Just say that I'm ready to get in, put up the money—and say nothing," Johnson said.[16]

Johnson's reference to Los Angeles came after the West Coast city took center stage, with various players pitching the Southern California Mecca. Griffith, the former Senators batboy, announced that he was going to act as a representative of a Los Angeles group that would shift the A's to Southern California. This was scoffed at, with one prominent baseball man saying that would be a $10 million deal. To pave the way for a Los Angeles team, Phil Wrigley, owner of the Chicago Cubs, but also possessor of the Pacific Coast League's Los Angeles entry, would need to be indemnified, possibly to the tune of $2 million. Officials from Los Angeles County appeared to announce imminent plans for the construction of a new facility to be built to Major League specifications.

Bill Veeck, out of baseball since unloading the Browns the previous year, announced that he owned the option to Phil Wrigley's Los Angeles Wrigley Field, home to Pacific Coast League baseball. The flamboyant ex-owner roamed the halls of the Blackstone, rumors abounding that he would lead a syndicate to buy the A's and take them west. Veeck was not allowed to speak to the owners and hovered on the periphery of the meeting.

Carrying the most weight for Los Angeles' hopes was the presentation made by Robert Thompson, associate of the Murchisons of Dallas. Clint Murchison Sr., who had made his fortune from investments in real estate, railroads, construction, and oil, and his son, Clint Jr., who would later achieve his own sports fame as owner of the Dallas Cowboys from 1959 to 1984, were ready to buy. Willing to match Johnson's $3.375 million offer "and close the deal tonight with cash on the barrelhead," the Murchison consortium planned to move the team to sunny California "as soon as humanly possible."[17] Their target was Opening Day 1955. However, if mandated by the league, Thompson said the group would be willing to stay in Philadelphia for one more year.

Johnson knew the owners were listening long and hard to the Murchison proposal and had to be a bit concerned. When it was his turn, the enthusiasm already on display in Kansis City was his focus. The ticket drive had been a resounding success, with 811,109 ordered at a total of $1,897,252. Most of the pledges had come from big businesses in the area. Playing to the sentiment felt by league executives for the Macks, Johnson said he was willing to allow Roy Mack to stay on board, even though Roy, who had arrived to the meeting late because a flood delayed his train, had been seen in conference with Calvin Griffith and Tommy Richardson, both Johnson opponents. To quell the palpable worries about his close Yankee relationship, he let it be known that he would be willing to sell Yankee Stadium if the club owners demanded. While Johnson had already explained that he did not violate any rules on the prohibition for one man to have financial interest in more than one club, he restated "all I own is the real estate, I don't have any connection with the baseball team."[18] Even so, he was willing to make this important concession. Johnson also mentioned that Nathaniel Leverone, chairman (and founder) of Automatic Canteen, would be involved with the baseball organization. The chances of Johnson's success, according to Mehl, were now 50–50.

Will Harridge had been clear at the outset that he wanted the matter resolved at this meeting. Before convening, Harridge claimed that neither the Richardson nor the DeOrsey–Tucci groups had been heard from. Additionally, Harridge mentioned that Johnson's was "the only bona fide offer we have received."[19] At meeting's end, the situation was more muddied than before. Richardson had seemingly fumbled his chance, while DeOrsey and Tucci had presented an offer, although most likely an insufficient one. The Murchison proposal was powerful money at hand, and a move to Los Angeles appeared to be in the best interests of the league as a whole.

When the vote was taken, it was announced as unanimous in favor of Arnold Johnson. The $3.375 million bid was in two parts. The team garnered a $1.7 million price, mostly going to the Macks, with Roy and Earle getting $450,000 each and Connie receiving $604,000. Connie Mack Stadium would cost the additional $1.675 million. As in the Yankee Stadium deal, when Arnold Johnson had most of the money set up with prearranged deals (Knights of Columbus sale, mortgages, loans) and the Kansas City stadium bond approval, which provided Johnson with necessary funds before he made a firm offer for the A's, Johnson had the Philadelphia stadium piece of the puzzle already covered. Johnson and Carpenter had already agreed on the sale of the stadium for $1.675 million. Johnson entered the select club of Major League owners for a mere $1.7 million. Blues Stadium renovations would cost around $3 million, but it seemed that was taken care of at no cost to Johnson. The new $2 million bond, coupled with excess money from previous bond issues would cover that. As to Blues Stadium itself, Johnson declared he would be willing to sell it to the city for $500,000, "hardly a third of its value."[20]

What did that revelation mean? If the Yankees could have sold Blues Stadium for $1.5 million dollars, why would they part with it for so much less, embedded within the entire Yankee Stadium–Blues Stadium transaction? While Topping, Webb, and Johnson were friends, did friendship alone entitle Johnson to, as he implied, something of a giveaway? What would the Yankee motivation be to do that for Johnson? Johnson's ownership of the ballpark gave him a leg up on competition, which was scrambling for playing fields.

Back to the vote, the unanimous decision was to apply to both the sale and the transfer to Kansas City, according to Harridge. Sales and relocations had different standards for approval—five of eight for a sale, six of eight for a move. Convenience was Harridge's driving force. He explained that the owners agreed to the move even before the Macks granted final approval to Johnson, so that the owners would not need to be called together at another time. Harridge, who asserted that Johnson would be paying the price in full, also relayed that Roy Mack was given an extension until 10 AM the following Monday to agree to the Johnson transaction. Though granted as a gesture of respect to the Mack clan, it added a bit of uncertainty to the process.

Howls of indignation were heard immediately. Walter Briggs, who had left the meeting before the final vote to attend a banquet for his newly appointed manager Bucky Harris, was furious. Although it could be argued that the fate of one of the eight league franchises was more important than a reception, Briggs did at least leave his proxy vote against the move admitting that he could "smell a plot" of the Yankees.[21] While Harridge had claimed that the Tigers and Senators had "jumped on the bandwagon," this was clearly not so.[22] The Senators were even more outraged.

Calvin Griffith officially protested the vote. He conceded that a vote was taken, but in no way did Washington see it as final. "No mention was made of specific provisos we entered," said the younger Griffith, "and any announcement that we favored Kansas City is full of misunderstandings. Let's set the record straight."[23] Griffith went on to set out the Senators' preferences for the A's. First, one more year in Philadelphia, second, a move to Los Angeles, and third, a move to Kansas City. The Capitol team was not alone in these wishes. It seemed that Joe Cronin shared the same desires. That there were three votes to deny the move seemed clear—Washington, Boston, and Detroit. Griffith was also planning on enlisting the support of Hank Greenberg and the Indians. "We have a lot more support around the league, and there may be more new developments before Monday's deadline," he cautioned.[24]

The octogenarian Griffith also spoke out. Still unsettled by the triumvirate of Johnson–Topping–Webb, Clark Griffith said, "I will definitely look into the financial affairs of Mr. Johnson. I know he owns the Kansas City stadium as well as Yankee Stadium. There's a definite rule in baseball [Rule 20] that no man can have any connections with another club directly or indirectly. I also have heard that Johnson and Dan Topping are business associates in a large corporation. I'm going to object if Mr. Johnson is going to own the ground the Yankees play on and then own a club in the same league."[25]

In fairness to Johnson, he had announced that he would sell Yankee Stadium and that he didn't own the ground, literally, as he had sold that to the Knights. "My position in regard to the Yankees has been fully disclosed to the league," said Johnson, "and the league is apparently satisfied."[26] Apparently not all members of the league were assuaged, and Griffith had a valid claim that these items should be looked into. While it was claimed before the meeting that the American League offices were looking into these business arrangements, it was apparent, based on Griff's remarks, that was not being done.

More objections were heard. A loud one came from Bob Carpenter of the Phillies. It had been clear all along that Carpenter did not want to buy Connie Mack Stadium, for the same reasons that Topping and Webb unloaded Yankee Stadium. Pressure, whether from the American League or Major League baseball in general, was applied firmly to Mr. Carpenter. "We weren't anxious to buy the park because we didn't want to get into the real estate business."[27] However, $1.675 million later, he had himself an old ballpark.

On a lighter note, Bill Veeck, who had not even been allowed into the meeting room, was stunned by Johnson's approval. Veeck had thought he had the deal "sewed up," although he never made a bid or spoke at the meeting. On a more serious note, a reporter thought that Veeck made it clear that Del Webb had blocked his efforts to get the A's to Los Angeles. As Shirley Povich had written, Yankee power was on the line, and on October 13, the line held.

The extension until Monday given to Roy brought to light the difficulties of separating the team from its kin. The A's were truly part, if not the sum, of the Mack family, and Roy was in emotional turmoil over the tide of events sweeping over him. One of Roy's overriding fears was the fate of his son, Connie III. Like his father before him, Roy wanted a job in the ball club for his boy. Harridge pointed out "that by the time his son was ready to assume operation of the club, there might not be anything left of it."[28] It wasn't clear what would happen if Roy and Earle did not sell their stock. It didn't seem plausible that they could continue on their own, and local backing seemed, at the moment, equally far-fetched. With no money in the coffers, declining attendance, and mounting debts, Earle was sure that without a sale to Johnson, his father would be broke. There seemed to be no other solution than selling. A league official confided that Roy had wanted the deal with Johnson done. There seemed little doubt that, come the deadline, the final sale would take place.

Povich summed up the meeting: once again, the Yankees demonstrated their control on league matters. As the tail "wagging the entire league," the Yanks put across one of "their own pet projects." Despite all the opposition that had been loudly expressed, the Yankees got their way. Besides putting their friend in the cozy position of owning a competitor, the Yanks were hoping to get a hefty price for their Kansas City holdings. Webb, "who fancies himself a king-maker" steered the owners to Kansas City and, although he had always been in the pro–Los Angeles camp, he did not support that proposition. It was this domineering manner that led Walter

Briggs to tell the press, "Anything the Yankees are for, I'm against."[29] In the Yankee-run world, even this no vote could become a yes.

---

1. Morrow, Art. "Richardson Group 'to Be Ready to Act,'" *The Sporting News,* October 6, 1954, p. 4.
2. Mehl, Ernest. *The Kansas City Athletics.* New York: Holt, 1956, p. 61.
3. Morrow, p. 4.
4. Mehl, p. 58.
5. Morrow, p. 4.
6. *The Sporting News.* "Johnson Offers Reasonable Payment for Kansas City Invasion," October 13, 1954, p. 11.
7. Prell, Edward. "Delay in Athletics' Sale Cools Johnson," *Chicago Daily Tribune,* October 17, 1954, p. D1.
8. *Los Angeles Times.* "Johnson Willing to Pay New York Yankees," October 8, 1954, p. C1.
9. Ibid.
10. Prell, Edward. "Delay in Athletics' Sale Cools Johnson," *Chicago Daily Tribune,* October 17, 1954, p. D1.
11. Memo from the Office of the Commissioner, Notice No. 25, June 1, 1953.
12. Povich, Shirley. "This Morning with Shirley Povich," *Washington Post and Times Herald,* October 12, 1954, p. 25.
13. Ibid.
14. Mehl, p. 73.
15. Addie, Bob. "DeOrsey, Joe Tucci Enter Bid to Buy A's," *Washington Post and Times Herald,* October 12, 1954, p. 25.
16. Prell, Edward. "Harridge Urges Decision Today on Athletics' Future," *Chicago Daily Tribune,* October 12, 1954, p. B1.
17. Povich, Shirley. "Pressure on Move to California Is Resisted," *Washington Post and Times Herald,* October 13, 1954, p. 29.
18. *Los Angeles Times.* "AL Owners Meet, Decide A's Plight," October 12, 1954, p. C1.
19. *New York Times.* "League to Discuss A's Plight," October 12, 1954, p. 32.
20. Prell, Edward. "League Votes A's Shift to Kansas City," *Chicago Daily Tribune,* October 13, 1954, p. B1.
21. Mehl, p. 70.
22. Prell, Edward. "League Votes A's Shift to Kansas City," *Chicago Daily Tribune,* October 13, 1954, p. B1.
23. *Chicago Daily Tribune.* "Senator Official Challenges A's Shift," October 14, 1954, p. E1.
24. Ibid.
25. Ibid.
26. Ibid.
27. *Chicago Daily Tribune.* "Phils' Owner Not Happy over Buying A's Park," October 14, 1954, p. E1.

28. *The Sporting News.* "American League Clears Way, but A's Shift to Kansas City Hangs Fire," October 20, 1954, p. 8.

29. Povich, Shirley. "This Morning," *Washington Post and Times Herald*, October 14, 1954, p. 61.

Chapter 6

TURNABOUT

Roy Mack was given nearly a week to get ready to accept Arnold Johnson's offer. American League President Harridge had no doubt that the Macks would approve the sale that had already received the league's imprimatur. Roy had already given Harridge that impression. While the opponents of Kansas City were outspoken in their resistance, it looked like a *fait accompli*. As Arnold Johnson understood it, Roy was handed this bit of breathing space to do nothing "except talk to his family." "It was never contemplated," said the winning bidder, "that Mr. Mack would be given an opportunity to look for other purchasers."[1] Never considered by Johnson and Harridge, perhaps, but certainly mulled over by Roy Mack. While Johnson was contemplating who would manage the Kansas City A's (Lou Boudreau's name was mentioned), Roy was busy looking for a new buyer.

Roy came out swinging after taking a day of rest after the late night of the October 12. "I have not sold my stock," said the second-generation Mack. From Connie III, Roy's son, came this statement: "Even the Supreme Court couldn't force my dad to sell his stock if he didn't want to."[2] Lee DeOrsey of the Washington bidding group also claimed that "from what Roy told me, it would seem the club may remain in Philadelphia."[3] Roy was obviously out hustling for prospects, talking to rejected bidders and fighting until the end to keep his beloved A's in their home.

Grudgingly, Harridge admitted that the American League could not force the Macks to sell. Although the impression was given at the Blackstone that Roy wanted to sell, the league "can't force him to sell. If he changes his mind, I suppose that is his prerogative."[4] Things became very unpleasant between the league president and the anti-Johnson forces.

Calvin Griffith never wavered from his disgust at the way Harridge handled the vote. Kansas City was the last choice of the Senators, and Griffith had voted in accordance with that aim. Harridge tersely responded, "The minutes of the meeting will show that Washington voted for Kansas City."[5] As Griffith had previously explained, the minutes would show that the Senators were in favor of Kansas City as a third alternative, after Philadelphia and Los Angeles. Further, Griffith firmly believed that Harridge was hasty in announcing the franchise shift. Detroit's Briggs had more to add. He was still stunned that his proxy, a no vote against Arnold Johnson and a move to Kansas City left with American League attorney Ben Fiery, was not counted. "The American League is not going to Kansas City, period," harrumphed Briggs. The whole idea for a Kansas City move, Briggs continued, was "a Yankee movement."[6] Joe Cronin defended Harridge, saying that Boston's vote was not conditional and that Griffith didn't understand what he was voting for.

Rebuffed suitors were still commenting on the situation. Tommy Richardson felt that his group had been given the bum's rush in Chicago and noted the incredible pressure he had seen placed on Roy to sell to the Johnson group. The DeOrsey–Tucci partnership was clearly still in contact with Roy Mack and, although their offer of less than $3 million was turned away as insufficient, their willingness to stay in Philadelphia, now for a year or longer, was, they thought, still an item in their favor. Then, on October 15 a blockbuster involving players both old and new was announced.

"Ten-Man Syndicate Pledges $3,750,000 to Keep Athletics in Philadelphia," the *New York Times* headline declared. Jack Rensel, disparaged previously by Ernie Mehl, was back, this time as spokesman for a Philadelphia syndicate willing to raise at least, if not more than, Arnold Johnson's $3.375 million final total. While some reports incorrectly cited a $3.75 million number, Johnson was not only matched, but also trumped by the new syndicate, which did not require a move. The group included the following players: Leonard Strick (truck trailer manufacturer), Paul T. Harron (owner of radio station WIBG), Barney Fisher, or Fischer (auto and oil executive), Arthur Gallagher (motor trucking executive and former Olympic rower), Joseph (also referred to as Morton) Liebman, (department store owner), Isadore Sley (of Raquet Parking), Arthur Rosenberg (vice president of the Food Fair grocery chain), William Anderson (heating and plumbing contractor), and one who chose anonymity. "The money was in the till," said one member of the group.[7] Enough money was put forth at the meeting, held in the boardroom of the Tradesman's Land Title & Trust Company, to buy the A's. It was stated that the group was oversubscribed and might need to hand back some of the pledges. If so, this was an advantage over Johnson, who still had a verbal agreement only and had not produced any money.

Meeting the Monday deadline of 11 AM (originally reported as 10 AM) was crucial to the negotiations, and they were proceeding hard and fast. A sticking point was Roy's status within the new ownership group. Negotiations could have been completed Saturday, October 16, following a secret nine-hour meeting on the 15th, the first between the Macks and the newly formed purchasing group. As all Athletics' business contained complications, this time the complication was that Saturday was also the wedding day of Roy Mack's daughter Kathleen. With the deadline looming, a recess was called for because of Roy's attendance at the nuptials. A stumbling block from the Friday meeting came with reports that Roy had insisted on a five-year contract for himself (dismissed later as "wild talk"),[8] as well as having Connie III in some way involved. The talks had involved the entire Mack family and, according to a witness to the meeting, the Macks were all pleased. Alfred Luongo, Earle Mack's lawyer, had informed Earle that he was to be ready on Sunday the 17th to pick up his father and drive to the attorney's Central City office.

There was even more action. Harry Sylk and Charlie Finley were still involved. Finley had no part in the syndicate and claimed he too had enough backers to match Johnson's offer. Along with Sylk, Finley could raise $1 million. Upon receiving word from two other potential cohorts, Sylk and Finley would be able to present a check for $2 million and get down to detailed negotiations.

From Chicago, Johnson's reaction to the latest news was one of shock and confusion. Attempts to salvage his deal were made, with offers to Roy of a five-year deal, stock in the new concern, and a place for Roy's son with the team. Feeling that the syndicate had played on family pride, Johnson was not willing to give up. In Kansas City, reaction was bitter. City manager L. P. Cookingham thought money to keep the team in

Philadelphia would be lost, and local residents said, "Maybe it would be the best thing—losing this deal," and "I'm fed up with Roy Mack."[9]

Back in Philly, the syndicate was going through some changes. By Saturday, the group had been whittled down to seven: Harron, Fisher, Gallagher, Rosenberg, Liebman, Sley, and, replacing Strick, T. R. Hanff, an investment broker. Rensel, who had once handled the public address system at Connie Mack Stadium, put this group together in less than two days. The deal being presented was not the same as Johnson's. While Johnson's $3.375 million was to purchase the whole concern (team, debts, stadium, etc.), the septet at first had $1.5 million on the table and in the bank to buy out only Connie and Earle's share of the team. Roy would then be able to stay on board. Although Earle had committed to Johnson, his overriding aversion to relocating the team made his decision clear. Said one member, "I think we're going to be successful. We've offered the Macks everything they want, more than they could get for the franchise anywhere else. I don't see how they can turn us down." A meeting set for 1:30 Sunday at the law office of Samuel Blank was arranged, and the deal was announced.

With great fanfare, the press proclaimed the syndicate's success. The group was now eight, with Harron dropping out and Rensel and John Crisconi, an automobile dealer, in. Roy Mack would stay on, and these nine men were all listed as owners, with equal shares in the team and the option of selling out some of their percentage with a limit of 25 total owners. The announcement read, "Roy Mack today announced that his father, Connie Mack, his brother, Earle, and he have sold control of the Philadelphia Athletics to a group of eight Philadelphia businessmen."[10]

Roy had telephoned American League President Harridge, alerting him to the sale and requesting league approval. The official sale was announced as $4 million, much more than Johnson's already approved payment. A total of $2.25 million was put toward the club itself, with Connie receiving $604,000, Earle garnering $450,000, and Roy getting $200,000, all in cash. Roy would reinvest $250,000 for his ownership rights. Rosenberg added that the group would assume the Connecticut General mortgage, now closer to $1.2 million after being paid down over the past four years. Bringing the package to the $4 million number was the assurance of another $550,000 to be used "as needed, and I think we'll need it," furthered Rosenberg.[11] Rosenberg added that on Sunday night, $3.375 million had been deposited in the bank, without difficulty. Johnson had never done likewise.

The end of Connie and Earle's baseball careers was at hand. While the first order of business of the novice owners was to unanimously vote Connie the title of honorary president, there was no such comparable move on Earle's behalf. As to his future, Earle said that he'd be a presence at the ballpark for a little while longer, willing to give advice if asked. He swore his support to the tyro owners and was overjoyed at the course events had taken, keeping the team in the city that once loved them and could, possibly, love them again.

Will Harridge's reaction was one of resignation. As far as he was concerned, the A's had completely new ownership, subject to approval by the league owners. Johnson had no recourse, as "it was a case of Roy Mack changing his mind after he told us he was willing to sell his stock to Mr. Johnson."[12] Harridge did have a few requests to make of Roy. Roy was instructed to send a telegram with complete details of the impending transaction. Harridge requested the names of each member of those associated with the new arrangement. When a meeting of league owners would be held could not be decided until all the details were in. Harridge's focus on the details of this major transaction was a change of course after the slipshod and rush job of the October 12 Johnson approval, but he did concede that, as of now, the Kansas City move was "as dead as a spitball."[13]

One overjoyed participant was Bob Carpenter. Upon hearing of the new arrangement, Carpenter could not have been more pleased. He did not want to buy Connie Mack Stadium and never did, but had Arnold Johnson's approved purchase held, Carpenter knew that he "wouldn't have had any alternative."[14]

Outraged and in a state of complete disbelief, Johnson scrambled to recover. Along with attorney Vollers, Johnson had hopped on a plane to Philadelphia in an attempt to preempt the syndicate, but the official announcement was made while he was en route. He had, as to be expected, nothing good to say about the new deal. "It doesn't sound good to me. Roy had a much better deal with me," which included an important vice president's role as well as a substantial salary.[15] While Roy was ecstatic about attaining his ultimate goal of keeping the A's in Philadelphia, Johnson was in the depths, having what he thought of as a completed sale swept out from under him in less than a week's time, 18 hours before the Monday deadline. Ernie Mehl felt that the city itself took the loss with grace, but, with the Mehl odds now set at 200:1, Johnson still had plenty of fight left in him. "It's not all over," he claimed.[16]

The messy and disorganized way that the baseball establishment conducted its affairs in general, and in regard to the A's specifically, was never more obvious than in these past few months. The lack of professionalism in their business decisions, whether seen in the continual reprieves given Roy Mack, the roller coaster ride of approval and rejection handed to Arnold Johnson, and the string-pulling generally understood to be happening at the hands of the Yankees, were all examples of the slap-dash methods of big league commerce. With Kansas City frozen out as a Major League city, and with citizens already on record as unsatisfied with Minor League Blues baseball, the Kansas City American Association franchise was probably worthless, and the Yankees might "just as well give it away."[17]

There was some gloating, too. Both Calvin Griffith and Walter Briggs, charging the Yankees "with trying to jam through a rush-act move to Kansas City,"[18] felt they had won the battle. Clark Griffith, in a clairvoyant moment, insisted that California was the place to be, and he was afraid that the National League would beat the American League to the punch, which they did (the Dodgers and Giants moved west before the 1958 season). The present American League owners were blind to the growth in California, averred Griffith. It was now to be seen whether the Yankees and their cohort Johnson would let this stand.

---

1. *Chicago Daily Tribune*. "Johnson Set to Sue A's Group," October 21, 1954, p. D1.
2. Associated Press. "Roy Mack Dims A's Transfer; Guards Stock," *Chicago Daily Tribune*, October 15, 1954, p. C2.
3. Ibid.
4. *Washington Post and Times Herald*. "League Can't Force Shift, Says Harridge," October 15, 1954, p. 35.

5. Povich, Shirley. "Detroit Head Joins Griffith in Dispute," *Washington Post and Times Herald*, October 15, 1954, p. 35.

6. Ibid.

7. United Press International. "Ten-Man Syndicate Pledges $3,750,000 to Keep Athletics in Philadelphia," *New York Times*, October 16, 1954, p. 20.

8. United Press International. "7 Put Up $1,500,000 to Buy Out Connie, Earle Mack of Athletics," *New York Times*, October 17, 1954, p. A2.

9. Associated Press. "Expect Verdict Today on A's Syndicate Deal," *Chicago Daily Tribune*, October 17, 1954, p. A2.

10. Associated Press. "Philadelphia Keeps A's; $4,000,000 Deal," *Chicago Daily Tribune*, October 18, 1954, p. C1.

11. Ibid.

12. Prell, Edward. "Harridge Asks Facts on Sale," *Chicago Daily Tribune*, October 18, 1954, p. C1.

13. Ibid.

14. *New York Times*. "New Owners of Athletics Mark Time Until League Approves Stock Purchase," October 19, 1954, p. 31.

15. Associated Press. "Johnson Says His Deal Better One for Macks," *Chicago Daily Tribune*, October 18, 1954, p. C1.

16. Mehl, Ernest. *The Kansas City Athletics*. New York: Holt, 1956, p. 87.

17. Daley, Arthur. "Sport of the Times—Philadelphia Story," *New York Times*, October 19, 1954, p. 31.

18. Povich, Shirley. "This Morning," *Washington Post*, October 10, 1954, p. 25.

Chapter 7

COUNTERATTACK

Sitting back and taking what came was not in the character of either Johnson or the Yankees. While Yankee power had been tested and seemingly vanquished, the story wasn't over just yet. On October 20 Arnold Johnson announced that he would be pursuing legal action against, not the Macks, with whom he felt he had an agreement, not the American League club owners, who he felt had voted firmly for a legitimate approval, but the Philadelphia syndicate for breach of contract. While Johnson had never had a contract with the Macks, as American League approval had been given before an agreement had been reached between the two parties, Johnson was claiming that the syndicate had induced Roy Mack to turn away from the Kansas City deal.

Claiming he had been maltreated by the new collection of buyers, Johnson engaged the services of Charles J. Biddle of the Philadelphia law firm of Drinker, Biddle, and Reath to study whether it was a worthwhile endeavor to sue for breach of contract and damages. "In view of the indicated advance ticket sales of almost two million dollars, the measure of my damages should be substantial," said the aggrieved Johnson.[1] Praising his own persistence, Johnson vowed to pursue the lawsuit with the same determination with which he had gone after the A's. Citing his costs in the thousands that had already been incurred in preparing Blues Stadium for the arrival of the Athletics, Johnson bemoaned the impending bills from architects (which Mehl reported as $40,000), engineers, traffic experts, and legal representation. Hoping to consolidate his support among the Kansas City faithful, Johnson said, "without the marvelous people of Kansas City, I would have given up long ago," but their enthusiasm forced him to honor his guarantee and justify the confidence placed in him.[2] He could not "break faith with Kansas City."[3]

Arthur Rosenberg, the most outspoken of the Philly syndicate, wanted his partners to consider the Johnson attack before comment, but a quick rebuttal emerged. Breach of contract was absurd, Rosenberg retorted, since there was no contract to breach. There had never been a final agreement of any sort between the Macks and Arnold Johnson. The reprieve given to Roy to consult with Mrs. Mack and the rest of the family was granted in the *hope* of achieving a contract between the family and Johnson. Johnson himself had admitted this was so. "It was a verbal agreement, true, but it stood with me as something unbreakable—and it is part of the minutes of the American League meeting, he confessed."[4]

As to the American League's view, Harridge would not comment until the syndicate signed the final documents for its purchase of the team. League approval was still needed for the new transaction, and, as of yet, no blessing had been bestowed. While Harridge had been quite willing to wrap up the vote for Johnson's purchase and transfer of the A's without a contract with the Macks, without Johnson's money in the bank, without an investigation into Johnson's partners, and without the promised scrutiny into the business arrangement between Johnson, Topping, and Webb, he now followed a cautious tack, waiting for all the papers to be in. This didn't slip by "The Old Fox."

Clark Griffith smiled slyly over what seemed to be a victory over Yankee supremacy. "There are a couple of fellas who think they're running this league. They're finding out different."[5] He named Del Webb specifically. In his folksy way, Griffith, soon to be the elder statesman of baseball with the exit of the 92-year-old Connie Mack, took credit for halting the speedy process of approving Johnson. Griffith related that Webb tried to "jam through a vote" at the New York meeting, and Griffith, although willing to assume that Johnson was "a good fella," needed to know much more about him. Although the Senators' owner thought he had impeded the Yankee onslaught, the results of the Commodore Hotel meeting proved otherwise. Griffith saw in Del Webb a nemesis, holding a grudge against the Yankee co-owner for his role in ousting former commissioner Happy Chandler in favor of present commissioner Ford Frick. In another veiled shot at Webb, and probably Johnson, Griffith said, "We've got a lot of promoters in baseball these days who are looking for a quick dollar instead of for the good of the game."[6]

League approval for the syndicate was necessary, but there was no hurry to deliver. Arthur Rosenberg, emerging as the sole spokesman for the syndicate, wondered what the holdup was. Having sent President Harridge a complete list of investors and their social and financial backgrounds, Rosenberg was unaware what more was needed, and no one was telling him. Wary of antagonizing with heavy pressure both the league president and the voting owners, who he would need for consent, Rosenberg promised that if approval was not granted on October 22, "two men will be sent to Chicago to talk with the American League president."[7] Having hammered out the final details of the contract on the 21st, it was announced that the completed agreement was now with the Macks, and it was fully expected that it would all be wrapped up the next day. More important to the syndicate was league approval.

Harridge was not bending over backward to accommodate the Philadelphians, as he had for Johnson. "We are awaiting definitive word from Roy Mack as to the signing of the contract consummating the deal and a request from him to approve the transfer of the stock and the new stockholders. Until then there would be no purpose in calling a meeting of league members."[8] Remember that for Johnson, there were no such details, and not only was approval given for his purchase, but it was also granted for his proposed move to Kansas City, *without any contract* with the Macks. Further, Harridge had pushed through the vote on transfer in order to not inconvenience his league's owners with an additional meeting, a rather flimsy rationale.

So, Harridge awaited the "bill of particulars" from Roy Mack and demanded much more. Unlike in the Johnson case, the league required the Macks to explain how current liabilities would be taken care of and how much the Macks were to be paid right now. Harridge also needed information on how the stock would be distributed among the new ownership group as well as the names of all likely officers of the syndicate and their duties. It was apparent that the demands put upon a group of unknowns without Yankee support was quite different than those put on an unknown who had the total backing of the New Yorkers.

While the syndicate insisted that quick approval was essential, only the seller could demand swift action. From Roy Mack came only silence. With an abrupt comment that the "proper time has not yet arrived" to ask for league approval, Roy once again contributed the one thing he had consistently added to the process begun in the summer—uncertainty. Working on Roy's fragile and indecisive nature was Arnold Johnson. Pushing Roy to compare the two deals, Johnson was planting doubt in Roy's head that perhaps the syndicate deal was not as good as he thought. Expressing his outrage, Johnson, dubbed "the nickel-in-the-slot tycoon" for his role in Automatic Canteen's vending business,[9] hammered home that Roy had "not lived up to the obligation"[10] he had committed to at the Chicago meeting. Catering to Roy's need to find a place within the A's for his son Connie III, Johnson was willing, of course, to give the lad a job and even offered a five-year baseball-training course. Like a cult leader breaking down a prospective member, Johnson was alternately cruel and placating.

Still, there was only one contract, and that was not between Roy Mack and Johnson. Johnson sent Mack a telegram that was harshly critical of his lack of consistent communication from the moment the syndicate entered the picture. Johnson harangued Roy, scolding him that it was "unbelievable that you would not talk to me or let me see you before you went off the deep end." Threatening Roy at the core, Johnson went on that "your future and your son's future are at stake."[11] Mrs. Katherine Mack, Connie's wife, was being swayed, agreeing that Johnson's deal was better, seemingly because he said it was.

Things were becoming a bit unsettled for the syndicate. The details of the contract were still being finalized, and attorney Luongo cited that the process, which would normally take months, could be completed in a matter of days. Though it was always possible that someone might not favor the final agreement, the chance of that occurring was one in a thousand. Despite any hang-up on the minutiae, Luongo reminded all that the contract was firm and "approved in writing by Roy, Earle and Connie."[12] Always wary of being too aggressive toward Harridge, Luongo said it was fine if league approval was delayed until everything had been worked out satisfactorily. Harridge was insisting on even more information from Roy Mack and instructed Roy that the league would definitely not act until a signed agreement was in his hands. Compare that with the double approvals for Johnson and Kansas City without Johnson having even the consent of the Mack family, let alone signed documents.

Legal action seemed to be on the back burner; little of Johnson's breach of contract suit was mentioned. Some lawyers wondered what his basis for suing was, while others felt he might have a legitimate claim if he could show "malicious interference with a contract," an actionable offense.[13] Yet Roy Mack's verbal commitment would only be valid if there were no conditions as part of the ownership transfer. There was one very big condition, though, and that was Johnson's need to move, rather than stay in Philadelphia.

Nothing was easy where Roy Mack was involved, and in a contentious meeting with the Philadelphia syndicate, the dreaded Mack delay reappeared. Roy granted the syndicate an extension until 3 PM Friday, October 29, giving the group until after American League approval to pay for the Mack stock. Upon acceptance of their offer, the syndicate's money would be transferred out of escrow to the Macks. With a genial, "Boys, you can have an extension to await league approval,"[14] the ticking time bomb exploded. Syndicate members were furious at Roy, and loudly so. Commenting within earshot of reporters, one member said he wouldn't be surprised if Roy wasn't trying to back out of selling the club. Said another, "If he [Roy Mack] wants to back out, let's give the story to the press." Another said irately, "I'm so mad I'd like to walk out of this thing right now."[15] It was obvious, said another, that Harridge's refusal to grant approval was an aid to Roy in his attempt to withdraw. Most importantly, while Earle and Connie had graciously been willing to extend the time for the benefit of the syndicate, Roy initially had shied away from doing so. Again, Roy Mack was having misgivings, and it was clear to one of the Quaker City businessmen that Roy's head was being spun back in the direction of Arnold Johnson.

At last, Harridge, who had received the signed papers of the proposed new owners on the 25th, declared that the American League owners would gather at 10:30 AM, October 28, in New York, this time at the Waldorf-Astoria, not to specifically address the sale of the A's to the syndicate, but more generally, "to consider the sale of the Philadelphia club stock,"[16] implying that there was more than one offer to be looked at. Without mention of a specific buyer, speculation was rampant that Arnold Johnson was back in the fray, and so he was. Defending his $3.375 million offer, and making sure that it was known that it still stood, Johnson insisted that the syndicate's offer of $4 million "equaled but did not exceed his bid."[17] Even more curious was that Johnson was "apparently fully informed of every move" of the past few weeks and was pointedly asked if any American League member had contacted him. He declined to answer, in no way assuaging the fears that Johnson and the Yankees went hand in hand.

Rumors flew on the day before the owners congregated. Jesse A. Linthicum, sports editor of the *Baltimore Sun*, claimed, "Roy Mack is reported to be backing out of the deal" to sell to the Philadelphia consortium, and furthermore, an anonymous source told Linthicum that "Kansas City seems certain now to get the franchise."[18] The syndicate was completely befuddled, and their chief counsel, Samuel A. Blank, noted that the contract was a standard one—nothing confusing that would result in rejection. Despite the hostility of the previous day's meeting at the Broad Street Trust Company, the relationship between the Macks and the eight-man group seemed harmonious. In an effort to scare Roy Mack, one rumor had it that if the syndicate was turned down, Arnold Johnson might not even be around to renew his offer, leaving the A's empty-handed.

On the eve of the meeting, when the league owners were ostensibly pondering both offers and looking at the entire A's problem, the deadliest rumor of all emerged. It was more than probable, according to gossip, that the league would veto the sale of the A's to the syndicate, leaving Johnson the only bidder left standing. Reliable sources were belittling the new ownership group and pointedly demeaning Arthur Rosenberg's Food Fair connection. Rosenberg's role as vice president of one of Philadelphia's largest food stores led to snide comments that the syndicate would be "more interested in peddling groceries than running a baseball club." An empty-headed worry that "contrary to the high professional standards of baseball," ticket giveaways at Food Fair stores would degrade the product, rather than bolster attendance, also became public.[19] It appeared that a potentially collusive arrangement between a Johnson ownership and the Yankees was less mortifying to American League owners than the horror of having tickets distributed by contest.

1. *Chicago Daily Tribune.* "Johnson Set to Sue A's Group," October 21, 1954, p. D1.
2. Ibid.
3. Mehl, Ernest. *The Kansas City Athletics.* New York: Holt, 1956, p. 88
4. *Chicago Daily Tribune.* "Johnson Set to Sue A's Group," October 21, 1954, p. D1.
5. Addie, Bob. "Sports Addition," *Washington Post and Times Herald*, October 21, 1954, p. 32.
6. Ibid.
7. *Chicago Daily Tribune.* "A's Group Presses for League Approval," October 22, 1954, p. C1.
8. Associate Press. "A's Group Ready to Seek Meeting," *New York Times*, October 22, 1954, p. 32.
9. *Sports Illustrated.* "Philadelphia Album," (Vol. 1, Issue 14), November 15, 1954, p. 14.
10. Mehl, p. 89
11. Ibid. pp. 92–93.
12. Associated Press. "A's Sale Details Still Unsettled," *New York Times*, October 23, 1954, p. 18.
13. Addie, Bob. "Sports Addition," *Washington Post and Times Herald*, October 24, 1954, p. C2.
14. Associated Press. "Mack Gives Extension to A's Syndicate," *Los Angeles Times,* October 26, 1954, p. C1.
15. Associated Press. "Syndicate to Pay Off After League Approval," *Washington Post and Times Herald*, October 26, 1954, p. 18.
16. Vaughan, Irving. "Johnson Re-enters Battle to Buy A's," *Chicago Daily Tribune*, October 27, 1954, p. B1.
17. Ibid.
18. Associated Press. "American League Meets Here Tomorrow on Sale of Athletics," *New York Times*, October 27, 1954, p. 37.
19. United Press International. "League May Veto A's Sale," *Los Angeles Times,* October 28, 1954, p. C1.

Chapter 8

FINAL SALE

Contradictions would abound in the third meeting to decide the destiny of the Philadelphia A's, Connie Mack, and Major League baseball. Dan Topping, who had loudly claimed that the Yankees were opposed to the Kansas City move unless they received proper compensation, while at the same time quietly not at all opposed to the relocation, now was solidly in Johnson's corner. "Our minor league franchise at Kansas City has been immeasurably harmed. It would be best for the league, as well as us, for the club to go."[1] An insight into the Yankee mindset was in the subtext. American League interests, while important, were somewhat secondary to the health of the Yankee organization, even down to its minor league holdings.

Johnson, though not officially invited to the meeting, was making his presence felt. According to Roscoe McGowan of the *New York Times*, Johnson "was not notified of the meeting by the American League but was in the city and available."[2] It was just as well that he wasn't in the room, as it seemed that Washington (Griffith), Detroit (Briggs), and Boston (owner Tom Yawkey) were still unenthusiastic about his proposal, with the Chicago White Sox a potential addition to this alliance. Also planning to attend was Connie Mack, lending an air of gravitas to what had, to this point, been a farce.

"I am in favor of the sale to the local syndicate. I talked to Roy and Earle and we are solidly behind the sale."[3] With those words Connie Mack made his feelings known, as Arnold Johnson had feared he would. Johnson had claimed that the syndicate had repeatedly phoned Connie, at least eight times, and insisted he make the trip up to New York. While Johnson thought this was a "stage play,"[4] the old master had sided unequivocally with the Philadelphia group, but his desire to decide to whom he would sell his stock was disregarded. This was just one of the many questionable happenings that day. Said Shirley Povich, "The suspicious thing about today's meeting is that a dozen times in the past the other clubs have been sold to new owners without occasioning any formal meetings of approval."[5] Just 16 days earlier, Johnson had been approved without the agreement of the Macks. Now, the Macks had a real contract with prospective buyers that Connie and the family preferred, but somehow that carried less weight in the league, or at least Will Harridge's eyes. The Mack family, it was clear, would have virtually no say in how their major asset would be disposed.

When the vote was announced, after six hours of discussion, the syndicate was shot down, in a deadlocked 4–4 vote. Initial reports had Detroit, Washington, and Cleveland for the syndicate and New York and Baltimore against. Chicago, Boston, and Philadelphia's ballots were unaccounted for. Charles Comiskey, White Sox vice president, said that the differences of opinion amongst the Macks themselves resulted in the refusal. It could be reasonably inferred then that the White Sox were anti-syndicate. Some owners put little stock in the credibility of Connie Mack, as he had already noted the support of his tribe for Philadelphia, which would have indicated a Philly yes vote, and, finally a Boston no vote. Johnson's offer was not discussed according to the American League director of public relations, Earl Hillegan. The Macks still had their stock, the team was still up for grabs to anyone, and no further meetings were called. Said the forlorn Earle Mack, "We're just waiting—for what I don't know, but we're just waiting."[6]

Interestingly, Johnson's attorney, Edward Vollers, said that, if his client made another offer, "no further action by the league" would be needed, because of the October 12 vote.[7] That Vollers would assume that no further meetings would be required shows that the Johnson group felt itself to be on firm footing and not subject to the rules imposed on other interested parties. For their part, the syndicate was completely befuddled by what they had witnessed. Arthur Gallagher, on behalf of his partners, said rhetorically that his group would "like to know what the objections were."[8] Rosenberg was disappointed and confused. Adding to the baffling developments of the meeting, Arnold Johnson was outside the meeting room and at one point was called into the anteroom and asked one question. Nobody would divulge what the nature of that query was.

Predictably, the aftermath of this meeting was chaotic and controversial. "Spike" Briggs was still in the forefront of the anti-Johnson movement, again pointing out that Kansas City was not a long-term solution to the A's problems and that other cities would fit the bill better. Briggs preferred at least another year or two in Philadelphia. The disregard paid to Connie, who appeared twice, once with Earle as his spokesman, the other, with Connie standing tall, albeit with the support of his chauffeur, Chuck Roberts, was cause for bitter feelings from Earle, who expressed shock at the league's turning their back on the Hall of Famer's plea. Cal Griffith objected to the implication made by Vollers that Johnson had the inside track and needed no further action. No sale could be completed without another meeting of the American League owners, and any "sale is subject to approval of the American League and there will definitely be a meeting before there is approval."[9]

Johnson, upon his return to Chicago, held court at his Merchandise Mart office. His offer of $3.375 million had *never* been withdrawn, despite reports that claimed otherwise. Finally, after Will Harridge had made his onerous demands of the Philadelphia syndicate to provide explicit details as to their names, backgrounds, and future roles in the A's, and three weeks after his initial American League approval, Arnold Johnson revealed the members of his group: Nathaniel Leverone, chairman of Automatic Canteen, where Johnson was the number two man, was named, as well as J. Patrick Lannan, Johnson's old replacement at Northwestern Terra Cotta, who had risen to director of more than 20 different companies, and Joseph H. Briggs, president of H.M. Byllesby and Co., a Chicago investment bank. The Johnson press was on to gain acceptance of the Macks and finally close the deal. Meanwhile, John Crisconi of the Philadelphia group was trying to keep their hopes alive. As for Harridge, he urged quick resolution; "definitive action is imperative."[10] Back in Philadelphia, Johnson and Vollers were in meetings with six lawyers, each representing a different Mack faction.

What happened on November 4 came complete with comedic chase scenes and melodramatic bedside scenes. Connie had been bedridden, unable to eat a substantial meal since the American League rejected his preference for the syndicate at the October 28 meeting in New York. His spirit broken as a result, his wife, Katherine, became his spokesman on this crucial day, but before the events at the Macks' Germantown apartment took place, Johnson was working on the rest of the family.

The night before, Johnson had dinner at the Warwick Hotel (which he and associates had purchased in 1953 in a capital gains deal similar to his Yankee Stadium purchase) with Roy and Earle Mack. *The Sporting News* had reported that Johnson had threatened to pull out of the bidding, although from Chicago Johnson denied it. Either way, it was enough to put the Macks "in a panic, lest they be forced into bankruptcy," and they were weaker for this.[11] The three talked all night and into the morning until, at 2 AM, Earle folded. Roy had already joined the Johnson camp. What turned Earle and Roy? Johnson's offer of three-year contracts to the brothers was soothing, as was Johnson's respectful offer to name Connie the honorary chairman of the board of directors. However, the granting of employment to Connie III (who would be going to Kansas City with the team) and Earle Jr. gave the fathers peace of mind as to the futures of their sons. With this part of the family wrapped up, Connie was needed and by no means assured.

Earle himself doubted that Connie would accept Johnson's offer and with it the creation of the Kansas City Athletics. Still in the hunt was the truncated syndicate, now composed of Crisconi, Hanff, Liebman, and Sley. A meeting was set for noon Thursday, but that time would end up meaningless. Johnson arrived at the School Lane dwelling at 9 AM, well in advance of the scheduled time. Earle, already having some second thoughts, called "Speed" Sley, who was just leaving Women's College Hospital. "Where are you fellows!" cried Earle, claiming that Mrs. Mack had said 10 AM, not 12.[12] The four dashed in a panic and arrived at 10 AM and encountered Johnson and Vollers in the lobby. While they waited for noon, Johnson got help from an unexpected source.

Ernie Mehl relates that Connie's chauffeur, physically supportive of his boss at the Waldorf, was now supporting Johnson. It seemed that Chuck Roberts was outraged that the syndicate had browbeat, in his estimation, the frail Mack into attending the October 28 meeting to preach their case. Now having sympathy for Johnson, Roberts literally snuck Johnson into Connie's bedroom via a back entrance. Johnson quickly realized that he had not brought a check of his own and hastily grabbed a check from his attorney, scribbled out Vollers' data and wrote in his own City National account number. With that, Johnson approached Connie, while the shrunken syndicate twiddled its thumbs in the hall.

His modified check in the amount of $604,000 in hand, Johnson spent two hours up in the Mack's quarters. Mrs. Mack questioned the validity of this form of payment, and Johnson beseeched her to call the bank for verification. She did and was satisfied. When he emerged from the apartment, he had gotten the job done, with Connie signing the papers from his sickbed. Ernie Mehl, always in Johnson's corner, reported in *The Sporting News* that the syndicate had not gotten together as much money as had been reported in the press, but this was not so. Rather than the scrawled-upon check from someone else's bank account that Johnson delivered, the syndicate had arrived with four separate checks, one each for Connie, Earle, Roy, and the four daughters of Connie and Katherine. While Mrs. Mack was surprisingly unwilling to accept four checks, one daughter was thrilled. The four checks, she noted, made it much easier to distribute the money among the family. What motivated Katherine Mack to accept Johnson's altered check is not clear, but that was her inclination. While the syndicate had arrived on time, Mrs. Mack cited their "dilly-dallying" as the reason they lost out to Johnson, a good man in her estimation. When it was all over, "Johnson was all smiles. He had won his fight and had every reason to believe he was now a major league magnate."[13] Earle Mack left his father's apartment sobbing, tears streaming down his creased face. With all the Macks signed, it was only left to gain league approval on the sale and move, approval that had been given to Johnson several weeks previously, before he had attained this level of firm accord with the Mack family.

The deal, now announced at an increased total of $3.504 million, was broken down into three pieces. The Macks would receive $1.504 million for their stake in the club ($604,000 to Connie and $450,000 for Earle and Roy), $800,000 would go to cover various debts, held mostly by Buffalo's Jacobs Brothers concessionaires, and $1.2 million was for an assumption of the remaining Connecticut General Mortgage. The cost of Connie Mack Stadium seemed embedded in the total. Reminiscent of the Yankee Stadium deal, the Athletics' deal would not result in much out-of-pocket money from the Johnson concern. *The Sporting News'* Art Morrow saw it clearly. "Actually, of course, it will cost Johnson far less"[14] than his $3.5 million. Mehl pointed out the great risk that Johnson incurred regarding Connie Mack Stadium, adding that there were rumors that the city was contemplating a new structure. This was not so, as it had already been arranged that Johnson would receive $1.675 million for the sale of the Philadelphia ballpark to Bob Carpenter. After subtracting that $1.675 million and the $500,000 he was expected to get from selling Blues Stadium to Kansas City, Johnson's outlay would be closer to $1.3 million. Johnson's three-month quest seemed near its end. He had purchased the largest block of stock, Connie's, and had agreements with Roy and Earle. Now all he needed was American League approval to seal the deal.

1. McGowan, Roscoe. "Fate of Athletics Is Awaited Today," *New York Times*, October 28, 1954, p. 49.
2. Ibid.
3. *Washington Post and Times Herald*. "Connie Mack Plans to Attend Meeting," October 28, 1954, p. 33.
4. Mehl, Ernest. *The Kansas City Athletics*. New York: Holt, 1956, p. 100.
5. Povich, Shirley. "This Morning with Shirley Povich," *Washington Post and Times Herald*, October 28, 1954, p. 33.
6. Vaughan, Irving. "Athletics' Status 'Still in the Air,'" *Chicago Daily Tribune*, November 2, 1954, p. B1.
7. *Chicago Daily Tribune*. "League Rejects Syndicate Bid for A's," October 29, 1954, p. C1.
8. Ibid.
9. *Chicago Daily Tribune*. "Griffith Holds Fast Against Shift of A's," November 5, 1954, p. B1.
10. *Chicago Daily Tribune*. "Johnson Presses Offer to Buy A's," November 4, 1954, p. D1.
11. Morrow, Art. "Inside Story of the Race for Possession of Athletics," *The Sporting News*, November 10, 1954, p. 6.
12. Ibid.
13. Ibid.
14. Ibid.

Chapter 9

THE LAST VOTE

Would Harridge wait until he had all the details, demanding from Johnson and his cohorts the same extensive particulars extracted from the Philadelphia syndicate? Of course not, and a meeting was called for the following Monday, November 8, a return engagement at the Commodore Hotel. An attorney for the syndicate was flabbergasted. "What? He [Harridge] called for a meeting without asking to see the agreement of sale?" he said indignantly.[1] The double standard was obvious, as it was only days before that Harridge had insisted on inspecting the signed agreements between the syndicate and the Macks as a prerequisite to calling a meeting of the American League owners. As to the whether the Yankee–Johnson link would provide an impediment to ultimate acceptance, Harridge claimed that league attorneys had thoroughly investigated the situation and would present their findings to the attendees. Ernie Mehl quoted the odds of success at even.

With the Senators still adamantly opposed, and additional dissent possible from Detroit and Cleveland, the one additional vote required to block the sale was potentially at hand. On the other side, Dan Topping, the period of his "opposition" over Yankee compensation notwithstanding said, "Our position has been quite clear all along. We hope this will finally bring the whole matter to a head."[2] The dramatis personae were virtually the same as on October 12. "Spike" Briggs brought legendary Tigers second sacker and present vice president Charlie Gehringer. Charles Comiskey left his White Sox general manager Frank Lane at home. Clarence Miles of the Orioles dropped Clyde Morris and arrived with Arthur Ehlers. All the Macks were there. Del Webb was not.

Johnson had returned to Chicago, weary from cajoling the Macks in Philadelphia, but went to New York optimistically. Having signed concords with the Macks gave Johnson more standing than had his verbal agreements the last time a vote was conducted, although even then his wobbly deal resulted in a favorable vote. While the syndicate bid and contract had been made to fail, it still, by its existence, had voided the October 12 vote. Johnson, confident that he would be approved as the new owner, would not comment on the possibility of getting only that sanction without subsequent endorsement of a move to Kansas City.

That scenario was quite probable, however. While there seemed to be consensus on the transfer of ownership, it was foreseeable that a move could be blocked. Supporting a move were New York, Boston, Baltimore, Chicago, and, of course, Philadelphia. Clark Griffith and Walter Briggs were seen as obstructionist. The key to it all might end up in the lap of the Indians. While Hank Greenberg pledged that he entered the meeting with an open mind and had voted for Johnson in Chicago (and for the syndicate in New York), his thought process was revealed with a reflection back on the American League's refusal one year before to grant Bill Veeck the right to send the Browns to Baltimore. Veeck and Greenberg had been close during their days as owner and general manager of the Indians, and Hank reminded all present that he had voted no in 1953 for "a friend;" why then would he vote yes "for a stranger."[3] Furthermore, Nate Dolin of the Cleveland Indians felt strongly that the Philadelphia syndicate was treated very poorly and brushed off unfairly.

Topping and Weiss chimed in. Topping felt that the October 12 vote was binding and that a 5–3 vote would be needed to approve its reconsideration. Any previous claims that the Blues were damaged irreparably and weren't worth a dime were patently false. Clearly, those were statements of expedience to be used to strong-arm the other owners. Now that the final vote was near, a different tune was played. Topping knew there were "more than half a dozen cities" clamoring for the Blues franchise.[4] There would be no trouble at all in selling the club, and general manager Weiss admitted that bidders were already extant. The Yankees' supposed issues, compensation for their territory and the resulting worthlessness of their minor league club, had all disappeared.

There were other interesting comments before the meeting. Information on Johnson's deal with Kansas City was brought out by city manager L. P. Cookingham. While Johnson had touted the pledges for Kansas City tickets as one of the main reasons that the American League should allow him to move the A's, he was hedging his bets. Cookingham reported that if the team did not average one million fans for a three-year period, Johnson would be allowed to leave the city, breaking the planned five-year lease. While very generous, it was not within the city manager's purview to permit another move; that was American League business. Cookingham thought attendance would be fine, as long as Johnson lived up to his commitment to invest money (cited as $1 million), present a quality product on the field.

Ford Frick, commissioner of Major League Baseball, had been remarkably quiet during the whole A's ordeal. While leagues did have more autonomy in this era, an absence of any remarks had been odd. When he did speak, the former New York reporter, broadcaster, and ghostwriter for Babe Ruth did not object to the conflict of interest Johnson might incur by owning the A's and Yankee Stadium. Citing that the Yankees' lease with the Arnold Johnson Corp. did not involve any percentage payment, just a flat sum, and that Johnson was only the Yankees' landlord, Frick commented, "I don't see how this could be regarded as irregular."[5] Topping agreed.

At 10:30 AM, the meeting began, and soon after, Arnold Johnson took center stage, hoping this would be the last time he would need to convince the American League owners that he was the right buyer for the A's and that Kansas City was the right location. Clark Griffith, while admiring Johnson's tenacity, inquired why Philadelphia needed to be abandoned. Johnson responded that he must live up to the promise he gave Kansas City. Aware of the ghastly performance of the A's in recent years, Johnson reaffirmed his guarantee that at least $1 million would be spent over three years to purchase quality ballplayers. Playing up the one million–fan guarantee, Johnson proved that the new Kansas City A's would have no problem packing Blues Stadium. As to the preparedness of that stadium, Johnson said construction work to expand the structure could start immediately.

Who would be in his corner, backing up his assurances that everything would be ready for the start of the 1955 season? Del Webb. The Del

Webb Construction Company of Phoenix had several engineers on the case. Another concern, Winn-Senter of Kansas City, was to work on the expansion project, although *The Saturday Evening Post* reported that Winn-Senter was Del Webb–owned as well. Ernie Mehl breezed past this barefaced conflict of interest, praising Webb to the skies, simply noting that Webb knew the ballpark, loved baseball, and could provide vital guidance. In a wonderful bit of understatement, Webb said, "I feel a personal interest" in this project.[6] How personally the Yankee co-owner was interested in the affairs of the A's was still a concern for some of the owners.

Forces were working on Johnson's behalf. Mehl maintains that Harridge was working to assist Johnson; his feeling was that Kansas City would be the American League's equivalent of the success of the National League's Milwaukee Braves. Frick's comments were an attempt, and apparently a successful one, to convince Clark Griffith that it was ethically up to standard for Johnson to own Yankee Stadium and the A's. In his presentation Johnson tried desperately to convince Greenberg and Cronin, possible unfriendly voters, "that he was not closely associated with the Yankees just because he owned Yankee Stadium,"[7] but his only real way to sway the American League owners on this was to agree to sell Yankee Stadium, and when Harridge asked point blank if he would, he consented. Johnson agreed that he would divest himself of that holding within 90 days of final approval of the A's transaction. Suspiciously, Dan Topping simultaneously waved off any compensation for his Kansas City territory.

The two votes were taken. As expected, Johnson was approved as the new owner, this time truly unanimously. It was revealed that Connecticut General was calling in their mortgage owing to "dereliction in interest and principal payments,"[8] contrary to reports all year that the Macks were on schedule. Even if this *Chicago Daily Tribune* report was accurate, and that this had forced the sale of the team, by no means did it need to result in a sale to Arnold Johnson specifically. For relocation he needed six votes, and that's all he got, with Washington and Cleveland voting no. What of Walter Briggs? Coming into the meeting hollering that he was unwaveringly opposed to Kansas City and wanted a Minneapolis or a West Coast move, as well as consistently and proudly claiming his anti-Yankee bias, Briggs completely reversed course. Johnson's acceptance of the league's request that he put Yankee Stadium on the market provided

Briggs with one less reason to oppose the deal. He also kidded that having a Briggs (Joseph, no relation) in his group worked to Johnson's favor.
"I wanted harmony in the league," the now placid Briggs reflected, "I
wanted to end all this wrangling."[9] Jokingly, Briggs said, "I am not so
anti-Yankee as I have been pictured."[10] Further, it was "plain bunk" that
Briggs felt that the Yankees were in any way involved with the Kansas
City endeavor.[11] While that picture had been painted with Briggs' own
statements, he ultimately ceded to the needs of the New Yorkers and even
made the motion for the A's transfer.

Slightly past 4 PM, Harridge announced the results. Reactions varied.
Of course, Kansas City was ecstatic, and Mayor Kemp, after working
for so long on the project, proclaimed it a great day in the city's history. Now that it was truly at an end, 84-year-old Clark Griffith, who
had held his ground unswervingly and suggested a last-second league
bailout of the A's, sadly shook his head. "The Washington club took a
beating today" was all he could say.[12] Mehl felt that Johnson's sincerity
led to his success, and went on to say, surprisingly, that payment to the
Macks was not conditioned on a move. J. G. Taylor Spink, in a *Sporting
News* editorial, was pleased that Johnson was forced to sell the Bronx
ballpark. "The average fan would not have liked the arrangement," he
wrote. "Landlord-tenant relationships are not necessarily chummy, but
the ordinary customer might have seen in this association a community
of interests which would have disturbed his conviction that club owners
are competitors, not partners."[13] Spink felt that the stadium sale would
be tangible evidence that nothing remained of the Johnson–Webb–
Topping entanglements, though Webb's company was involved in the
Blues Stadium job.

"He had gambled," said Mehl of Johnson's sticking to Kansas City.
An investigation of the deal showed that any chances he may have taken
were nominal at best. In the spring of 1955 Arthur Mann wrote an exposé
describing Arnold Johnson's way of doing business. In "How to Buy a Ball
Club for Peanuts," Mann rehashed the Yankee Stadium deal as a model for
Johnson's purchase of the Athletics. Kansas City Athletics, Inc. was formed
as a Missouri corporation on November 15 to hold Johnson's A's stock.

While the deal was indeed valued at $3.5 million, the amount of
out-of-pocket cash was negligible. Yes, Johnson paid $1.504 million for

the Mack stock, settled the Connecticut General Mortgage in the exact amount of $1.225 million, and assumed the $800,000 in debt. That's the outgoing side, but a great deal was coming in, mostly prearranged. Connie Mack Stadium had been sold for $1.675 million to Bob Carpenter, and the $800,000 owed to Jacobs Brothers concessions was not an out-of-pocket expense. The Jacobs Brothers were given a long-term lease in Kansas City and were happy to take payment out of future profits. Kansas City paid $650,000 for Blues Stadium, not the $500,000 that was earlier reported. As to the remaining $400,000, Roy Mack was reported to have plowed back a chunk of his $450,000, and other investors in the new entity, Leverone, Lannan, Briggs, Vollers, and Johnson's brother Earl, also paid their way in. Talk from the Chicago financial world was that Johnson had pulled the deal off "without a dollar of fresh money appearing on the table."[14]

Figure 9.1

Finances of the A's Purchase.

It wasn't enough that Arnold Johnson gained a Major League franchise for less, probably much, much less, than $400,000. That merely scratched the surface of the money that would be thrown at Johnson. The 1 million–fan guarantee would return approximately $750,000 to Johnson. There were also radio rights and, more importantly, a speedy

Treasury Department decision in regard to player investment. Private attorneys had sought to have players be amortizable. With about 200 owned by the major and minor league clubs now in Johnson's possession, this decision would have a huge impact on team profits. With amazing haste, it was ruled that players were an "extraordinary expenditure, which if expensed in the year of acquisition would distort net income."[15] This judgment, along with the attendance assurances and broadcast fees would provide a windfall for at least three years. It's no wonder Johnson never gave up, and his experience at City National, looking for potential profit in distressed businesses, came in quite handy.

Mehl protested, perhaps too much. "How ridiculous this is!" he wrote derisively. Using the original sale price, Mehl would only concede the Connie Mack Stadium sale as worth taking off the total. "All bills were paid in full as Johnson [had] kept his commitment as soon as possible after the closing. The Saturday Evening Post author to the contrary not withstanding."[16] Conveniently slipping Mehl's mind was that the sale to Carpenter was a done deal. Mehl chided Arthur Mann for criticizing Johnson for his sale of Blues Stadium. This was not a windfall, but a return on investment to which Johnson was entitled. Mann never said Johnson didn't deserve his profit; he just pointed it out. How wrongly Mann gave the "impression that the Chicagoan . . . had turned a slick profitable deal, that he expected to profit from the enthusiasm engendered in K.C."[17] Mehl was outraged that any person would dare puncture the myth of the benevolent Johnson, patron saint of Kansas City baseball, with something as venal as monetary motivation. Regardless, this phase was completed, and it was time to build a ball club.

The new team needed new executives. Lou Boudreau, the star shortstop of just a few years back, who led the Indians to a World Series title in 1948 as a 31-year-old player–manager and Red Sox manager through the 1954 season, had always been the top candidate for the manager's role. On November 17 he received a two-year deal and cautioned against too much optimism on the field.

Off the field many of the hires in charge of baseball operations had a shared background. They had all been in the employ or in some way connected to the New York Yankees. One candidate mentioned for the general manager position was Bill DeWitt, who had been an assistant to

Yankee general manager George Weiss. The person ultimately chosen was Parke Carroll, who would act as business manager and vice president, as well as sit in on any prospective player deals. Not only had Carroll been a Yankee employee as general manager of the Blues since 1950, but he would serve as the consultant to the Yankees during the Blues' relocation while a member of the A's staff. The incestuous Yankees–A's relations did not stop there.

Ray Kennedy, former general manager of the Newark Bears, another Yankee minor league club, was hired as the new director of player personnel, and Harry Craft, Blues manager in 1953 and 1954, was named as an A's coach. Lee MacPhail, supervisor of the Yankees' farm system, saw his brother Bill hired by the A's as head of public relations. The A's front office had all the appearances of a Yankees branch office. In December, Ford Frick commented that "of course, there is nothing to prevent the Kansas City and Yankee clubs from making as many player deals as they desire."[18] The deck was stacked to ensure that this would occur.

The hardcover copy of *The Kansas City Athletics* by Ernest Mehl at the A. Bartlett Giamatti Research Center at the National Baseball Hall of Fame and Museum in Cooperstown, New York, contains an inscription. Written boldly is a message from the author to Yankees general manager George Weiss. "To George Weiss with Deepest Regards," wrote Ernie Mehl, expressing his profound thanks for all Weiss and the Yankees had done to help create the Arnold Johnson's Kansas City Athletics. In the next five years Arnold Johnson would show his gratitude in a much more significant way.

1. Morrow, Art. "Inside Story of the Race for Possession of Athletics," *The Sporting News,* November 10, 1954, p. 6.
2. *Chicago Daily Tribune.* "Griffith Holds Fast Against Shift of A's," November 5, 1954, p. B1.
3. Mehl, Ernest. "Persistence Won Obstacle Race for Kaycee," *The Sporting News,* November 17, 1954, p. 4.
4. Associated Press. "Report Hints Indians Hold Key to League Approval of A's Deal," *New York Times*, November 6, 1954, p. 21.
5. Associated Press. "Kansas City Is Certain Athletics Will Attract 1,000,000 Yearly," *New York Times*, November 7, 1954, p. S1.

6. Mehl, Ernest. "Hammers Ring in Rebuilding of K.C. Park," *The Sporting News,* November 27, 1954, p. 21.

7. *Chicago Daily Tribune*. "It's Official! A's Move to Kansas City," November 9, 1954, p. B1.

8. *Chicago Daily Tribune*. "A's Sad Secret—Foreclosure," November 9, 1954, p. B1.

9. *Chicago Daily Tribune*. "It's Official! A's Move to Kansas City," November 9, 1954, p. B1.

10. Drebinger, John. "Athletics Transfer to Kansas City Wins Final American League Approval," *New York Times*, November 9, 1954, p. 33.

11. Mehl, Ernest. "Persistence Won Obstacle Race for Kaycee," *The Sporting News,* November 17, 1954, p. 4.

12. *Chicago Daily Tribune*. "A's Sad Secret—Foreclosure," November 9, 1954, p. B1.

13. Spink, J. G. Taylor. "All's Well That Ends Well for K.C." (Editorial) *The Sporting News,* November 17, 1954.

14. Mann, Arthur. "How to Buy a Ball Club for Peanuts," *The Saturday Evening Post*, April 9, 1955, p. 106.

15. Ibid.

16. Mehl, Ernest. *The Kansas City Athletics*. New York: Holt, 1956, p. 192.

17. Ibid.

18. *The Sporting News*. "Frick Denies More Time Sought to Sell Yankee Park," December 22, 1954, p. 9.

III

THE TRADES

Part III Timeline

March 30, 1955: K.C. sends $50,000 to N.Y. for Ewell Blackwell, Tom Gorman, and Dick Kryhoski.

April 28, 1955: K.C. sends $10,000 to N.Y. for Lou Sleater.

May 11, 1955: K.C. sends Sonny Dixon and cash to N.Y. for Enos Slaughter and Johnny Sain.

June 14, 1956: K.C. sends Bill Renna, Moe Burtschy, and cash to N.Y. for Lou Skizas and Eddie Robinson.

July 11, 1956: K.C. sends Tom Lasorda to N.Y. for Wally Burnette.

August 25, 1956: K.C. sends Enos Slaughter to N.Y. for the waiver price.

October 16, 1956: K.C. sends cash to N.Y. for Bob Cerv.

February 19, 1957: K.C. sends Bobby Shantz, Art Ditmar, Wayne Belardi, Jack McMahan, and players to be named later to N.Y. for Irv Noren, Milt Graff, Mickey McDermott, Tom Morgan, Rip Coleman, Billy Hunter, and a player to be named later.

April 4, 1957: K.C. sends Curt Roberts to N.Y.

April 5, 1957: N.Y. sends Jack Urban to K.C.

June 4, 1957: K.C. sends Clete Boyer to N.Y.

June 15, 1957: K.C. sends Ryne Duren, Jim Pisoni, and Harry Simpson to N.Y. for Billy Martin, Woodie Held, Ralph Terry, and Bob Martyn.

July 18, 1957: A's owner Arnold Johnson appears before the Antitrust Subcommittee of the Committee on the Judiciary House of Representatives, 85th Congress.

June 15, 1958: K.C. sends Virgil Trucks and Duke Maas to N.Y. for Harry Simpson and Bob Grim.

August 22, 1958: K.C. sends Murry Dickson to N.Y. for Zeke Bella and cash.

April 8, 1959: K.C. sends Jack Urban to N.Y. for Mark Freeman.

April 12, 1959: K.C. sends Mike Baxes and Bob Martyn to N.Y. for Russ Snyder and Tommy Carroll.

May 9, 1959: K.C. acquires Murry Dickson from N.Y. for the waiver price and sends Mark Freeman to N.Y. for the waiver price.

May 26, 1959: K.C. sends Ralph Terry and Hector Lopez to N.Y. for Johnny Kucks, Tom Sturdivant, and Jerry Lumpe.

December 11, 1959: K.C. sends Roger Maris, Kent Hadley, and Joe DeMaestri to N.Y. for Norm Siebern, Hank Bauer, Marv Throneberry, and Don Larsen.

March 10, 1960: Arnold Johnson dies of a cerebral hemorrhage.

Chapter 10

A MAJOR LEAGUE FARM TEAM

There's only two kinds of people: the caught and the uncaught.
—Ralph Terry, quoting a Texas judge[1]

G ive us three years, five at the outside, and we'll build a winner,"[2] Kansas City Athletics owner Arnold Johnson boldly declared in the spring of 1955. By the time of his untimely death as a result of a cerebral hemorrhage on March 10, 1960, the A's were in shambles, consistently at the bottom of the league standings. During these five years, all the Cassandran warnings expressed by Clark Griffith, and, for a time, Walter Briggs, were realized, and the A's were widely perceived as a Major League farm team for the New York Yankees. From 1955 to 1959, the A's and Yankees traded with an unparalleled constancy, 16 transactions involving 61 players, with some players riding the Kansas City–New York express more than once.

Lee MacPhail, head of the Yankees farm system during this period, acknowledges, "There was a relationship between the clubs. But it was nothing inappropriate."[3] It was at minimum inappropriate. The A's front office was littered with ex-Yankee employees, including those in charge of player personnel—Parke Carroll and Ray Kennedy. While collusion is hard to prove, the circumstantial evidence points to Arnold Johnson as the Yankees ace in the hole.

How else can the sale of Blues Stadium be explained? While Kansas City was clamoring for the Yankees to come up with a price to enable them to buy Blues Stadium and pursue their own independent access to

Major League baseball, Dan Topping and Del Webb kept pushing the city off and giving them false hopes that they would be cooperative in delivering the ballpark to the city. Meanwhile, they were negotiating to sell the park to their business ally Johnson. What did this do? It gave Johnson a leg up on any future ownership group looking for a big league franchise by allowing Johnson to have a stadium ready at hand.

How else can the sale of the Philadelphia A's be explained? While Johnson was the first bidder, he never had more than a verbal commitment on the table or a written agreement with the Macks until the very end. The Philadelphia syndicate had at least as much money, if not more, than Johnson, yet was held to a different, more exacting, standard of disclosure by American League president Will Harridge and was swiftly rejected. Did the Yankees exert their power over the American League, as Shirley Povich had said they would? That impression was certainly broadcast through quotes from Griffith, Briggs, Bob Carpenter, and others; they felt the Yankees called the shots. Indisputably, a close business partner of Yankee ownership, as well as the owner of their stadium, was permitted entrance into the select group of Major League owners, despite clear conflict of interest. Now that the Johnson matter was closed, the owners voted to shut down future Johnson–Yankee types of affairs in a December vote that declared no one could own stock in two clubs or "any other proprietary interest or financial interest" in any other club.[4] Clearly, there was enough discomfort with Johnson and the Yankees to create a rule to outlaw this type of relationship in the future, although why that unease did not prevent a vote of approval one month before is a mystery.

That the A's were merely another minor league team in the Yankee organization rankled all concerned in Kansas City—players, sportswriters, and fans. It was clear to players at the time that the A's were under the control of the Yankees. Whitey Herzog, later hugely successful as manager of the Kansas City Royals and St. Louis Cardinals, was an Athletics' outfielder for two seasons, 1959 and 1960. "The players knew it," Herzog reported. "We knew that if we had a good year, we'd be in New York by August."[5] *New York Times* sportswriter George Vecsey summed it up perfectly: "The Brother-In-Law League allowed the Yankees to dip into the A's roster and take whatever they needed."[6] A Kansas City writer cited that fans were "sore" that the A's were seen as "just part of the Yankee farm system."[7]

An argument repeatedly used by Yankee ownership to deflect this criticism took this form: no one else would trade with the Yankees; therefore they had no choice but to deal with the A's. On its face, that alone would be suspicious; if no other club would engage in transactions with the Yankee pennant juggernaut, why would the A's? George Weiss made the claim repeatedly. At the 1953 Minor League convention in Atlanta, Yankee skipper Casey Stengel cried, "It is silly to talk about a deal, because it looks like nobody wants to deal with us. Maybe they got together and decided not to make a trade with the Yankees."[8] Poor Yankees. In December of 1953 the Yankees had recently defeated the Brooklyn Dodgers, again, in the World Series, the fifth consecutive championship for Stengel's stars. It was simply not the case that the Yankees were pariahs in the world of player swaps.

In the five years from 1950 to 1954, when the Yanks won four of the five titles, Bronx brass traded 28 times with the other Major League clubs. Of these deals, only two (7.14 percent) were conducted with the Mack-led Philadelphia A's. During the five-year reign of Arnold Johnson, 1955–1959, the Yankees made nearly the identical amount of trades (29)—a bit weighted toward the Johnson A's, though. Of these 29 transactions, 16 were with Kansas City—a whopping 55.17 percent. Adding fuel to the fire, after the sad death of Arnold Johnson before the 1960 season, the Yankees–A's pipeline shut down. From 1960 to 1964, the Yankees engaged in 18 deals, only two with the now Charles Finley–owned A's. The parabolic trading between New York and Kansas City occurred only during the Johnson years.

What of the A's? As a team low on talent and short on success, they must have made plenty of deals. That was so, and from 1955 to 1959, the A's were extremely active in the market. Looking for help, the A's made 47 total trades, the 16 with the Bronx Bombers being slightly more than a third of the total. No other team was within shouting distance of the quantity of trades the A's conducted with the Yankees. The Pirates, Tigers, and Indians were tied for second, with 5 trades each, a long way from 16. After Johnson's demise, the A's were active with 38 transactions from 1960 to 1964, the aforementioned two with the Yankees being about 5 percent of their total.

Were the A's a farm team? A Major League team uses its minor league clubs mostly in two ways. There's the mid-season call-up, when the Major League team needs help from below, whether because of injury or unacceptable performance. Also, there's the late-season call-up, when rosters expand. These minor leaguers are brought up less to aid the team's performance on the field and more to give these youngsters a taste of the big time—the proverbial "cup of coffee." How did the Yankees' dipping into their lower levels change during the Johnson era in Kansas City?

When the Kansas City Blues were the Yankees' top level (AAA) minor league squad, they supplied New York with 71 players from 1950 to 1954. During this half-decade, 62 percent of the call-ups were the end-of-the-year option recall, the late-season moves that are of less significance. During the Johnson years, the years of the accusation that the A's served as a Yankee farm team, nearly 84 percent of Yankee minor league transfers were of the "cup of coffee" variety. With AAA clubs in Richmond and Denver at various times during the 1955 to 1960 period, 80 players were brought to Yankee Stadium, 67 at the end of August.

The decrease in non–end-of-the-year call-ups, coupled with the increase in trading with the A's during the years of Johnson ownership, is damning empirical evidence. Using the minor leagues less during the season for their needs, and turning to Kansas City more, does show transference of the minor league role from Richmond or Denver to the Kansas City Athletics. The A's management, former Yankees all, seemed to have a hard time releasing themselves from the grasp of their former boss, Yankee general manager George Weiss. Parke Carroll had voiced his view on the trading process in June of 1953, more than a year before he went from a Yankee to an A's executive. Said Carroll, "The idea of a trade or sale isn't to hurt one club at the expense of another but rather to help two clubs, each swapping a player it doesn't need for a player it needs."[9] George Weiss said, "The Yankees and Kansas City have faith in each other."[10] For Kansas City, that faith was blind.

---

1. Conversation with author, summer 2005.
2. Holland, Gerald. "The A's Find Friends in Cowtown," *Sports Illustrated*, April 25, 1955 (Vol. 64, Issue 7), p. 22.

3. Letter to author, summer 2005.

4. Associated Press. "Majors Veto Radio-TV Curb; Minors Gain Financial Aid," *Chicago Daily Tribune*, December 8, 1954, p. C1.

5. Schwarz, Alan. "The Man Behind the Myth," *Sport*, October 1998, p. 80.

6. Vecsey, George. "Roger Maris: No Asterisk," *New York Times*, December 16, 1985, p. C11.

7. Daniel, Dan. "Daniel's Dope," *The Sporting News*, March 11, 1960.

8. Daniel, Dan. "Cries of 'Hate Yankees' Stir Case to Yelps About Rivals," *The Sporting News,* December 8, 1953, p. 17.

9. Mehl, Ernest. "Sporting Comment," *Kansas City Star*, June 14, 1953, p. 2B.

10. Shecter, Leonard. *Roger Maris: Home Run Record.* New York: Bartholomew House, 1961.

Chapter 11

THE DEVIL'S IN
THE DETAILS

March 30, 1955: K.C. Sends $50,000 to N.Y. for Ewell Blackwell, Tom Gorman, and Dick Kryhoski

By the tail end of 1957, when it was now firmly in baseball fans' minds that the A's–Yankees relationship was a mite too cozy, one of Arnold Johnson's justifications for the continuous trading between the two clubs was that "we have traded with the Yankees because the Yankees have had young players who figured to help us."[1] So many of the problems with the New York–Kansas City trades were exemplified by this first trade. The A's received Ewell Blackwell, one of the best pitchers in the National League—in 1947! Not only was the string bean Blackwell years past his fearsome fastball throwing, sidearm-delivering form, but he was just coming off the voluntary retirement list. At 32 years old, "The Whip" had been out of the game for nearly 18 months because of a sore arm. Applying for reinstatement in February 1955, the 6'6" Blackwell did nothing to impress manager Stengel after his three spring outings. In 1947 Blackwell had come within two outs of hurling consecutive no-hitters, á la teammate Johnny Vander Meer. Now, eight years later he was damaged goods. He would last through two appearances with the fledgling Kansas City squad, allowing three runs in four innings and garnering his release on April 30.

1953 Ewell Blackwell.

Johnson had promised to spend money on improving the A's roster. What did he get besides a broken-down old righty? In Tom Gorman, another sidearmer, the A's received a 29-year-old who, in parts of the three campaigns with New York, had never pitched more than 77 innings and whose performance was always average. He had been sent to minor league Kansas City for part of 1954, and there were no plans to use him in 1955. Not only did the Yankees have no use for Gorman in the upcoming year, but they had little use for him during spring training, where he was used sparingly. He would stick with the A's for parts of the next five years, posting numbers consistent with a second-tier starting pitcher.

1956 Tom Gorman.

Dick Kryhoski defined *journeyman*. Since his debut for the Yankees in 1949, Kryhoski, a first baseman, had seen action with the Detroit Tigers, St. Louis Browns, and Baltimore Orioles. At 30, he was no longer a prospect. Returning to the Yankees in the trade that brought Don Larsen and Bob Turley to New York after the 1954 season, Kryhoski did not appear with the Yankees this second time around. It was clear before he was sold to Kansas City that he "never quite lived up to expectations,"[2] and he mercifully came to the plate only 47 times, hitting .213 with zero home runs. He never played in the Major Leagues after his sole year of service with Johnson's A's.

The first deal bode ill. While Gorman's middling performance may have been worth $50,000, it is hard to argue that the A's gained much from the trade. Blackwell was not even a truly active player, while Kryhoski was already a has-been that never was; there was not a young prospect in the bunch. Later, after several trades were made, the consensus was that the New Yorkers sent players they felt were of no use to them. It was clear from the outset that Yankee castoffs were to be the pool from which the A's could choose.

April 28, 1955: K.C. Sends $10,000 to N.Y. for Lou Sleater

A waiver transaction, the A's picked up left-hander Lou Sleater, a pitcher already in his late 20s who had seen time with the Browns and Senators and had been purchased by the Yankees from Toronto in the International League in October of 1954. With a weak record over parts of three seasons in St. Louis, Sleater, whose main pitch was a knuckle ball, did a slightly better job in his one year in Washington. The Yankees were obviously unimpressed and never gave him a chance. They did manage to exact another $10 thousand from Johnson, bringing their total receipts to $60,000 in their first month of trading (or selling) with their partner.

During the wrangling over the future of the Philadelphia A's, the Yankees had clamored for compensation for losing their minor league territory when the A's moved from Philadelphia. It turned out to be a mere smokescreen, a false showing of opposition to their friend's ambitions to join the ranks of Major League owners. Ironically, Milwaukee had been paid $50,000 for the loss of their minor league rights. In just two trades, the Yankees had recouped slightly more in transactions created, quite possibly, to send the Yanks some cash for their troubles.

May 11, 1955: K.C. Sends Sonny Dixon and Cash to N.Y. for Enos Slaughter and Johnny Sain

Sain, of the legendary rhyme, "Spahn and Sain and pray for rain," was seven years removed from that glorious year when the Boston Braves won the National League pennant. Sain, a 20-game winner four times between 1946 and 1950, threw a steady stream of curveballs, earning him the sobriquet "The Man of 1000 Curves." He had put in a few quality years for the Yankees as bullpen ace and spot starter. Leading the team in saves and appearances in 1952 and 1954, Sain contributed greatly to Yankee success. He won 11 games in 1952 and 14 in 1953, helping the Bombers to two World Series titles. After a poor start to the 1955 season, a 6.75 ERA in 5-1/3 innings, he was shipped to Kansas City, a 37-year-old past his prime. He pitched an unimpressive 44-2/3 innings for the rest of the year, giving up nearly 5.5 runs per game. It would turn out to be Sain's farewell season, after which he would embark on a very successful career as a Major League pitching coach.

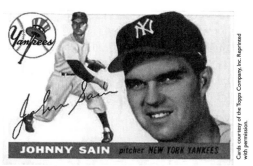

1955 Johnny Sain.

Enos "Country" Slaughter continued the "youth" movement of the A's. Slaughter was a great prospect—two decades earlier. He was 39 years old when the Yankees sent him to the Midwest. A true great who roamed the Cardinals outfield from 1938 to 1953, a 10-time All-Star and author of one of baseball's signature moments, his mad dash to home to defeat the Red Sox in the World Series of 1946, Slaughter was nearing the end of a career that would earn him induction into the Baseball Hall of Fame in 1985. Slaughter had performed poorly (.248 AVG, 1 HR, 19 RBIs) in limited service with the 1954 Yankees, a broken wrist resulting in an abridged season. Not given a real chance to start the new season (only one hit in nine at-bats), Slaughter was sent packing. While the Yankees felt they were sending a wrecked, older ballplayer to the A's, Slaughter performed well over parts of the next two seasons and was the first example of another Yankee–A's trend.

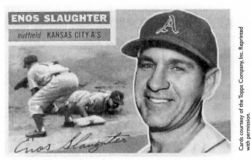

1956 Enos Slaughter.

A recurring theme in Yankee and A's trades was that the Yankees could pick and choose whoever they thought was of use to them from the A's roster. The Yankees thought they were sending a has-been out west, consistent with the likes of Blackwell and Sain. At the time of the deal, Slaughter's career seemed at an end. Much to everyone's surprise, he saw a resurgence as an A, and the deal worked out well for Kansas City. That only paved his way back east. Gil McDougald, a five-time Yankee All-Star infielder from 1951 to 1960 noted that he can "remember Casey asking who on the KC team could help us?"[3] when canvassing Yankee players on whom the team should pursue in trades. Stengel gave the impression that anybody on the A's roster was for the taking, just like making a shopping list before going to the store. Hitting for a .302 average during his stay in Kansas City (.322 in 1955), Slaughter piqued the Yankees' interest again in 1956 and, when they needed late-season help, he was sent back to New York.

At the time, Ernie Mehl conceded that the Yanks "had little use"[4] for the two aged stars. Again, Yankee hand-me-downs were all Kansas City was permitted to receive. John (Sonny) Dixon, a near 30-year-old righty was summarily sold to the Yankees' top minor league club in Denver, although he was called up later in the year to pitch four and one-third innings. Again, for the third consecutive transaction, the A's sent an undisclosed sum to the Yankees. It is more than interesting that Arnold Johnson was consistently sending cash New York's way. After three deals, the A's had received six players whose average age was over 32 and had sent over $60,000 to the already wealthy New Yorkers. It was hard to see how these initial swaps fit the Parke Carroll mold of two teams helping each other. It seems like the Yankees were helping themselves to Kansas City dollars.

June 14, 1956: K.C. Sends Bill Renna, Moe Burtschy and Cash to N.Y. for Lou Skizas and Eddie Robinson

A minor league deal, another older player and more money for the Yankees. First baseman Robinson had been a four-time All-Star, most recently in 1953, when he drove in 102 runs for the Philadelphia A's. He was a key part of the trade between the pre-Johnson A's, along with Harry Byrd, to the Yankees on December 1953, the day before the Yankee Stadium sale was completed. That trade, though overwhelmingly in the Yankees favor, did not pan out as they thought it would. Robinson's poor initial play, .268, 3 HRs, 27 RBIs in 1954, followed by a .208, 16 HRs, 42 RBIs season in 1955, hastened his exit. When he started 1956 with a .222 average, he was gone. The A's, once again, had the good fortune of receiving a player past his prime. Now 35, Robinson would hit .198 with two homers the rest of the year. Cast off by the A's, Eddie Robinson played for three clubs (Detroit, Cleveland, and Baltimore) in 1957 before leaving the big leagues.

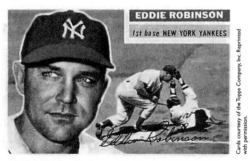

1956 Eddie Robinson.

Lou Skizas, Bill Renna, and Ed "Moe" Burtschy were all involved via minor league franchises. In Skizas, the A's finally received a productive player in a Yankee trade, although for a short time. At 24 years old, he was the first young player that the Yankees sent to the A's and, for the duration of the 1956 campaign, led the A's with a .316 batting average. He also had some pop in his bat, with 11 homers in 83 games. The following year he would slump to .248 and be traded in November of 1957 to the Tigers. Playing sporadically in Motown, he also saw limited action for the White Sox in 1959 before his career ended.

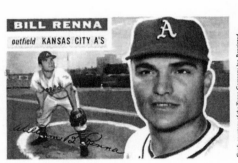

1956 Bill Renna.

1957 Lou Skizas.

Skizas had been brought up by the Yankees from their Richmond Triple A Minor Leagues right before being moved to Kansas City. Renna and Burtschy were sold directly from the A's to Richmond. "Big Bill" Renna, an outfielder who was also part of the 1953 trade involving Eddie Robinson, never saw time with the Yankees, although he re-emerged with the Red Sox in 1958 and 1959. Burtschy, a right-handed pitcher, also never played for New York. He never appeared in a Major League uniform again. It is assumed that the Yankees put the cash they received from the A's (again an undisclosed amount) to better use than they did Renna and Burtschy. Clearing Robinson's spot on the roster was of the utmost import to the New Yorkers, who brought up 23-year-old slugging outfielder Norm Siebern from Richmond. Ironically, the powerhouse

Yankees were getting younger, while the struggling A's were going older, thanks to the graybeards who were sent to them from the east. Siebern would later factor in the most egregiously lopsided Yankees–A's trade.

July 11, 1956: K.C. Sends Tom Lasorda to N.Y. for Wally Burnette

The A's bought Burnette from the Yankees' Denver affiliate, selling Lasorda from the A's roster to the Yankee minor league team. Wally Burnette was a knuckleball-throwing right-hander who had never pitched for the Yankees but managed to put in a serviceable performance for Kansas City. For 1956, Burnette's ERA was 2.89 in 18 games, 14 as a starter. While he only won six of those games, it was enough to be the fourth highest in a weak group of hurlers. Used mostly in relief the following year, Burnette's ERA shot up to 4.30 runs per game. On his last legs in 1958, Wally pitched 28 1/3 innings before leaving the majors. He gave the A's more quality than the pitcher they gave up. Score one, quite modestly, for Kansas City (two, if the short-term "loan" of Slaughter is counted).

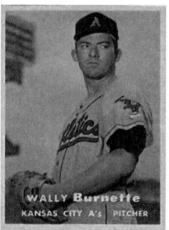

1957 Wally Burnette.

Lasorda, elected to the Hall of Fame after his 20-year stint as Dodgers manager, was finishing off a decidedly un-Hall of Fame career in 1956. With no wins and four losses, the lefty curveballer was not likely to find a spot on the defending champ's squad, and he didn't. The Dodgers, for whom Lasorda started a career that was highlighted by being sent to the minors before the 1955 season to make room for a "bonus baby" named Koufax, bought him from the Yankees in May of 1957. Not able to crack the Dodgers staff, Lasorda was given his release in 1960, soon to go on to bigger and better things.

August 25, 1956: K.C. Sends Enos Slaughter to N.Y. for the Waiver Price

Now 40, Slaughter had regained his usual high level of play in Kansas City. After his injury-filled first tour with the Yankees, he had played his way back into form, second on the A's in 1955 with a .322 average and still hitting a respectable .278 at the time of the deal. Now that he was a productive player again, the Yankees, suffering from a spate of outfield injuries, needed him back. The A's were willing to oblige for the waiver price, although there were reports of additional money, the usual mysterious undisclosed sum. As no trades could be made after June 15, waivers, where one team releases a player and the other teams all get a chance to pick him up for the waiver price (at that time $20,000), were a way to skirt around that rule.

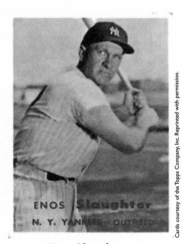

Cards courtesy of the Topps Company, Inc. Reprinted with permission.

ENOS Slaughter
N. Y. YANKEES OUTFIELD

1957 Enos Slaughter.

None too pleased about heading back to New York, Slaughter, never shy about expressing his view, proclaimed "I'm sick all over" about the deal.[5] Johnson professed his sincerity in looking out for Slaughter's best interest. The A's only wanted to give Slaughter another shot at appearing in the World Series. Of course, this would entail helping the Yankees get there. Clearly, the aging outfielder felt differently, and it was hard for him to leave Kansas City, where he had been the clear favorite of the fans, who had voted him the most popular player on the team in 1955.

For the Yankees, it was in with the old and out with the old, as stalwart pin striper and 1950 Most Valuable Player shortstop Phil Rizzuto was released on the same day to make room for the returning flycatcher. Slaughter would be an extremely useful fourth outfielder and pinch hitter until September of 1959, when he would be put on waivers and picked up by the Milwaukee Braves. As the oldest Major Leaguer in 1958 at 42, he hit .304 and led the American League in pinch-hit at-bats with 48. The A's were on their way to a last place, 100-loss season and had no business giving up one of their more useful players, as well as a longtime Missouri fan favorite. But the Yankees were calling and were not to be denied. Arnold Johnson announced that the A's would later receive a player who was presently a Yankee regular and who would be a regular for the A's as well. Certainly any player who could be a regular for the front-running Yankees would be assured a starting job with the cellar-dwelling Kansas Citians. For now, at least the A's got some of their money back.

October 16, 1956: K.C. Sends Cash to N.Y. for Bob Cerv

At last here was a good transaction for the A's. More than likely, the player the A's were expecting in the Slaughter waiver deal, Cerv was not a regular in the Yankee outfield in 1956. Cerv served as an extra outfielder, sharing playing time with a raft of others, while Mickey Mantle and Hank Bauer pulled down full-time duty. A great pinch-hitter, Cerv hit .328 in that role from 1954 to 1955 (20 hits in 61 at-bats). The delayed delivery of Cerv to Kansas City allowed him to participate in the World Series, garnering a winner's share of $8,714.76.

As an A, Cerv returned to the scene of some of his finest minor league seasons and produced his greatest Major League years. He was without a doubt the team's most productive player during his time there. A moderately successful 1957 season saw the ex-Yankee hit for a .272 average with 11 home runs and 44 runs batted in. Nothing here would signal his upper echelon feats of 1958. That year Cerv was a first-time (and only time) All-Star, hitting .305. His power numbers zoomed as he clubbed 38 home runs and drove in 104 runs. He finished fourth in homers, fourth in RBIs, and when the season ended, fourth in the MVP voting. While his numbers dropped in 1959 (20 HRs, 87 RBIs, .285 AVG), the slugging Nebraskan was still the top player in Kansas City. By early 1960 the Yankees needed him back, and back he went, but for a time, the A's had actually acquired a stellar performer.

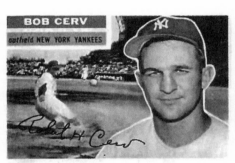

1956 Bob Cerv.

1957 Bob Cerv.

February 19, 1957: K.C. Sends Bobby Shantz, Art Ditmar, Wayne Belardi, Jack McMahan, and Players to Be Named Later to N.Y. for Irv Noren, Milt Graff, Mickey McDermott, Tom Morgan, Rip Coleman, Billy Hunter, and a Player To Be Named Later
   • **April 4, 1957: K.C. sends Curt Roberts to N.Y.**
   • **April 5, 1957: N.Y. sends Jack Urban to K.C.**
   • **June 4, 1957: K.C. sends Clete Boyer to N.Y.**

"Nobody's ever gonna trade unless they think they can rob you,"[6] said Skipper Stengel on the heels of this 13-player blockbuster, the largest trade in the major leagues since a 17-player swap in November 1954 between the Yanks and Orioles. While Stengel may have been right about most teams' motives when they entered into a trade, this transaction spoke loud and clear as to how the A's viewed their trading with New York and their willingness to be taken.

The minor league part of the trade involved Belardi, McMahan, Roberts, and Boyer. Wayne Belardi was a first baseman with some pop in his bat and had spent time with Brooklyn and Detroit from 1950 to 1956. In three of those years he had reasonable production in limited play—11 home runs and 34 runs driven in during the 1953 season in only 163 at-bats for the Dodgers. His power numbers were virtually the same the following year for the Tigers, although it took almost 90 more at-bats to achieve them. In 1956, when his numbers were half of 1953s (6 HRs and 15 RBIs), the signs pointed to a lessening of his strength at the plate and warranted a trade. The Yankees top farm club in Denver was the recipient of his waning skills in the February deal, and Belardi never surfaced again. Likewise, McMahan, a lefty twirler who had originally been signed by the Yankees as an amateur free agent before the 1952 season, went straight to the American Association. After splitting 1956 between the Pittsburgh Pirates and A's and racking up 0 wins, he went straight from Kansas City to Denver, his Major League career over.

In exchange for Belardi and McMahan, the Yankees sent 26-year-old Milt Graff, Denver's projected second baseman. Graff, coming off a league-leading 207-hit campaign along with a .317 showing in the lower minors in Birmingham of the Southern Association, would now be part of a new double-play tandem with Billy Hunter. Stengel touted this duo as a long-term solution to Kansas City's infield problems. Things went a bit awry for the A's, though, as Graff hit only .181, with not one shot clearing the wall in 155 at-bats. A single at-bat, and a hitless one to boot, comprised Graff's entire 1958 season for the A's before he disappeared from the big league scene. Casey's powers of prognostication were as unsuccessful as the short-lived Graff–Hunter keystone combo.

The early April moves that nearly completed the huge February trade were also of the bush league variety. Roberts had put in a full season with the cellar-dwelling Pirates in 1954, hitting .232. His position as a regular was due solely to Dick Groat's absence for military service, and when Groat returned, Roberts was virtually done, playing sporadically for the next two seasons. He too would never again play in the major leagues. Urban, on the other hand, put in a decent performance for the A's, winning seven games in 1957 and 8 in 1958. Once the Yankees saw that the 5'8" righty could produce on a Major League level, he was summoned back to the Yankee organization in April of 1959, similar to the cases of Slaughter and Cerv. Finding no use for him, the Yanks sold him to St. Louis. After eight appearances for the Cardinals in 1959, he too was gone.

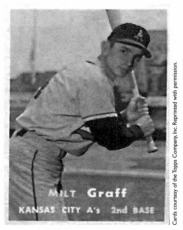

1957 Milt Graff.

Those were the lesser lights in the trade. The Yankees wanted pitching, and in Shantz and Ditmar they got two hurlers who would help them for years. Shantz, the 1952 American League MVP, had been suffering from a sore shoulder in recent years. While Yankee brass such as Stengel and Weiss were, for public consumption, spouting that Shantz was a gamble, word around the league was quite different. Although a winner of only two decisions in 1956 while sporting an ERA of 4.35, the pint-sized (5'6") port-sider was clearly regaining his form, and people were talking. Vice president Charles Comiskey of the Chicago White Sox was well aware that Shantz could help the Yankees, and the White Sox management agreed. "From our angle, I'd have to say the Yankees got the better of it," commented Comiskey.[7] Senators manager Chuck Dressen went further. "I'll let you in on a secret," he confided to Bob Addie of the *Washington Post*. "I told Calvin [Griffith, Senators president] to grab him from Kansas City because I think he can still pitch. He showed me in a series we had with Kansas City last summer. Bobby pitched three straight days in relief against us and *you don't do that if your arm is bad.* (author's emphasis)."[8] If Dressen knew that, so did Stengel, who slyly said, "If his arm comes through, I've got a good deal."[9] It did.

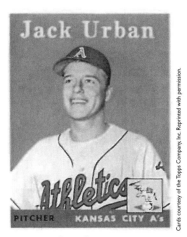

1958 Jack Urban.

For the next four years, Shantz was a huge presence on the Yankees staff, as both a starter and reliever. He burst out of the gate in 1957, making the All-Star team, leading the American League in ERA with a 2.45 ERA, and winning the first Gold Glove Award for excellence in fielding, when only one was handed out for each position across the whole Major Leagues. Shantz would go on to win the American League Award when each league's best were recognized starting in 1958 and every year he was on the mound for the Yankees (he would also win four straight in the National League from 1961 to 1964). Whether as fourth starter (1957), spot starter and long reliever (1958), or relief ace (1959 and 1960), Shantz contributed greatly to the Yankee success of the late 1950s. A starter (and loser) in Game 2 in the Yankees' World Series loss to Milwaukee in 1957, Shantz rebounded to save Game 2 of the 1960 Series. He nearly closed the door on the Pirates in Game 7 with five strong innings and was gone before the devastating blow off Bill Mazeroski's bat ended Yankee hopes. While the Yankees let Shantz go in the 1960 expansion draft to the new

Washington Senators, they got enough out of his service alone to make the trade worthwhile. As to the suspicious nature of the A's–Yankees trades, Shantz said, "I'm just glad I was part of one of those transactions!"[10]

Ditmar was more of a sure thing. At 6'2", 185 pounds, the lanky right-hander had won 12 games in both 1955 and 1956, years when the Athletics won only 63 and 52 times, respectively. "A practitioner of proved ability,"[11] Ditmar would only make things tougher for those clubs trying to play catch-up with the Yankees. Charles Comiskey admitted as much. For the next four plus years, Ditmar, with one of the best fastballs in the league according to *The Sporting News*, was a mainstay on the Yankees staff.

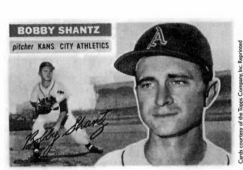

1956 Bobby Shantz.

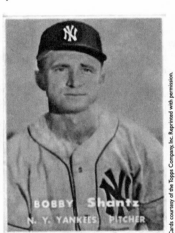

1957 Bobby Shantz.

As the Yankees' second-best reliever in 1957, behind Bob Grim, Ditmar put up an 8–3 record and a 3.25 ERA and was tied for the team lead with 46 appearances. After a similar performance out of the pen in 1958, Ditmar pitched three and two-thirds innings in Game 6 of the World Series, holding the Braves scoreless in a must-win situation for the Yankees, who ultimately prevailed in seven games. Ditmar's mix of inside fastballs and sliders elevated him to the starting rotation in 1959, and he led the Yankees with an ERA of 2.90 while compiling 13 victories. He followed this with the best year of his career, 1960. That season, the Winthrop, Massachusetts, native led the American League pennant winners with 15 wins, an ERA of 3.06, innings pitched with 200 and complete games (eight—tied with Whitey Ford). A stellar season ended on a sour note as Ditmar was shelled in the World Series by the potent Pirate bats, losing both games he started. His ERA of 21.60 bode ill for the 1961 campaign, and when Ditmar got off to a rough start with 3 losses while giving up 4.67 runs per game, he was traded to the Kansas City Athletics.

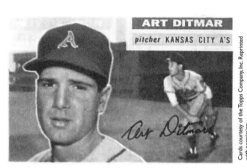

1956 Art Ditmar.

Cards courtesy of the Topps Company, Inc. Reprinted with permission.

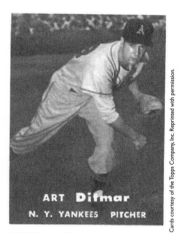

1957 Art Ditmar.

Cards courtesy of the Topps Company, Inc. Reprinted with permission.

For four years, the two pitchers the Yankees got from the lowly A's were major contributors to their success. Winning three pennants and one world championship with Shantz and Ditmar comprising one-fifth of their pitching staff, the Bombers were hard to beat. The A's gave up pitchers who were among the best on the best team in baseball. What did the A's get? Lou Boudreau crowed, "Now we have a pitching staff. This deal gives us three young pitchers, none of whom has reached his peak."[12] Mickey McDermott, Rip Coleman, and Tom Morgan would produce 12 wins combined for the A's. Art Ditmar alone would win 47 in his Yankee career, and Bobby Shantz another 30.

Mickey McDermott was a high-flying Red Sox prospect, an 18-game winner in 1953 at the age of 24. McDermott happily admits to a 100-mile-per-hour fastball and a wicked curve, although his fastball was in reality a respectable mid-90s. He also admits in his autobiography to a fast life style and wicked drinking problem. When he arrived in New York by way of Washington in 1956, his alcohol problem was drowning his career. After posting two wins in limited work and causing manager Stengel untold headaches for curfew breaking, he was included in the monster trade. In Kansas City, as one of the "three young pitchers," the 28-year-old, washed-up alcoholic pitcher won two games and was dumped on Detroit in 1958. After pitching two innings that year, McDermott would resurface briefly in 1961, putting in a few innings for the Cardinals, before wrapping up a once promising career with five and two-thirds innings and an ERA of over 14 for, once again, the A's.

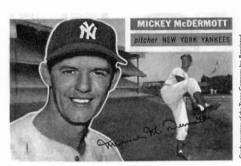

1956 Mickey McDermott.

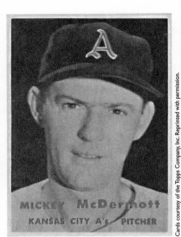

1957 Mickey McDermott.

Rip Coleman, nearly 26 at the time of the trade, was a sporadic member of the Yankees pitching crew in 1955 and 1956. Appearing in a total of 39 games during that period, Coleman produced an ERA slightly over 4 and was unable to prove to the Yankees executives that he was worth keeping, so he was sent to Kansas City, where he was unable to prove that he was worth keeping. With a 0 win, 7 loss season, and an atrocious ERA of 5.93, the second of the A's staff of the future was a complete bust. A trip to the minors for all of 1958 did nothing to right the Coleman ship. When he returned in 1959, he clearly showed that his 1957 season was no fluke and went 2–10. In fairness, his ERA improved a great deal, dropping to 4.56. That was all the A's could take, and he, like Mickey McDermott before him, was tossed. Coleman was put on waivers, and the Baltimore Orioles claimed him. He would throw four innings for them in 1959, then four more in 1960, and then he was finished as a Major League hurler.

1957 Rip Coleman.

In Tom Morgan, the A's got a valued member of the Yankees staff. After pitching 25 scoreless innings in spring training, Morgan made the staff in 1951 as a 21-year-old and produced nine wins as well as two shutout innings as the Yankees beat the New York Giants in the World Series. After missing part of 1952 and all of 1953 because of military service, Morgan returned for 1954 and notched 11 wins at the tail end of the Yankee starting rotation. He even tied for the team lead in shutouts with 4, remarkable in that he started only 17 games. For the next two years Morgan was a top-level relief pitcher, putting in 81 appearances and, in the pre-closer era, tallying 21 saves, both numbers pacing the Yankee relief corps. "Plowboy," so named by Mel Allen for his lengthy stroll to the mound from the bullpen, threw a hard sinker and had an average year with the A's. However, it was only one year, and after a nine-win, 4.64 ERA showing, Morgan was sent to the Tigers along with McDermott and others. Morgan would pitch for six more years, even garnering a few MVP votes as one of the pitching leaders of the 1961 expansion Los Angeles Angels. While McDermott and Coleman were useless, Morgan was serviceable in his only A's year. As Calvin Griffith commented in regard to Morgan, "Kansas City had to get something."[13]

1953 Tom Morgan.   *1957 Tom Morgan.*

What of the position players the A's received? While the pitchers were a disaster, did the A's at least get, as Yankee general manager George Weiss crowed, "a nucleus of major league players?"[14] The futility of Milt Graff's career has already been shown, but what of Billy Hunter, the other side of the double-play team that Casey Stengel said would help the A's? Hunter was the regular shortstop for the Browns in 1953 and kept that role when the team moved to Baltimore in 1954. Slight of bat, Hunter hit .219 and .243 in those years, with virtually no power. With the Yankees in 1955, Hunter played less and hit worse, his average dropping to .227. When the six-foot shortstop got his batting average up to .280 in limited time during the 1956 campaign, perhaps, like the groundhog from his Punxsutawney, Pennsylvania, birthplace, the A's foresaw an early end to his cold batting, but Kansas City proved to be a long winter for Hunter, as his offensive performance was truly bleak. An emergence of power, with eight home runs, was buried by a dismal .191 average in 116 games. When things got worse at the start of the 1959 season (.155 BA), Hunter was traded to Cleveland, where he improved to .195 before leaving big league ball for good.

1957 Billy Hunter.

Irv Noren had been a helpful member of the Yankees since he was acquired from the Senators soon after the start of the 1952 season. A superb defensive player, Noren served as a fourth outfielder in his first two years with New York. He became a regular in 1954 and 1955, putting up his best numbers in 1954. That year, Noren led the team with a .319 average and was leading the circuit in batting until a September slump knocked him down to fourth. Still, it would turn out to be his one all-star year, as knee surgeries would begin to hamper his play. When the A's acquired the now 32-year-old hobbled veteran, there was serious doubt that his knees would hold up, particularly after operations on both knees had limited his 1956 contribution to 29 games. Plus, Noren hated the idea of descending the ladder from the top-rung Yankees to the lowly A's. From his Pasadena home, Noren told United Press International that he would "consider retiring" unless the A's paid him "substantially what I received last year."[15] A grumbling and gimpy Noren played 81 games for the A's in 1957, hitting .212 with 2 home runs and 16 runs batted in before he was waived. He left the Major League scene in October 1960, released by the Los Angeles Dodgers.

1956 Irv Noren.

1957 Irv Noren.

The A's gave up two quality Major League pitchers and in return got seven players, none of whom would play more than two years with the A's and none of whom would play well. The minor league swaps of Belardi, McMahan, and Roberts were of little consequence. Arnold Johnson had claimed that this trade was "the most important since the Athletics were transferred from Philadelphia."[16] It was a disaster. On a curious note, the A's had been offered a similar trade from the White Sox, but they made greater demands. Comiskey claimed, "They wanted Billy Pierce or Jack Harshman included in the deal. Well, they didn't get a pitcher of that class from the Yankees."[17] Harshman had been a 15-game winner in 1956, while Billy Pierce had won the Pitcher of the Year Award from *The Sporting News*. From the Yankees, the pitchers the A's needed were Mickey McDermott, Rip Coleman, Tom Morgan, and Jack Urban. This willingness to accept the Yankees dross was troubling and suspicious. If the career paths of the 12 men dealt showed a clear triumph for the Yankees, what transpired in regard to Clete Boyer demonstrates a contempt for league rules, disdain for the feelings of Kansas City fans and, quite likely, a true collusive relationship between Arnold Johnson's A's and the New York Yankees.

The Clete Boyer part of the story begins with the "bonus baby" rule. Starting in 1947 (and ending in 1965 with the advent of the amateur draft), Major League owners were gripped by phenom fever, the symptoms of which caused great piles of money to be thrown at teenage prospects. Paul Pettit was handed $100,000 in 1950 and in return pitched 12 games in his entire Major League tenure with the Pirates. In 1953 the Phillies bestowed $100,000 on infielder Ted Kazanski, who hung on for six seasons, with an unremarkable .217 batting average. The Yankees first bonus baby was to be the next Lou Gehrig. Frank Leja, a 17-year-old from Massachusetts, had negotiated with each of the 16 Major League teams. While the Yankees did not announce his signing bonus, it was well known that Leja was asking for at least what Pettit and Kazanski got. Hardly the "Iron Horse" that Gehrig was, Leja would bat seven times in his Yankee career. These three examples of big money, low productivity were the norm for bonus players, and the Major Leagues tried to clamp down on the wild spending.

1957 Clete Boyer.   *1959 Clete Boyer.*

In 1954 the owners decreed that any player signed for a certain bonus (the amount changed over the years) would have to remain on the Major League roster for two years, and that each team could have no more than two such players. Rather than hit the owners with a cap on spending, it was thought that having unproven teens sit on the bench would prevent owners from lavishing prospects with piles of cash. The result was that many talented athletes were ruined; they could not learn their trade in the minor leagues, yet they were not good enough to play big league base-ball. The most notable of this class were Harmon Killebrew and Sandy Koufax, whose progress was impeded by lack of minor league instruction. Their talent was so great that they surmounted this difficulty and went on to Hall of Fame careers. Entering the 1955 season, the Yankees were at their maximum, with the aforementioned Leja and shortstop Tommy Carroll riding the pines.

Clete Boyer was a star shortstop at Alba High School in Missouri. "Not bragging," Clete proudly said, "but the best athlete always played short."[18] With Major League scouts from all over the country hovering around Boyer, the offers rolled in. He remembers several offers; the Red Sox, Cardinals, and Orioles all came calling. It was the Kansas City A's that ultimately signed the 18-year-old Boyer on May 30, 1955. When the A's tried to send the young prospect New York's way in February of 1957, they were in violation of the rule mandating that a bonus signer had to put in his two years with his original club. It took the American League office to intervene and prevent the transfer, and Boyer was sent to New York on June 4, once the deadline had passed.

This story is troubling in many ways. It would strain credulity to think that George Weiss, the preeminent general manager in all of baseball, who had signed two bonus players himself, would be unaware of the two-year requirement. As to what the A's knew, one can conclude that when the Yankees made any request, that was enough for them. It's puzzling why the A's would be in such a rush to send Boyer to New York that they were willing to violate Major League edicts. Why the A's would invest nearly two years' time on the young infielder and then not allow him the opportunity to learn his trade in the A's minor league organization after May 31 is a mystery. He had just turned 20 and had great potential.

Collusion between the two clubs was possible. With the Yankees at their bonus limit, could the A's have been convinced to sign the high school star with the understanding that he would end up in New York in two years, when the Yankees would not have to keep him on the big league roster and could send him to the minor leagues? In 1955 George Weiss told A's general manager and former underling Parke Carroll, that he would have to sign Boyer. Many baseball people believed that Boy-er's bonus of $35,000 was paid with Yankee money. According to Joe

Reichler, the A's signed Boyer "on behalf of the Yankees with the understanding that he would be turned over to New York as soon as the two-year period was through."[19]

Boyer recalled this period of his career with disgust. Although initially coy, he became very angry when the subject of his controversial signing and Arnold Johnson was broached. "I hate those guys," he fumed. It seemed, Boyer recollected, that he had been paid his $35,000 over three years—15, 10, and 10 as his total yearly compensation. There was no salary. He had expected the $5,000 minimum plus his bonus in the first year, and this had not panned out. At first, Boyer was unwilling to talk but later delved into the history of his signing.

Eventually Boyer was chatty and cooperative. When asked if it was true that the A's signed him on behalf of the Yankees, he acknowledged that he had been aware of the talk. "I heard about it later, " he acknowledged, "and there's one reason why I believe it." As a high school star, Clete was well known to baseball scouts. Tom Greenwade, the legendary Yankee scout most known for signing a young Oklahoman named Mantle, lived in nearby Willard, Missouri, about an hour's drive from Alba High. According to Boyer, Greenwade "knew how good I was." Oddly, the Yankees never approached Boyer or made an offer. Over 10 years later, Greenwade made a clubhouse visit to the Yankees. Boyer teasingly shouted, "How come you used to come to my house every day and eat dinner? Every day, Tom. You never made an offer, you just ate." Greenwade conceded the gist of the jibe, "Aw, you're exaggerating," he sheepishly replied.[20] Boyer didn't know for sure if the A's had signed him with the intent of shipping him to New York, but there was the "feeling the Yankees were gonna wait on me." Greenwade was inadvertently more revealing. In the same clubhouse stopover, Greenwade looked back on his signings, the players that he referred to tenderly as "his boys." The name he mentions right after Mickey Mantle is Clete Boyer.

As to the trade itself, Boyer had heard the gossip and in terms of the too comfortable relationship between the A's and Yankees, noted that it "felt like that was the way it was." "Who did they [New York] want that they didn't get?" he posited. The Yankees got the men they needed and provided Kansas City with "stop gap type of guys." "All you gotta do is look at the trades," he went further and brought up another point. The

A's were a miserable club on the field, who needed to rebuild. However, they received older players from the Yankees with regularity. What could the fans look forward to in the future if there were no prospects to anticipate? The A's only real prospect was this local boy who could provide hope for the coming years. Yet he was just a throw-in in a 13-player deal. It didn't add up.

Now that the Yankees had Boyer and were not obliged to keep him on the bench, he was sent to Binghamton and then promoted to Richmond (International League) to learn the trade of a Major League baseball player. He would reemerge in 1959, still spending some time at shortstop but soon to be firmly entrenched as the Yankees third baseman. While consistently in the shadow of Brooks Robinson, Clete Boyer was one of the finest hot corner defenders in the history of the game. A quick glove, vast range, and a gun for an arm, Boyer led the American League in assists three times and in double plays once. Though unable to crack Robinson's Gold Glove domination, Boyer's lifetime fielding percentage compares favorably. His breathtaking play at third in the 1961 World Series is still talked about today.

While the cavernous dimensions of Yankee Stadium and his low placement in the order prevented Boyer from putting up great offensive numbers, he had some pop and put up double-digit home run totals six times, tying for the team lead in triples on three occasions. A key contributor to the 1962 defeat of the San Francisco Giants, Boyer was second to Tom Tresh, posting a .318 average. His home run in Game 1 off Giants' lefty Billy O'Dell gave the Yankees a lead they would never relinquish. Another home run came in Game 7 of the 1964 Series, although it could not prevent sibling Ken Boyer's Cardinals from defeating the Yankees. Upon his trade to Atlanta, Boyer showed what he could have produced in a ballpark of more reasonable proportions, slugging 26 home runs and driving in 96 runs in 1967. Boyer played into 1971 and then left Atlanta and headed to Japan. Reflecting on his career, Boyer knew that his time in the minors, the time he was deprived of in Kansas City but given the luxury of in the Yankee organization, helped make him the player he became. "I was so happy the Yankees waited on me."

The multiplayer trade of February 1957 was so obviously to the disadvantage of the A's, that Cleveland general manager Hank Greenberg, who had opposed the Johnson shift of the A's to Kansas City, saw the dreadful implications. "It must be nice," Greenberg bitingly commented, "to have your own farm system in the same league."[21] More was to come.

June 15, 1957: K.C. Sends Ryne Duren, Jim Pisoni, and Harry Simpson to N.Y. for Billy Martin, Woodie Held, Ralph Terry, and Bob Martyn

The Copacabana incident was a unique moment in 1950s Yankee history, as the public got to see the real people behind the stolid, businessman-like corporate reputation the Yankees were labeled with during this decade of supreme success. The hard-drinking, hard-playing off-field activities were little known to the average fan, spoon-fed the image of the ultra-professional Yankees of the ball field. It also paved the way for this trade, another pro-Yankee transaction that allowed general manager George Weiss to dispose of one of his least-favorite players.

One month before the deal, on the night of May 15, a group of Yankees—Mickey Mantle, Whitey Ford, Yogi Berra, Johnny Kucks, and Hank Bauer, along with their wives—took their popular teammate Billy Martin out on the eve of his 29th birthday. The Copa was one of the premier nightspots in New York, showcasing top-notch performers. That night, Sammy Davis Jr. was playing the club. After dinner at Danny's Hideaway in mid-town Manhattan and a stopover at the Waldorf Astoria to see chart-topping singer Johnny Ray, the group made their way to the Copacabana, where they were seated at one large table. As the night of the 15th became the morning of the 16th, trouble began to brew.

A rowdy group on the other side of the room, later revealed as a crowd of bowlers and their wives, were spewing racial taunts at Davis, variously reported as "Sing this, Black Sambo," or "You Jungle Bunny," or both. Davis was a bit unnerved, and Hank Bauer took his part, telling the hecklers to shut up. Upon seeing Bauer and realizing their adversaries were a table full of Yankees, the bowlers began directing their invective toward the players. After 30 minutes of abuse, Bauer challenged one harasser, Edward Jones, a 40-year-old delicatessen owner from New York, and they headed toward the men's room. Whitey Ford recalls Bauer and

Martin following Jones, but by the time they arrived, Jones was sprawled out on the floor. Ford says that his teammates could never have been in the fight, as they never left his view, and later it was clear that two Copa bouncers had administered the beating.

Although Jones' suit against Bauer and the Copacabana for $250,000 was thrown out by a Manhattan grand jury for insufficient evidence, Weiss had the pretext he need to unload Martin, whom he saw as a bad influence on the club. Martin's supposed "bad influence" included rooming with Berra, Mantle, and Phil Rizzuto in years when each won the MVP Award. He also compiled a .333 average over five World Series and knew the real reason for the trade: "Weiss hated me."[22] When a team is desperate to trade a player, they usually will accept anything in the mix, as long as they are rid of that player. However, Weiss once again got the best of the A's in the Martin trade, some of it immediate, some of it deferred.

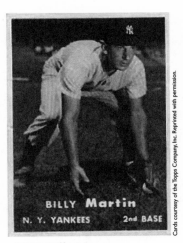

1957 Billy Martin.

In Martin, the A's received a versatile infielder with some pop in his bat. In 1956 Martin had achieved All-Star status, but he would always be known for his World Series heroics. Putting in one of the more memorable performances in postseason history, Martin had clouted a three-run home run in Game 2 of the 1952 set, leading the Yanks to victory. His most famous moment on the field came in Game 7, when Martin, sprinting at peak speed, rushed to grab a wind-blown pop-up for the third out with the bases full. It put another nail in another Dodger coffin. As if that was not enough to place him in the pantheon of Yankee postseason heroes, he followed that in 1953 with a .500 average and 23 total bases to win MVP as the Yankees sent the Brooklynites to yet one more defeat.

Despite a late-inning home run against his former teammates on the day after the trade, a certain fire left Martin when he was banished from New York. On that day the A's, snidely but accurately referred to as "the Yankee juniors (or seniors),"[23] fielded seven ex-Yankees. Martin played out the string in Kansas City before being sent north to Detroit in the same November deal that involved Mickey McDermott and Tom Morgan. From then on, "Billy the Kid" floated around the Major Leagues, spending time with Cleveland, Cincinnati, Milwaukee, and Minnesota. As division, pennant, and World Series winning manager from 1969 to 1988, with many firings in between, Martin became one of the most colorful characters in baseball history. For the Kansas City A's, he was a bust, and, what was worse, he was the cornerstone of this trade.

Bob Martyn, a minor league outfielder and American Association All-Star in Denver, would see action through 1959 for Kansas City but did little to make anyone notice. Hitting .263 over that span, Martyn had some speed and little power, hitting 3 homers and driving in 35 runs over 154 games, the equivalent of a full season. Sent back to the Yankees in 1959, Martyn's only service in the majors was to be the years he spent with the A's. On the other hand, Woodie Held, who went to Kansas City via the Yankees' Denver farm club, had a long Major League career as a slugging shortstop and part-time outfielder. Alas, only one of these years would be in the service of the Kansas City A's. In what amounted to a single full-season spread over 1957 and 1958, Held stroked 24 homers in 139 games, driving in 66 runs. Dealt to the Indians as part of the trade to acquire Roger Maris exactly one year after coming to the A's, Held would average nearly 20 home runs, 60 RBIs, and 100 strikeouts as a starter until 1964. After stints with Washington, Baltimore, California, and the Chicago White Sox, Held was released. Although not a key factor for the A's, Held was instrumental in their ability to get Maris, which is another story.

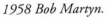
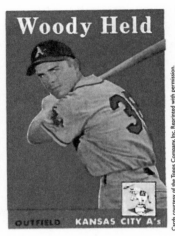

1958 Bob Martyn.   *1958 Woodie Held.*

The last player shipped to Kansas City was right-handed pitcher Ralph Terry. From the start, Terry, signed as an 18-year-old by Yankee scout Tom Greenwade, became involved in controversy. The Cardinals claimed that they had signed the talented Oklahoma teen, and it was up to Commissioner Ford Frick to decide where he should be assigned. Frick ruled for the Yankees, who sent him to Binghamton. From 1954 to 1956, Terry would pitch for Binghamton and Denver. A 13–4 mark in 1956 got him a late-season look, and after seven appearances in 1957, Terry was sent to the A's. It was certainly odd to have the Yankees send a highly touted prospect to the A's, a pitcher of potentially great value. Here lies the rub. With little chance to hone his array of fastballs, curves, sliders, and changeups for the Yankees, Kansas City was a place where Ralph Terry could mature and learn his craft against Major League hitters. In 1957 he pitched 130 2/3 innings, winning 4 and posting a respectable ERA of 3.38. He showed even better in 1958, when he won 11 games for a seventh-place team, logging in over 200 innings and emerging as one of the league's best in strikeout to walk ratio, with 134 strikeouts against 61 walks. It was a more seasoned hurler that was sent on a return trip to New York in May of 1959, and from then until 1964, Ralph Terry would be a leader on the Yankees staff and a World Series MVP. Terry, like Clete Boyer before him, were truly products of a Kansas City Athletic farm team, as they served on the big league roster until they were ready to come to New York.

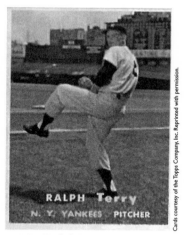

1957 Ralph Terry.   *1958 Ralph Terry.*

Having Terry get more work was not the only benefit derived by the Yankees. Harry "Suitcase" Simpson was a 31-year-old veteran outfielder who had a banner year in 1956, an all-star year in which he placed fourth in the circuit with 105 RBIs. With 21 home runs and a .293 average, Simpson was far and away the number one offensive force on the ball club. While his numbers were only slightly behind his 1956 pace, Simpson was a valuable member of the A's outfield, hitting .296 at the time of the trade. Simpson performed below expectations in New York before he was sent back to the A's a year later. Simpson's acquisition again proved that the Yankees could get anyone from the A's roster they deemed useful, regardless of how well he was playing in Kansas City.

Ryne Duren would gain fame as a wild flame-throwing, coke-bottle-glasses wearing leader of the Yankees bullpen from 1958 until his trade to the Los Angeles Angels early in the 1961 season. Though the blazing Duren had little Major League experience, he impressed the Yankees with an eight-strikeout performance over seven innings as the A's lost to New York 3–1 on May 2. The fearful Yankee batters had good reason to avoid digging in at the plate. A fifth inning heater sailed over Yogi

Berra's head, causing him great consternation. Duren, in a conversation with the author, felt this showing was his ticket to the Yankees. An obvious talent on an A's staff, that would rank second to last in the league in pitching, a shocked Lou Boudreau told Duren, "I had nothing to do with this."[24] The A's manager went on to explain to his promising righty that Duren was the last person the ball club who he would want to trade.

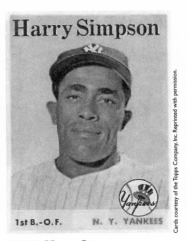

1957 Harry Simpson.   *1958 Harry Simpson.*

With the Yankees, Duren would blossom, taking the American League Rookie Pitcher of the Year honors from *The Sporting News* in 1958. As an All-Star in 1958, Duren was the leading fireman, pacing the league in saves with 20. The Yankee leader in saves and games pitched in 1958 and 1959, Duren would repeat as an All-Star in 1959, finishing second in the American League, with 14 saves. After his trade to the Angels, Duren would once again head to the mid-season classic, but it was a poor year, and by the end of 1965 he was out of baseball, with an admitted alcohol problem.

1958 Ryne Duren.   *1957 Jim Pisoni.*

The last player in this mix was Jim Pisoni, a good glove in center field, but not much with the bat. After playing a bit with Kansas City, he went straight to Denver. He was drafted from the Yankee organization in December of 1958, only to be returned to New York in May of 1959. He played briefly for the Yankees in 1959 and 1960. While not changing teams, Milt Graff, the A's infielder of the future according to Stengel, was sent back to the Yankees Triple A Minor League franchise in Denver. While still a member of the A's organization, Graff was a reminder of just what kind of bounty the A's had been receiving from the Yankees. This trade showed increasingly definable themes: the Yankees could get the best players from the A's roster, get prospects from a team desperately in need of the same, send their youngsters to gain experience in Kansas Ciy before being brought to New York, and drop on the A's their unwanted or troublesome players. By late 1957, 16 of the 25-man roster of the A's were once Yankee-held. It was so noticeable that a Congressional committee sought to find out exactly what was the nature of the A's and Yankees relationship. Arnold Johnson came to explain.

1. Mehl, Ernest. "A's Rap Rep That They Will 'Trade Only with Yanks,'" *The Sporting News*, December 4, 1957, p.19.
2. Associated Press. "A's Purchase Blackwell, Two Others," *Los Angeles Times*, March 31, 1955, p. C1.
3. Letter to author.
4. Mehl, Ernest. *The Kansas City Athletics.* New York: Holt, 1956. p. 175.
5. Associated Press. "News 'Sickens' Slaughter," *New York Times*, August 26, 1956, p. S1.
6. *Washington Post and Times Herald.* "The Big Switch," February 23, 1957, p. A10.
7. *Chicago Daily Tribune.* "Trade Helps Yanks, View of Comiskey," February 20, 1957, p. B3.
8. Addie, Bob. "Dressen Calls Shantz Key in Yanks' Deal," *Washington Post and Times Herald*, February 21, 1957, p. D1.
9. Associated Press. "McDermott, Noren Go to K.C. Club in 13-Man Deal." *Washington Post and Times Herald*, February 20, 1957, p. C1.
10. Letter to author.
11. *Washington Post and Times Herald*, p. A10.
12. Prell, Edward. "Yanks Acquire Athletics' Ditmar in 13 Man Deal," *Chicago Daily Tribune*, February 20, 1957, p. B1.
13. Addie, Bob. "Griffith Still Hopes for Yanks Trade," *Washington Post and Times Herald*, February 20, 1957, p. C1.
14. Briordy, William J. "Noren, Coleman Go to Kansas City," *New York Times*, February 20, 1957, p. 39.
15. Ibid.
16. Associated Press. "McDermott, Noren Go to K.C. Club in 13-Man Deal," *Washington Post and Times Herald*, February 20, 1957, p. C1.
17. *Chicago Daily Tribune,* "Trade Helps Yanks, View of Comiskey," February 20, 1957 p. B3.
18. Interview with author.
19. Reichler, Joseph L. *The Baseball Trade Register.* New York: Macmillan, 1984, p. 349.
20. Vecsey, George. "He's the Man Who Discovered Mick," *Newsday*, July 26, 1966.
21. Golenbock, Peter. *Dynasty.* Englewood Cliffs, NJ: Prentice-Hall, 1975, p. 193.
22. Ford, Whitey, Mantle, Mickey, and Durso, Joseph. *Whitey and Mickey.* New York: The Viking Press, 1977, p. 100.
23. Addie, Bob. "Martin Hits Two-Run Homer Off Kemmerer," *Washington Post and Times Herald*, June 20, 1957, p. C1.
24. Interview with author, March 5, 2005.

Chapter 12

CONGRESS CALLS

Since 1922, when Supreme Court Justice Oliver Wendell Holmes ruled that baseball was exempt from antitrust laws because the interstate travel necessary to play the games was not the essential object of the industry (*Federal Baseball Club of Baltimore, Inc. v. National Baseball Clubs*), baseball has been viewed more as a game than a multimillion- (now multibillion-) dollar business. Periodically, the House of Representatives holds hearings to look at the exemption specifically, and baseball business in general, to keep watch on any potential unlawful monopolistic activities. On July 18, 1957, Arnold Johnson appeared before the Antitrust Subcommittee and its chairman, Emanuel Cellars (Democrat, New York), at his own request, accompanied by attorneys Edward Vollers and Paul Porter.

All evidence to the contrary, Johnson defended his actions *vis-à-vis* the Yankees. In his opening comments Johnson swore his love of baseball was his sole reason for buying the A's. Making money was not his aim, said the banker and financier. As to the aspersions cast his way, Johnson was firm in his defense. "I want to say that we are not anybody's 'farm' club. We are not anyone's 'country cousin.'" Further, "the only interest I have in the New York Yankees or any other major league club is beating their brains out every time we play them, and I mean that."[1]

With Johnson's protest on record, Julian Singman, the counsel to the committee, had a few questions regarding Johnson's short-lived ownership of Yankee and Blues Stadiums. After delineating the trail of payments, leases, and first and second mortgages (see Chapter 1), Singman noted that the cash outlay by Johnson was only $600,000 and inquired how much Johnson received in his sale of Blues Stadium to Kansas City less than one year later. When Johnson answered $650,000, committee counsel pointed out that within a year, Johnson had recouped all cash laid out and was still in possession of all the physical assets as well as the Yankee lease payments for use of Yankee Stadium, which outstripped the money due to the Knights of Columbus. Johnson pointed out that he did lose Blues Stadium (the tiniest piece of the deal), but Singman made it clear that Arnold Johnson had ended up with ownership of prestigious Yankee Stadium and a lucrative income stream with no money down.

Moving on to the potential Rule 20 conflict posed by his ownership of the Yankee ballpark and subsequent purchase of the Philadelphia A's, Johnson reiterated that he never felt a conflict truly existed. Though Singman mentioned that Commissioner Frick felt such a conflict was cause for concern, Johnson believed it was only an American League matter and that Frick was not in the mix. Singman pressed the issue. As Johnson, or Arnold Johnson Corp., had a "debtor relationship" with the Yankees, wasn't it conceivable that if the loan ($2.9 million from Topping and Webb to Johnson) were in need of refinancing or extension, the Yankees could be "in a position to influence or exert pressure on the team [the A's]?"[2] Johnson responded only that the Yankees paid rent and that his debt was on the stadium real estate, somewhat off the point in that it would still leave him in a position of debtor.

The questioning turned to the divestiture of the Yankee Stadium property. A condition to the approval of Johnson's purchase of the A's on November 8, 1954, was that he would put the stadium on the market and finalize a sale within 90 days. On March 22, 1955, 134 days later, it was announced that Chicagoan John W. Cox, president of General Package Corporation, had purchased the stadium from his longtime friend Arnold Johnson. From West Palm Beach, Florida, the deal was made public, although the price was not. Said Johnson at that time, "I have been paid in full, either in cash or real estate and thus my connection with Yankee Stadium is completely and permanently severed."[3] Cox, a native Texan and Rice University graduate, had been a practicing attorney when he joined General Package about 15 years previous, ultimately climbing to the presidency in 1953. He had been a friend to Arnold Johnson for over two decades, and the two had been involved in real estate transactions over time. Had Johnson talked to other potential buyers than his friend and sometime business partner? Johnson told the committee that "Undoubtedly I did. I cannot recall."[4] A businessman of such acumen would surely be able to unload a property of world renown, with a positive revenue stream attached, with little trouble, even considering the short time allotted.

Considering that the Yankee Stadium piece of the December 1953 real estate deal could be set comfortably at $3.35 million (the $6.5 million Johnson paid minus the $2.5 million the Knights of Columbus paid him for the land and the $650,000 Kansas City paid for Blues Stadium), and throwing in that the original package had been appraised for even more ($8 million), it was likely that Yankee Stadium was worth at least a few million dollars. Cox paid $385,000. Not only was the price substantially below market value, but the proof of the sale was questionable. Literally, a scrap of paper, a memo dated February 25, 1955, was the only document of transfer. On this fragment were the following itemized entries:

Figure 12.1

Cash on transfer of all stock	$30,000
Assume Lannan Agreement	$60,000
Assume balance on bank loan	$245,000
Real estate	$50,000
TOTAL	**$385,000**

In addition, was a line about changing the name of the corporation from Arnold Johnson Corp., accompanied by a question mark.

Much inquiry followed and Johnson explained the memorandum in greater depth. The total payment was "subject to a presently outstanding second mortgage,"[5] the mortgage received from Yankee owners Dan Topping and Del Webb. The Lannan money was to buy out the 20 percent interest held in Arnold Johnson Corp. by J. Patrick Lannan. Singman cited a letter from Vollers to American League president Will Harridge dated March 17, 1955, notifying the league that Johnson had sold all of his shares in Arnold Johnson Corp. (Harridge, in his own testimony, would confess that the American League had not investigated whether the sale was bona fide.) There were no written agreements of any kind that showed Johnson would not repurchase his interest in the future. As seen in the note, the only money going directly to Johnson for Yankee Stadium was the grand sum of $80,000 in cash and securities.

Was that possible? Could that be the total worth of Yankee Stadium? Johnson said that he estimated the value "as accurately as I could tell," and that this deal "was very speculative," not to mention that he "was under great pressure" to sell.[6] Singman wasn't buying it. He ran through the Johnson Corp.'s assets, now under the ownership of Cox's Yankee Stadium Corp. They were the stadium itself (subject to lease), a 28-year leasehold on the land and parking lots, options to repurchase the land and lots at specified prices, options to renew the lease for a total of 45 years, and the sizeable rents from the Yankees' lease, a 30-year net total of $11.5 million. After subtracting the liabilities of payments to Knights of Columbus for the land lease, Atwell & Co. for the mortgage, and the $2.9 million loan from Topping and Webb, the net profit would be $2.73 million over 28 years, in addition to the physical ownership of the stadium.

Johnson minimized all of this. The profit was small change when held against such a long period of time, and the stadium itself could be worthless. He cited that Ebbets Field was presently a drain on the Dodgers' finances. Even so, Singman reiterated the peculiar nature of selling a concern that was worth at least $3 million for $30,000 in cash. The Chicago financial wunderkind had proven himself countless times to be an ingenious handler of money and creative dealmaker, but not this time. To Singman, Johnson said, "Apparently you feel that I made a poor deal. Maybe I did make a poor [deal], but I was pushed into it."[7]

A one-year snapshot of income and payments drew the next set of questions. For 1955, Yankee Stadium Corp. collected $600,000 from the Yankees for use of the park, while paying the Knights $125,000 for land supporting the ballpark. Singman continued with additional Johnson liabilities such as monies owed annually to Topping and Webb ($50,000) and Atwell & Co. ($65,000). Johnson, though unable to confirm these numbers, acquiesced. The net of this was a positive return of $360,000 in one year. Johnson suggested that bank loan payments of $204,000 needed to be added. When Singman objected that those numbers were already included in the $385,000 purchase price as the assumption of said bank loan, Johnson demurred and insisted they were to be added again. Singman conceded, as, even if the $204,000 of bank payments were re-added, it would not take away from his point that Cox was left with a return of $156,000, well over the $30,000 in cash he paid out. Having earned five times his investment in the first year of ownership, Cox seemed to have achieved a financial coup.

This was not so, pleaded Johnson. First, there was the additional $50,000 in real estate securities that Cox used as payment, although even bringing Cox's purchase to $80,000 in cash and securities only reduced his return to twice his investment price in the first year of operation. Johnson continued the theme of how tough it was for Cox. He was in a very high tax bracket and would have to pay a dividend, and it was very difficult to get money out of a corporation—poor Mr. Cox. As suspicious as the finances were, though, even more important was whether the sale was for real.

Chairman Cellars was finding the whole Johnson–Cox transaction hard to swallow. "Wait a minute," he said, "You sold this property as described without a written contract of sale, and the only evidence of sale is that paper with the pencil notation."[8] Was it genuine? Singman followed up. With no written contract, how could either the commissioner's office or the American League know what all the terms of the transaction were, such as a possible later repurchase date? The question was fair enough, but Johnson became indignant. "My integrity as a businessman over the last 30 years" should be sufficient evidence of good faith.[9] With some braggadocio, Johnson noted that he was "independently wealthy" and would have no need to pull a fast financial deal. He claimed that his assurances were enough, more weighty, in fact, than an actual contract. Attorney Vollers said, "Mr. Johnson is not that character of man" and shrugged off the flimsy proof of sale as just "the way Messrs. Cox and Johnson do business."[10] Johnson's final words on the matter were "and that is really true,"[11] the use of the word *really* pointing to other statements perhaps less truthful. The committee backed off from this line of questioning. After some more inquiries into the matters of trades and Arthur Mann's article that Johnson bought the A's for "peanuts" (which Johnson refuted), the hearings were closed, Johnson expressing his thanks for being allowed the chance to clear his name amidst the buzz of collusion with the Yankees.

Yankee Stadium would change hands again, and its path reveals the truth behind the sale to John Cox scribbled on that fragment of paper. An alumnus of the Rice University Class of 1927, John Cox made a gift of the stadium to his alma mater in the summer of 1962. The piece of property that Arnold Johnson had told Congress in 1957 was highly speculative and likely to become a liability to its new owner was most gleefully accepted by Rice officials, who expected more than $1 million in rentals over the next two decades. Cox was not nearly so conservative, saying that the totals might actually be in the $3 million range—all this from an outlay of $80,000 in cash. "Rice has helped a lot of poor boys get started," said Cox benevolently. "Rice now owns Yankee Stadium lock, stock and barrel."[12] The 59-year-old Cox had been in ill health in recent years and had an eye on his legacy. His health had made him relinquish his title of President of Automatic Canteen, a position he assumed upon Arnold Johnson's death and held from March of 1960 to December of 1961—Automatic Canteen, the place where all the major players, Dan Topping, Del Webb, Arthur Friedlund, John Cox, and Arnold Johnson—converge.

Flash forward 10 years. Yankee Stadium, now in need of a complete facelift, has, in New York City, an interested buyer. After some negotiations, Rice sold the historic venue for $24 million in 1972 according to one source.[13] Legal papers show that payment to Rice was a result of condemnation, totaling a little more than $3 million. However, when the Rice and New York City lawyers got together to hammer out the details, they were surprised by exactly what Cox had given. It turned out the school received no lock, no stock, and no barrel. What was bestowed upon the Houston University was not John Cox's ownership of Yankee Stadium, but his right to acquire the stadium. John Cox never owned Yankee Stadium.

In a January 17, 1973, letter to L. S. Shamblin, Rice treasurer, the law firm of Baker & Botts described what they had found out about their valuable "gift." At the beginning, what was termed a gift was found out to be, "as the matter progressed," something different. "It developed that Cox was in fact giving to Rice *his right to acquire stock* (author's emphasis) of the existing Yankee Stadium Corporation for an agreed price." While the right to the stock certainly had value, it did not carry with it ownership until exercised. After finding that the original corporation had a note against it held by the Knights of Columbus, which Rice subsequently acquired, he had to form an entirely new Yankee Stadium Corporation to hold the stadium and leasehold.[14] Five years later, in another letter from the Houston legal concern, this time to the Rice comptroller, further details were revealed. To receive this donation, Rice had spent $425,000 for the option to buy the stock of the corporation. In addition, Rice retired Yankee Stadium Corp.'s debt in the amount of $1,574,761. The January 10, 1962, deed of gift from Cox to Rice was for *his option* to purchase stock, not outright stock. The right gives the option of ownership, and ownership itself is not present until that right is exercised. It seems to have never been exercised by John Cox, who, it follows, never acquired the stadium in any concrete way. Without an actual buyer, it's hard to have a real seller. Major League Baseball's order that Arnold Johnson divest himself of Yankee Stadium does not seem to have been followed and contradicts a letter from Edward Vollers to City National Bank that "all the outstanding shares" in Arnold Johnson Corp. were transferred to Cox.[15]

In 1958 Commissioner Ford Frick testified before the same Congessional committee, and the issue of Johnson and his financial ties to the Yankees was by no means a dead one. Mr. Singman was very curious about whether Johnson was still in debt to New York ownership. In all of the papers submitted as evidence, there was no mention of the $2.9 million and whether that debt had been extinguished. Frick was stumped, but not enough to prevent him from feeling satisfied that there were no problems between Topping, Webb, and Johnson. As to how deeply the commissioner's office looked into the veracity of the sale of Yankee Stadium to John Cox, Frick confessed that he "didn't conduct a serious investigation of that," but he "had assurances that there was no connection" to Rule 20 and that the conflict of interest had been settled.[16] Singman was incredulous that Frick, aware of the close friendship and ties between Cox and Johnson conducted no investigation.

The perception (or reality) of the Kansas City A's as the Yankees' farm club in the American League persisted. Again in 1959, Frick had to fend off a slew of inquiries. Ironically, on July 29, the day of Frick's appearance before the board, the A's had just sneaked past the Yankees into fourth place, before their ultimate descent into seventh place. Frick crowed, and, to defend the A's trading with New York, claimed that, "when Kansas City went into the American League a few years ago, they had no players."[17] Tennessee Senator Estes Kefauver wasn't buying it, and it was impossible to ignore that the Kansas City squad was not an expansion team. "They took Philadelphia with them when they went out," Kefauver pointed out.[18] Minority counsel Peter N. Chumbris made clear the predicament posed by the shuttling of players between the A's and Yankees. The Yankees had 425 players wallowing in their organization. "Instead of bringing them up," Chumbris argued, "they're going to Kansas City and buying there, and instead of bringing them up from the minors they are making trades."[19] Between Johnson's showing before Congress in 1957 and Frick's in 1959, the two teams had made six more trades, involving 19 players, with the worst to come.

---

1. *Hearings Before the Subcommittee (Subcommittee No. 5) of the Committee on the Judiciary House of Representatives.* 85th Congress, First Session, Part 2, p. 2082.

2. Ibid, p. 2086.

3. *Chicago Daily Tribune.* "John Cox of Chicago Buys Yank Stadium," May 23, 1955, p. C3.

4. *Hearings Before the Subcommittee (Subcommittee No. 5) of the Committee on the Judiciary House of Representatives.* 85th Congress, First Session, Part 2, p. 2089.

5. Ibid., p. 2089.

6. Ibid., p. 2091.

7. Ibid., p. 2093.

8. Ibid., p. 2095.

9. Ibid., p. 2099.

10. Ibid.

11. Ibid.

12. Phillips, McCandlish. "Yankee Stadium Given to Rice U," *New York Times*, July 20, 1962, p. 27.

13. Robinson, Ray and Jennison, Christopher. *Yankee Stadium: Drama, Glamour and Glory.* New York: Viking Studio, 1998.

14. President's papers, Norman Hackerman 1970–1985. Courtesy of Woodson Research Center, Fondren Library, Rice University.

15. Ibid.

16. *Hearings Before the Subcommittee (Subcommittee No. 5) of the Committee on the Judiciary House of Representatives.* 85th Congress, Second Session, Part 2, p. 148.

17. *U.S. Senate on Antitrust and Monopoly Subcommittee of the Committee on the Judiciary.* 86th Congress, First Session, Part 2, p. 78.

18. Ibid.

19. Ibid., p. 81.

Chapter 13

THE DEVIL'S IN THE DETAILS, PART 2

By mid-1957, all parties were exasperated. The fans, initially frenzied by Major League ball, were discouraged, and attendance by season's end would be almost 400,000 fewer than just two years before. The sportswriters, at first blind boosters for Johnson and the A's, had removed their rose-colored glasses and now saw the reality of the situation. It was depressing. Some blame for the horrendous trades was being placed at the feet of manager Lou Boudreau, who was shown the door on August 6. Ryne Duren's recounting of Boudreau's sadness and shock at the time of his trade points to a different story of responsibility. Clearly, with or without Lou Boudreau, the A's were going to continue to be at the service of the Yankees as long as Arnold Johnson was in control.

June 15, 1958: K.C. Sends Virgil Trucks and Duke Maas to N.Y. for Harry Simpson and Bob Grim.

The first trade of the post–Congressional hearing period was minor but in the same mold as the rest. The Yankees would get a valuable player "while shucking off little to the A's."[1] One year after heading east, Harry "Suitcase" Simpson had proved himself of little use to the Yankees. Stengel played Simpson sparingly for the balance of 1957, and his offensive numbers were below average (.250, 7 HRs, 39 RBIs). Hitters dread the inevitable batting slumps, but nothing can be worse than experiencing a drop in production in October during the World Series. Simpson went 1 for 12 against the Braves for a .083 batting average as the Yankees fell in seven games. This did nothing to bolster Casey's confidence, and, when Simpson's 1958 season got off to a poor start (.216), the now 32-year-old veteran had shown that he was on the way out. Kansas City seemed like a good spot for him. By the end of 1959, Simpson was out of the Major Leagues entirely.

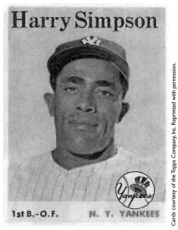

1958 Harry Simpson.   *1959 Harry Simpson.*

Bob Grim, sporting what Stengel, Berra, and pitching coach Jim Turner referred to as an exceptional "sneaky fastball," burst out of the gate in 1954 as a 20-game winner and American League Rookie of the Year. The onset of arm trouble in 1955 resulted in a drop in velocity, and Grim was shifted to relief beginning in 1956. From the bullpen, the former phenom had some success, particularly in 1957, when he led the loop in save (19) and relief (12) wins and was granted an all-star game appointment where he registered the last out, but a World Series bombing at the hands of the Braves pointed out that the end was near, and, after a poor spring, Grim lost his role to the new guy in town, the A's, Ryne Duren. Grim won six games for the sixth place A's in 1959 with an ERA over 4 and was sent to Cleveland in April of 1960. From there he was sold to Cincinnati, then St. Louis, and then released. Two years later, in 1962, Grim resurfaced in Kansas City, pitching 13 innings with an ERA of 6.23, and his Major League career was over.

1958 Bob Grim.   *1959 Bob Grim.*

In 1952 Virgil "Fire" Trucks, then of the Detroit Tigers, had the rare distinction of throwing two no-hitters in one season against the Senators and Yankees. Possessor of one of the preeminent fastballs in all of baseball, zipping in at, according to Trucks himself, over 100 miles per hour, the near-6-foot Alabamian was a two-time All-Star and consistently placed in the leaders of strikeout artists. A 20-game winner in a 1953 season split between the Browns and White Sox, Trucks' performance, like fine wine, improved with age. At 37 he won 19 games for the White Sox and was still effective in 1957, at 40. That year, as the A's leader in ERA (3.03) and games (48) and coleader in wins (9) and saves (7), Trucks was arguably the most valuable member of the Kansas City staff, but, as so many trades have shown, it didn't matter how important a player was to the A's. If the Yankees felt the need for the A's best, they got him. While Trucks would end his 17-year career after 1958, it is less important what he did for the Yankees than that the Yankees could acquire the cream of the A's crop whenever they so chose.

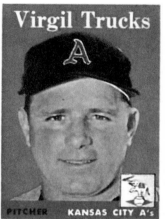

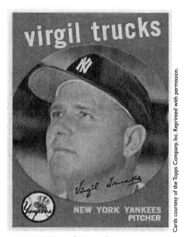

1958 Virgil Trucks.   *1959 Virgil Trucks.*

The key to the trade, and the most helpful to the Yankees, was Duke Maas. Having won 10 games for the Tigers before heading to the A's in the November 1957 deal that saw the A's unload some of their ex-Yankee stock (Martin, Morgan, McDermott), the Utica, Michigan, native won four games before being shuttled to New York. Immediately after getting the win over the Red Sox in the second game of a June 15th doubleheader, Maas headed to Cleveland to join his new teammates. Seeing work as a starter and reliever, the versatile Maas went on to chalk up seven more wins in 1958. He came into his own in 1959. Though a fourth starter, Maas was second in victories with 14, behind Whitey Ford's 16, in a rare non-pennant winning season. While Maas was almost exclusively used in relief in 1960, he had contributed mightily to the Yanks in his one year as a starter. An original draftee of the nascent Los Angeles Angels in the 1960 expansion draft, Maas would return to New York for one-third of an inning in 1961 in his career finale. During his time in New York, Maas' winning percentage was a remarkable .684, with 26 wins and 12 losses. Sadly, Maas passed away in 1976 at the age of 47. Maas' Yankee legacy showed that, even in a relatively low-profile trade with the A's, the Yankees were firmly on the plus side.

1958 Duke Maas.   *1959 Duke Maas.*

August 22, 1958: K.C. Sends Murry Dickson to N.Y. for Zeke Bella and Cash

As summer marched on, the Kansas City A's found themselves in a rare position—near the first division. Three games out of fourth place and tasting the World Series money that would trickle down to the top finishers, the fans who were still coming out were cheering loudly, and no one was more firmly in their hearts than Murry Dickson, who at 42 was the second oldest player in baseball. Stan Musial noted that Dickson was referred to as "Tom Edison" on the mound, a pitcher who was always experimenting. In his arsenal were fastballs, curves, sinkers, sliders, screwballs, and, at this point in his career, a notable knuckleball.[2]

After three seasons of double-digit victories with the Cardinals, Murry moved to the Iron City. In the early 1950s the Pittsburgh Pirates were the laughingstock of baseball, consistently in the cellar, usually compiling about 100 losses, yet Dickson found a way to win there, even reaching 20 wins in 1951. An All-Star in 1953, Dickson moved across state to Philadelphia, and after a return engagement with St. Louis, the A's shrewdly picked him up as a free agent. Quickly assuming hero status for the success-starved A's fans, Dickson, born in nearby Tracy, Missouri, was the most consistent A's pitcher. Effective as both a starter and reliever, the ageless wonder had picked up nine wins and a save when the Yankees came to get him. For the Yankees, Dickson lost his edge and was largely ineffective, but a small bit of hell broke loose in Missouri.

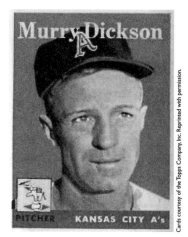

1958 Murry Dickson.   *1959 Murry Dickson.*

The fan and press criticism was directed exclusively at Arnold Johnson. Finally, with the A's in a position to show great improvement, one of their best was sent packing without a replacement in return. The dependably supportive *Daily Star*, newspaper home to Ernie Mehl and Joe McGuff, had no choice but to jump ship. McGuff wrote bitterly that this deal was "unjustified" and that its effect on the club's psyche was devastating.[3] Players had complained to him anonymously that now their hope of any share in postseason cash was snatched away. Other critics of the trade felt that the A's had suffered a setback that they could not overcome. This was borne out on the field as they lost whatever momentum they had and closed out 1958 in seventh place. Dickson was put on waivers in order for New York to claim him, but an A's spokesman assured the upset multitudes that a "satisfactory player" would be sent to the A's for the spring of 1959, along with cash.

What bounty did they receive for one of their top hurlers? Besides a few pieces of silver, the A's accepted delivery of John "Zeke" Bella. Bella had been signed by the Yankees as an amateur free agent in 1951 and finally had a small taste of life in the majors six years later. Called up in

1957 at 27 years of age, Bella went 1 for 10 and did not resurface for all of 1958. Given slightly more playing time with Kansas City, Bella roamed the outfield in 25 games and appeared in 47 all told, hitting .207 and clouting but a single home run. Bella's big league career ended after the 1959 campaign. Once again, the A's were given little or nothing in return for an important member of their team. In Dickson, the Yankees acquired a mainstay of the A's staff and gave them a part-time flycatcher half a year later. Like the Trucks and Maas deal, the Dickson trade showed that even the small deals swung strongly the Yankees way, but this time, the loud outcry was heard.

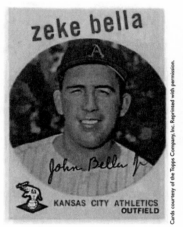

1959 Zeke Bella.

April 8, 1959: K.C. Sends Jack Urban to N.Y. for Mark Freeman.

Hardly worth a mention, this transaction's importance lies in that it followed the Slaughter pattern. Urban, who had been sent sans experience to Kansas City in the 1957 blockbuster that involved Clete Boyer, now had some experience and wins under his belt. In 1958 Urban was the number three starter in the A's four-man rotation (along with two other ex-Yankees, Ralph Terry and Bob Grim) and had pitched well in spring training. While not up to Yankees standards and sent directly to Richmond in the International League, Urban was more accomplished than the player the A's were given. Mark Freeman, a right-hander who had spent time at Louisiana State, did give the A's more height, as Urban was 5'8" to Freeman's 6'4". His A's tenure was brief, making it into three games, pitching a scant three and two-thirds innings. His ERA of 9.82 did not help manager Harry Craft gain any confidence in his skills. Interestingly, Freeman was sent back to the Yankees a month later for the waiver price, while Urban was sold to the Cardinals from the Yankees three days later. Perhaps the Yankees made a bit of money on these cash transactions, as, by getting Freeman back, the deal boiled down to the Yanks simply paying the waiver price to Kansas City and receiving an unknown cash price from St. Louis for Urban.

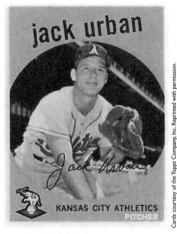

1959 Jack Urban.

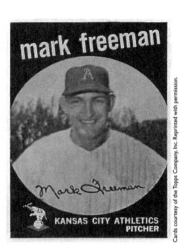

1959 Mark Freeman.

April 12, 1959: K.C. Sends Mike Baxes and Bob Martyn to N.Y. for Russ Snyder and Tommy Carroll

The second inconsequential deal in a row. Perhaps both teams were lying low after the deluge of hostility and bad press as a result of the Dickson deal of the previous summer. By now, every trade between the Yankees and A's was tainted, and snide comments directed the A's way were prevalent, for example, "balked in their efforts to swing a deal of major proportions," the Yankees turned to "their old Kansas City trading partners."[4] In this case, the old partners were no help to New York.

Mike Baxes, had seen part-time service in the A's infield during the 1956 and, skipping a year, the 1958 seasons. Wielding a slight bat, Baxes managed to hit .217 over the two seasons with inadequate power. Unlike his brother Jim, an infielder for the Los Angeles Dodgers and Cleveland Indians, Mike saw no Major League action during the 1959 campaign or ever again. Bob Martyn was a strapping six-footer who had managed to hit in the .260 range during sporadic play stretched over 1957 and 1958 after being sent to Kansas City from New York in the Billy Martin trade. The fleet outfielder placed sixth in the American League with seven triples in 1958, and, although placing ninth in the circuit in intentional walks (five), he lacked the power commensurate with his frame. Baxes and Martyn's only service on the Major League level was with the A's, and they never would appear in the big leagues with New York, heading straight for Richmond upon the completion of the trade.

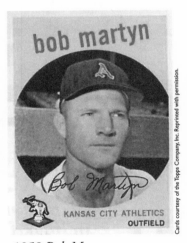

1959 Mike Baxes.   *1959 Bob Martyn.*

Tommy Carroll, one of the bonus babies that precluded the Yankees from signing Clete Boyer, had come out of Notre Dame with great acclaim. For their $40,000 investment, the Yanks got a teenager who would appear in 50 games in his two required seasons on the Yankee bench. Carroll hit .348 during his Yankee residency, but all eight hits were singles. Finally getting some minor league experience, Carroll put up decent offensive numbers, splitting 1958 with Denver (.289) and New Orleans

(.278). Carroll departed, as so many had before him, on the Kansas City–New York shuttle. However, his stay in Kansas City was a short one, with seven at-bats resulting in a .143 average and a quick exit from the Major Leagues at the age of 23.

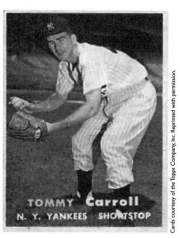

1957 Tommy Carroll.   1959 Tommy Carroll.

In Russ Snyder, the A's gained a quality fourth outfielder. Sent from the Yankees farm club in Richmond and optioned by the A's to their Portland franchise in the Pacific Coast League on May 4, Snyder would reemerge and make a fine showing, hitting .313 with 3 HRs and 21 RBIs stretched over 73 games. The following year, the Nebraskan outfielder would put up similar power stats in 59 more at-bats, but with his average slipping to .260, was shuffled to Baltimore, where he would spend the next seven seasons, hitting over .300 two times (1962 and 1966) and swiping 18 bases in 1963, the third highest total in the American League. Two years after appearing with the World Champion Orioles of 1966, Snyder bounced around from the White Sox to the Indians to the Brewers, ending up in Milwaukee for their inaugural 1970 season before bowing out after 12 Major League seasons, only the first two spent in Kansas City. Overall, this trade meant little in terms of Major League service, with Baxes and Martyn's nonexistent and Carroll's brief. While Snyder had a commendable Major League career, he spent only a small piece of it in Kansas City.

1960 Russ Snyder.

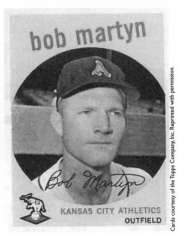

1959 Bob Martyn.

May 9, 1959: K.C. Acquires Murry Dickson from N.Y. for the Waiver Price and Sends Mark Freeman to N.Y. for the Waiver Price

Freeman, at first sent straight to Seattle in the Pacific Coast League, returned to the Yankees and did get a chance to pitch in Yankee Stadium. He found himself starting a late-September game against the Orioles and fared well, yielding two runs in seven innings that resulted in a no-decision. Traded to the Cubs in May of 1960, Freeman left the majors that September. The popular Dickson, exiled to New York in August of 1958, proved that his 42-year-old magic was finite. While still a major contributor upon his departure from Kansas City, Dickson hardly pitched for the Yankees, appearing in six games for the duration of the 1958 season, his ERA a lofty 5.75. Although he pitched in training camp, Dickson would see no action for New York in 1959. Heading back to the A's was the end of the line for the mound magician, as he picked up two wins with an ERA of 4.92. Ironically, Zeke Bella, who had been sent to the A's for the high-riding Dickson in 1958, was optioned to Shreveport to make room for Murry's return.

May 26, 1959: K.C. Sends Ralph Terry and Hector Lopez to N.Y. for Johnny Kucks, Tom Sturdivant, and Jerry Lumpe

With their usual flippant claim that nobody else would trade with them, the Yankees raided their old pals. As the June 15 trading deadline grew near, they surprised no one by turning to Kansas City, "who had been so amenable to Yankee transactions."[5] In giving up three players who were either surplus or fizzling owing to lost talent or poor health, as well as promising that they would send one more man at a later date, the Yankees acquired two mainstays of the next dynasty, the 1960–1964 Bombers who made five consecutive World Series appearances, winning two. The Yankees, destined to finish in third place in 1959, were in need of a shot in the arm, and they got it, courtesy of Arnold Johnson.

As a 6'3" sinkerballer, Johnny Kucks had proven success in four seasons twirling for the Yankees. At 19, Kucks made a splash in his first professional season. He blew through the Piedmont League (Class B), winning 19 games for Norfolk while holding opponents to 2.55 runs per game. Military service halted the Hoboken native's progress, and when he hit New York in 1955, his eight victories as fifth starter and long reliever were a herald of good things to come. He exploded with his best season in 1956, winning 18 games, for second-most on the staff (behind Ford's 19), while leading the team in games started (31) and shutouts (3) and earning a place on the American League All-Stars. It was his three-hit shutout against the Brooklyn Dodgers in Game 7 of the 1956 World Series that would bring Kucks his lasting fame as a Yankee. He excelled in the postseason, with an ERA below 2 in 19 innings over four World Series. A sudden slump to eight wins in both 1957 and 1958 bode ill, and by 1959, the wind had gone out of his sails. His rapid descent led to the inevitable trade to Kansas City, where he would again win eight, and he finished with an ERA over 4 for the A's, leading the league in the dubious category of hit batsmen (12). The 1960 season was worse, with half the wins and an ERA that ballooned to 6.00. That was it; at 27, Johnny Kucks, four years removed from the unsurpassable glory of a World Series–clinching whitewashing of the Dodgers, was out of the major leagues.

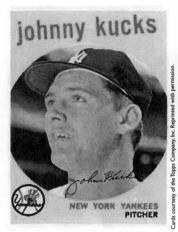

1960 Johnny Kucks.

1959 Johnny Kucks.

Tom "Snake" Sturdivant had been another quality prospect scouted and signed by Tom Greenwade. While in the minors, he was converted from the field to the mound, bringing a two-pitch repertoire of knuckleballs and fastballs. After a fine debut out of the bullpen in 1955, Sturdivant played a key role the next year, winning 16 games from the fifth spot in the starting rotation, as well as relieving. The 6'1" ex-position player still wielded a potent bat, hitting .312 that year. Like Johnny Kucks, Tom Sturdivant was crucial to the Yankees 1956 championship, beating the Dodgers in Game 4 with a six-hit complete game. That season, Sturdivant wistfully reflected, "was like a dream fulfilled."[6] Moving to the number one spot in 1957, Sturdivant again won 16, his ERA dropping to 2.54. It was downhill from there. Missing part of spring training because of a contract holdout, Sturdivant found himself with a sore arm and a mere three wins. A terrible start in 1959 led to his exile, and in Kansas City he was mostly a mop-up man, and a poor one at that, yielding 4.65 runs per game while notching only two wins. From that point on, the former Yankee stalwart journeyed from team to team, with stops in Boston, Washington, Pittsburgh, Detroit, then back to Kansas City, before closing out his Major League service in New York, back with Casey "The Old Perfessor" Stengel, as a member of the 1964 Mets.

1959 Tom Sturdivant.

A week before this deal was struck, "The Old Perfessor," in frustration with the team's inadequate play and the thinness of his pitching corps, had warned, "Some of these pitchers aren't going to be around long."[7] Clearly, the Yankee manager hinted at the fate of Kucks and Sturdivant, who combined could not muster a single victory. What made Arnold Johnson so keen to add these pitchers to the A's is puzzling at the least. If Jerry Lumpe, a light-hitting infielder batting at a .222 clip at the time of the trade, was the major reason for the A's to conclude the transaction, that makes it only more difficult to understand.

Lumpe was never going to crack the double-play pair of Bobby Richardson at second base and Tony Kubek at shortstop and gain starting status. After hitting a superb .340 in a platoon role in 1957, Lumpe's numbers slumped to .254 in 1958 and further at the start of 1959. In comparison to what the Yankees had historically dumped on Kansas City, Lumpe was a valuable addition to the A's, and not in an abbreviated stay. For over four seasons, he was the regular second sacker, patrolling the Municipal (formerly Blues) Stadium infield, while also seeing some time at shortstop. Offensively, the tall shortstop averaged single digits in home runs and 50 RBIs. His breakout year came in 1962, when a 20-game hitting streak helped propel him to a .301 average. His power numbers soared as he ended up with 10 home runs and 83 RBIs. Traded to the

Tigers in November 1963 as the key to acquiring slugger Rocky Colavito, Lumpe would turn in his lone all-star performance in his first year in the Motor City. He was released after the 1967 season, his 12th.

1959 Jerry Lumpe.

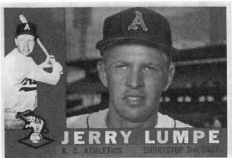

1960 Jerry Lumpe.

The A's finally got a multiyear contributing player in this, their 15th time doing business with the Yankees. Of course, the Yankees got so much more. Hector Lopez, a hard-hitting Panamanian, had come off a fine 1958 season (17 HRs, 73 RBIs) and was in the midst of a torrid hitting streak at the time he was dealt, having gone 6 for 12 with two doubles, two triples, and two homers. Also, Lopez had to this point in the season driven in more runs than any Yankee hitter. Upon arriving in the Big Apple, he was immediately inserted into the lineup as the regular third baseman, replacing Andy Carey. Lopez would finish out the year with 93 runs driven in, coupled with 22 home runs and a .283 average, toward the top of the Yankee leader board in those categories. Always versatile, Lopez would see time in the infield and outfield during his time on the Yankees. The main player off the Yankee bench, Lopez, a jack-of-all-trades, served as fourth outfielder, pinch-hitter, and platoon player. As a member of five straight pennant winners, the native of Colon hit well in the World Series, delivering a .286 BA with 1 homer and 7 RBIs. A link to the glory years of the early 1960s, Lopez remained popular in New York until the end of 1966, a year in which the Yankees finished in last place. Undoubtedly Lopez, like so many others before him, was thrilled to go to New York from the hapless A's. Any incestuous relationship between the two clubs was of no matter.

1960 Hector Lopez.

1959 Hector Lopez.

The return of Ralph Terry was most alarming to onlookers. As previously described, Terry was a bright prospect who needed more work on the big league level, and, while the Yankees couldn't provide the opportunity, the A's could. In his only full season in Kansas City, Terry was the second biggest winner on the staff in 1958 while serving his apprenticeship as a quality Major League pitcher. Stengel tried to diminish Terry's growth, stating, "I understand that after we traded him to the A's Harry Craft [the A's manager] never was quite satisfied with him."[8] Any reservations Craft had did not preclude him from trotting his 22-year-old talent to pitch the most innings for the A's. Terry did get off to a bad start in 1959, but it's hard to swallow that a struggling team would give up on such a young prospect. Bill Veeck, owner of the White Sox, on their way to the World Series that year, cried foul. This trade was "a definite disservice to baseball," the unconventional owner contended. It was obvious to Veeck that the Yankees had used the A's as a farm team in the case of the young hurler. "They had Ralph Terry out on option," he said.[9] Indians general manager Frank Lane had been cautioning other clubs against dealing with the struggling Yankees and was no doubt apoplectic about another A's gift laid at the feet of the Yankees.

During the next phase of Yankee success, Ralph Terry would win 73 games, their best starter behind Whitey Ford. His first full year back in New York found him in the fourth starting slot, and he garnered 10 wins, which led to a promotion to number three in 1961. That year he had a stunning winning percentage of .842, going 16–3 for one of the legendary teams in Yankee history. In 1962 he would pace the American League with 23 wins, his great control and assortment of fastballs, curves, changeups, and sliders (taught to him by pitching coach Johnny Sain) being the keys to his stellar, all-star year. At the head of the American League in games started (37) and complete games (18) for 1963, Terry led the Yankees in strikeouts on two occasions.

Terry also figured in two memorable World Series. On the downside, he was the unfortunate who served up the pitch that Bill Mazeroski hit for his World Series winning home run in 1960, propelling the Pirates over the Yankees in one of the game's greatest moments. Two years later he was a two-game winner and Series MVP. A four-hit, 1–0 shutout in Game 7 went down in history as a result of a blazing shot off the bat of Giants giant Willie McCovey that Bobby Richardson snagged for the final out. Terry's career would end after the 1967 season and two games with the cross-town Mets.

1959 Ralph Terry.

1960 Ralph Terry.

With hindsight, it is an appalling trade. The Yankees got vital members of their last dominating period, all for a spare infielder and two pitchers who were past their prime. Shirley Povich of the *Washington Post* wondered *at the time* what was "the compulsion of Kansas City to make the deal." It was "baffling" to Povich why Johnson would do it.[10] There wasn't a prayer that this could turn out any other way than it did, the vampire-like Yankees growing stronger with the blood of the A's. It was impossible for anyone not to be suspicious of the A's–Yankees intermingled business relations, as it consistently surfaced with these egregious trades. Johnson, Povich went on, was most unpopular with American League owners, except for those who owned the Yankees. The growing heat, made hotter by the Dickson and Terry–Lopez deals, would erupt with the last trade of the Johnson era seven months down the line. In December of 1959, Roger Maris would become a Yankee.

December 11, 1959: K.C. sends Roger Maris, Kent Hadley, and Joe DeMaestri to N.Y. for Norm Siebern, Hank Bauer, Marv Throneberry, and Don Larsen

Even those lingering few who did not suspect collusion between Arnold Johnson and the Yankees jumped ship after the Maris trade. As the everlasting symbol of the troubling relationship that resulted in the cream of the A's organization being shipped to New York, the trading of Roger Maris drew intensely negative reaction from the press and executives around the league. In retrospect, the players couldn't pretend that the Yanks and A's simply traded with each other. In Ralph Terry's opinion, all previous transactions were "dollar for dollar" transfers and were all "fair until the Roger trade."[12] One player who traveled the well-worn path from Kansas City to New York surmised, "The only reason the Yankees and K.C. worked together was no one else wanted to make the Yankees stronger than they were." Arnold Johnson had no such objection.

Marv Throneberry was a husky first base prospect who had filled in for the injured Bill "Moose" Skowron during the 1959 season. A below average hitter with power that fell short of his stature (6', 197 lbs), Throneberry hit .240 with 8 homers and 22 RBIs. For Kansas City he would play more and accomplish nearly the same. A repeat of this middling performance led to his being sent to Baltimore in June of 1961, and on May 9, 1962, Throneberry had his date with destiny as he was sent to the 1962 Mets, one of the worst and most amusing teams in Major League history. At the end of a 110-loss season, "Marvelous Marv" had become legend, the symbol of futility. As a key figure in the "Can't Anybody Here Play This Game" Mets, immortalized in Jimmy Breslin's book, Marv was best known for hitting a triple vs. the Cubs and being called out when he clearly missed both first *and* second base in his trot around the bases. After an abbreviated 1963 season that saw his average plummet to .143 in 14 at-bats, Throneberry was gone but used his comic legend to become a beloved figure in baseball history and beer commercial star. Receiving a baseball joke as 25 percent of the deal did not promise a good outcome for the A's.

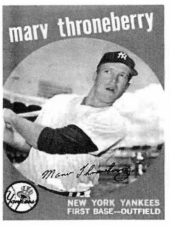

1959 Marv Throneberry.

1960 Marv Throneberry.

Don Larsen was the author of the most improbable feat in the annals of the game. After two seasons racking up big losses with the Browns and Orioles, including 21 defeats in 1954, Larsen was sent to New York as part of an 17-player blockbuster trade that November, the largest in baseball history. General manager Weiss saw some potential in Larsen and, after splitting time between Class AAA Denver and New York, the towering righty employed his blazing fastball as the fourth starter in 1955 and 1956. His moment of glory came in the 1956 World Series, when the

11-game winner hurled the one and only perfect game in Series history, throttling the Dodgers in a 2–0 Game 5, possibly the finest achievement the game had ever seen. He was rewarded with the Babe Ruth Award as Series MVP, as well as *Sport Magazine's* MVP trophy. Larsen continued his postseason pitching, putting up fine performances with his no-windup delivery against the Braves in both 1957 and 1958.

The onset of arm troubles began with an injury to his elbow in 1958, a soreness that continued through 1959, dropping his win total to 6 and lifting his ERA to 4.33. Larsen's damaged right arm and unimpressive record were made worse by his penchant for late-night carousing. Jimmy Dykes, his manager during his sole year in Baltimore quipped, "The only thing Larsen fears is sleep."[12] Horrid in his one full year with Kansas City, Larsen would go 1–10, his ERA skyrocketing to 5.38. After 15 innings in 1961, Larsen began a trek that would take him to five teams over seven years, the Cubs serving as his last stop after four innings in 1967.

1959 Don Larsen.

1960 Don Larsen.

Like Larsen, Hank Bauer had seen better days, but he had seen more of them. There was the possibility that Larsen had some magic left, as he was only 30 when the deal was made, but Bauer was 37 and on his last legs. A consistent presence on the Yankee juggernaut, Bauer had been called up in 1948 and took part in nine World Series. Signing with the Yankees in 1941, Bauer's first year in pro ball found him deep in the minor leagues in Grand Forks, North Dakota. One month after Pearl Harbor, Bauer, who had the tough visage of a Marine, became one officially when he enlisted. Encountering fierce fighting, Bauer was injured on Okinawa. After the war, mega-scout Tom Greenwade came through again when he suggested the New Yorkers resign Bauer for a $200 bonus, Bauer worked his way up to the big time and a September call-up late in 1948. The highly touted prospect did well, and for the next 11 full seasons, he was a key to the Yankees attack. The man who had "a face like a clenched fist," (a term first employed by fabled sportswriter Jim Murray),[13] had good power at the plate but like so many right-handed batters in Yankee annals suffered because of the cavernous dimensions of left center field at Yankee Stadium, "Death Valley." Still, Bauer led the team in triples on three occasions and led the American League in 1957 with nine. An American League All-Star from 1952 to 1954, Bauer was an all-around athlete and great leader. If that wasn't enough, Bauer hit in 17 straight World Series games and clouted 4 home runs in the 1958 classic.

The 1959 campaign showed that the end of the line was near for the Yankee great, as he collected his fewest at-bats since his first full year. His .238 average was the lowest of his career, and his production had slumped to 9 home runs and 39 RBIs. It was this Hank Bauer who the A's would receive, not the fabled Bauer of old. Heading out to pasture, in this case his home and restaurant near Kansas City, Bauer was "of course sorry to leave the Yankees. But very happy to join the Athletics."[14] Bauer, who would turn 38 during the 1960 season, raised his average to .275, but he played less and had very little pop, clubbing a mere three homers. The following March he announced during spring training that 1961 would be his farewell, wistfully citing that "the legs ain't what they used to be anymore."[15] While the A's would lose a player, they would gain a manager, as Bauer succeeded Joe Gordon on June 19 and remained active until July 21, smacking two hits against the Tigers. Always able to inspire younger players, Bauer would find great success as a manager, although not with the A's. From 1964 through part of 1968, Bauer was at the helm for the creation of the great Orioles dynasty, overseeing a four-game sweep over the L.A. Dodgers for the 1966 World's Championship. For his achievements that year, Bauer was awarded *The Sporting News'* Manager of the Year. He returned to the A's fold, this time in Oakland, and guided them to a second-place finish in 1969. A return to the minor leagues was also triumphant, as Bauer won Minor League Manager of the Year as the steward of the Mets' AAA Tidewater club in 1972. Unfortunately for Kansas City, the A's had traded for a baseball player, not a baseball skipper, and Bauer's career from 1960 on was mostly from the bench.

1960 Hank Bauer.

1959 Hank Bauer.

The key acquisition for the A's was Norm Siebern. A stellar prospect, the imposing outfielder won the James P. Dawson Award as the outstanding Yankee rookie of 1956's spring training. Siebern was ill suited for the majors that year and, after hitting a paltry .204 in 54 games, was sent back to the minor leagues after the World Series. He tore through the bushes in Denver, winning the 1957 Minor League Player of the Year. The extra work paid off as Siebern hit .300 with 14 HRs and 55 RBIs. His fielding abilities were a huge asset, and he would win his only Gold Glove that year, yet it was his glove work that betrayed him in the 1958 World Series rematch against the Milwaukee Braves, as he lost two fly balls in the glaring October sun that made it near impossible to pick up a ball headed toward Yankee Stadium's left field. Unfairly pinned with the blame for a Yankee loss to a stingy Warren Spahn (who hurled a two-hit shutout), Siebern was quickly relegated to a seat on the bench and in Casey Stengel's doghouse. The unkind criticism directed his way seemed to rattle the youngster, and his performance dropped in 1959. Although he kept his power numbers in line with 1958, the former phenom's average sunk to .271. A change in scenery would help.

Norm Siebern would prove to be the best player the A's would receive in this, their 16th deal with the Yankees. Over four seasons, he would average 19.5 home runs, nearly 92 RBIs and a .269 average. A two-time All-Star for the A's, Siebern would post his career best in 1962 (25 HRs, 117 RBIs, .308), finishing a distant seventh in MVP voting, well behind ex-teammate Mickey Mantle. Traded to the Orioles in November of 1963, Siebern would see his offensive numbers drop noticeably (although he would make the All-Star team) and, after stops with the California Angels, San Francisco Giants, and Boston Red Sox (for whom he would appear in the 1967 World Series), would end his 12-year Major League run after the 1968 campaign.

1959 Norm Siebern.

1960 Norm Siebern.

Siebern's success in Kansas City stuck out in this mostly typical Yankees–Athletics trade. A sore-armed Larsen, an over-the-hill Bauer, and a nonprospect Throneberry were more in line with past deals. Surprisingly, the A's, who had been promised another player from New York in the May Ralph Terry trade, felt that what they had received was sufficient in the current transaction to discharge the Yankees from that obligation. Most would disagree that the A's were not in need of another body in light of what they gave up. In Roger Maris, the Yankees received one of the towering figures in their hallowed history.

The other two figures in the Maris deal were Kent Hadley and Joe DeMaestri. Hadley was Marv Throneberry without the comedy. At 6'3", 190 lbs., Hadley was not as powerful as one would expect from a man of his frame. He hit 10 home runs in 288 at-bats for the A's in 1959, and in his abbreviated stint in New York, hit .203 with four circuit blasts, appearing in 55 games before leaving the Major Leagues for good. De-Maestri had more to his credit, slapping six consecutive singles in one game against the Tigers (July 8, 1955) to tie a current record held by many. An All-Star shortstop for the A's in 1957, DeMaestri was, when it was his turn to go to the Yankees, the third best shortstop in the loop in the estimation of White Sox owner Bill Veeck. The two ahead of him were most certainly Veeck's own future Hall of Famer Luis Aparicio and Tony Kubek of the Yanks. While the A's were relinquishing their starting shortstop since 1955, the Yankees had little use for him, and he served as Kubek's caddy from 1960 to 1961, appearing in 79 games over the two-year span. Remarkably, the A's had no one better to replace DeMaestri, as the forgettable Ken Hamlin took charge in 1960 before being let loose in the 1960 expansion draft. Characteristically, the A's handed over a useful player who had no function for the Yankees.

1959 Joe DeMaestri.

1960 Joe DeMaestri.

Roger Maris was different. A superior multisport star at Fargo Shanley High School in North Dakota, Maris, still holds the high school record of four touchdown returns (kick, punt, and interception) in one game. Maris was signed by the Indians in 1953 and tore through the minors, winning Rookie of the Year at Class C Fargo. The fans in Keokuk, Iowa, saw Maris conquer Class B the following year, as he hit .315, while knocking 32 over the wall and swiping 25 bases. Maris, born Maras, changed his name in 1955 to quell the chants of "Mar-ass," but no taunting could deter his path. Climbing up the ladder with solid turns in Tulsa, Reading, and Indianapolis, Maris made the majors in 1957.

It was a promising first year. Maris showed his potential with 14 HR and 51 RBIs, but he could not duplicate his high minor league batting averages at the big league level, as he hit only .235. Where people stood on their views of Roger Maris as a person depend on whether they were a friend, teammate, writer, or executive. Maris was his own man, his comments always true to himself, and the honest approach with which he conducted himself would ruffle feathers throughout his career. Fifty-one games into the 1958 season, the Indians shipped their promising outfielder to the A's after friction developed between Maris and manager Bobby Bragan. Indians general manager Frank Lane had a gut feeling that Maris's future was bright, but Lane loved to deal, and the troubling relationship Maris had with management made a trade easier to swallow.

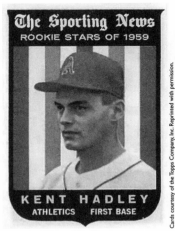

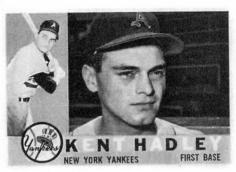

1960 Kent Hadley.

1959 Kent Hadley.

The A's knew what they had gotten. The willingness to trade All-Star first baseman Vic Power for a still unproven youngster showed the esteem in which they held the powerful right fielder. Ernie Mehl, sensing a savior for the beleaguered A's, wondered, "Have the A's found in Roger Maris the outstanding performer they have been searching for ever since the franchise moved here [Kansas City]?"[16] For the remainder of 1958, Maris showed his strength with 19 home runs and 53 RBIs, but it was the following year that he demonstrated his impressive ability. By late May, Maris's average was .328, and then appendicitis struck. A quick recovery saw Maris resume his assault on league pitching and, now a first-time All-Star, he was atop the leader board in late July with a .344 average, one point ahead of the Tigers' Harvey Kuenn. Everything unraveled quickly, whether because of the bout of ill health or just an old-fashioned batting slump. Whatever the cause, from July 27 on, Maris was horrendous, hitting .165, with 2 HRs and 19 RBIs. Finishing the year off with a .273 average and 19 home runs, Maris said at season's end, "I still don't know what happened."[17]

Unbeknownst to Maris, he was being watched. The Yankees were hot on the North Dakotan since he piqued George Weiss' interest during his time in Reading. Tom Greenwade kept tabs on Maris during his Cleveland time, and Cleveland executive Hank Greenberg recounted that Yankee director of player personnel Lee McPhail was always asking him about Maris. Frank Lane knew the Yankees "had their eye on him for years. I'm not at all certain they didn't tell Johnson to get Maris from us [Indians]."[18] Lane was on to something. George Weiss said, "I told Johnson that if he ever landed Maris, I'd make him a *real deal* [author's emphasis] to bring Roger to the Yanks."[19]—a real deal, as opposed to the other 15 deals in which Kansas City was consistently flimflammed, with what seemed like great willingness.

It was clear to many that once the A's got hold of Maris on June 15, 1958, he was not long for the Midwest. While Frank Lane conceded that Maris would eventually head to New York, he exacted a promise from Arnold Johnson to wait a year before the inevitable trade. During the negotiations for the Philadelphia A's, Lane had said that Arnold Johnson was the "sort of a man we need in this league."[20] Now, after nearly five years of watching him serve Yankee needs, Lane was wary of Johnson "passing him [Maris] to New York right away."[21] It's puzzling why Lane would trade him to Kansas City at all. From the Kansas City clubhouse, outfielder Whitey Herzog knew that a good year ensured a trip to New York. "Everyone knew Roger wasn't going to be there long."[22] Back in pinstripes, Ralph Terry said the players "always had the idea that the deal was part of something bigger, and since so many players in those days went back and forth to New York we thought sure that would happen."[23] Ryne Duren, another Kansas City expatriate, remembers the scene inside the Yankee clubhouse. When the A's obtained Maris from Cleveland, he vividly recalls senior Yankees such as Gil McDougald, Hank Bauer, and Yogi Berra shouting, "Well, we just got Maris."[24]

Maris was happy in Kansas City but aware of these rumblings. He had heard of a deal to the Big Apple, but was reassured this would not be so when he heard Arnold Johnson would only trade him if one of the Yankee players he received was Mickey Mantle, but, as usual, when the Yankees called, Johnson answered. Weiss tried to land Cincinnati's Gus Bell, one of the top outfielders in the National League, but he found that Reds general manager Gabe Paul was not in the same mold as A's general manager Parke Carroll and would not be put under his spell. When other teams such as the Cubs and Braves would not see things the Yankees' way, "they had to turn to their old country cousins, the A's."[25] Stengel was brought into the loop from his California home, Parke Carroll was called, and the deal was done.

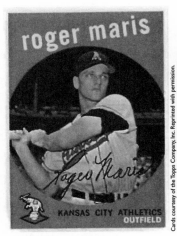

1959 Roger Maris.

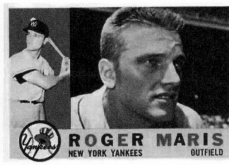

1960 Roger Maris.

It didn't take long for the flood of criticism to begin. While Weiss expected some "ribbing,"[26] no one was laughing. Said Hank Greenberg, "If it [the trade] didn't actually violate baseball rules, it violated the spirit of them."[27] Veeck went wild. He saw that Maris would be a long-term presence in the Yankee outfield, his left-hand power tailor-made for the short porch of the stadium's right field. As to the double standard that Arnold Johnson employed between his New York friends and other league owners, Veeck went deeper. "Whenever Johnson talks to us, his players are suddenly more valuable," he protested. "Only this morning Detroit asked for Maris, and was told he was too valuable to put in any transaction that didn't include Harvey Kuenn,"[28] the Tigers' seven-time All-Star, 1953 Rookie of the Year and reigning batting champ. From the Yankees, Norm Siebern would do. This trade was "conduct detrimental to baseball," and Veeck hoped his fellow owners would band together to stop these "brutal transactions" that resulted from the "unholy alliance" between New York and Kansas City.[29]

The Yankees pulled out the clichés they turned to when criticized for raiding the A's roster. They used the time-honored "no one would trade with them" cliché. Besides being untrue as proven by the frequency of activity in the five years before the Johnson era, this complaint also contained the truth that no other team was willing to kowtow to the Yankees' view of what they needed. The A's might, in effect, trade Siebern for Maris, but no other owner was going to part with their most promising star for some of the Yankees' excess. As in the Shantz trade, the Yankees cited the great risk they were taking in going after Maris. First, before his late season slump, Maris had shown on a big league level the vast potential he had. Second, the Yankees gave up nothing that they needed from their own roster. Also reminiscent of the Shantz trade was how the A's asked for greater talent from other teams. For Shantz and Ditmar, the A's asked the White Sox for stars like Jack Harshman and Billy Pierce. For Maris, they asked the Tigers for Kuenn. From the Yankees, the A's accepted much, much less.

The press was appalled. Jack Lang of the *Long Island Press,* called the trade "another heist," where the Yanks "got what [they] wanted" and the A's "got what New York didn't want."[31] Another scribe wrote, "New York seemed to retain some under-the-table hold on the A's."[32] Shirley Povich saw it as a further example of the "cross-business relationship" between Topping, Webb and Johnson.[33] The A's were clearly at the beck and call of the Yankees and owner Arnold Johnson and General Manager Parke Carroll were seen as obliging, in the former's case, and mesmerized by George Weiss, in the latter. *The Sporting News* went so far as to suggest a five-year ban on the return of any of the players involved in the Maris deal. There was a feeling in the air, one based on the Ralph Terry experience, that Siebern was out on loan, to spend time in Kansas City until his aforementioned fielding problems were ironed out. Once cured, he'd head back to New York. A few weeks later, George Weiss protested, once again citing that no other team would abet the Yankees pennant chances.

Maris, like Enos Slaughter before him, was sad to leave the Midwest. Having learned about his impending relocation from a customer in an Independence, Missouri, supermarket, Maris expressed his mixed feelings about heading to the pressure cooker that was New York, but he made it big there, and his place in baseball history was soon established. His debut season was spectacular, as he topped the American League in multiple categories: slugging percentage (.581), RBIs (112), and extra base hits (64). Maris was also runner up with 98 runs scored and 39 home runs, but those hitting numbers didn't tell the whole story. Seven triples, for second place in the loop, demonstrated his speed afoot, and a Gold Glove in right field was awarded for his excellence with the glove and his rifle-armed throws. Manager Stengel was impressed by the completeness of his new star's skills. Gil McDougald, a teammate for this one season, remembers Maris as an "outstanding ballplayer who could run, hit, throw and field and should be in the Hall of Fame," a sentiment echoed by many of his teammates.[33] By the end of 1960, Roger Maris was the reigning Most Valuable Player in the American League, and the trade of December looked ridiculously lopsided. A year later, it would look worse.

Roger Maris' assault on the single season home run record of 60, set by Babe Ruth in 1927, has been told and retold many times. The first man in history to hit his 50th homer in August, Maris set the baseball world on its ear in 1961, as his battle with Mickey Mantle to break Ruth's record fascinated fans and nonfans alike. Maris' quiet honesty set the New York press against him, making him wistful for his A's days. He told Mantle that during his 1959 slump he was never booed in Kansas City. Ford Frick, in his view protecting the Babe's legacy, ruled that if Maris broke the record, it would have to be in 154 games, rather than the new 162 schedule, a result of the 1961 expansion of teams to include the L.A. Angels and Washington Senators—no asterisk, but a separate line in the books.

Finishing with a new record of 61 homers, Maris also led the league in runs scored (132), total bases (366), and RBIs (142) as he led the monstrous Yankee hitting attack all the way to a World Series. Though Maris hit poorly in the five-game Yankee win over the Reds, it would not mar his monumental year. The hardware he was awarded was legion. Again, he won the MVP, as well as *The Sporting News* Player of the Year, the Associated Press Male Athlete of the Year, the *Sports Illustrated* Sportsman of the Year, *Sport Magazine's* Man of the Year, and the Hickok Belt as the Top Professional Athlete. His fame was such that in April 1962 he was featured in a movie along with Mickey Mantle entitled *Safe at Home*, as well as a cameo role in the Doris Day–Cary Grant vehicle, *That Touch of Mink*. Nearly 40 years later, comedian Billy Crystal would recount the triumphs and sadness of Maris's fabled year in the movie *61**.

A fine year followed and in 1962 Maris was named to his fourth consecutive All-Star team. His 33 homers were fifth in the league, his 100 RBIs good for eighth. Though similar to his 1960 MVP numbers, Maris was unfairly expected to produce Ruthian statistics, and when he didn't, the fans turned on him. The press, never a great fan, raised the level of negativity. From 1964 to 1966, Maris was a shell of his earlier form and often injured. Unfair management now joined unsympathetic fans and unfriendly media. With the game no longer a source of pleasure, Maris notified manager Ralph Houk that 1966 would be his last season. Houk beseeched Maris to wait, and now-general manager Lee MacPhail told Maris he would not be traded from the Yankees. On December 8 he was shipped to the Cardinals in one of the worst trades in team history. The Yankees received third baseman Charley Smith, whose only top-10 finish in 1967 was the 10th spot for most strikeouts.

His return to the friendly Midwest was happier for Maris. In two years with St. Louis, he would hit .258, better than average in those years of pitiful league-wide offensive production. His power numbers were low, totaling 14 home runs and 100 RBIs for 1967 and 1968 combined. Fortunately, Maris was able to go out a winner, appearing in the World Series two more times. In the 1967 victory over the Red Sox, Maris was second on the team, with a .385 average, behind Lou Brock's .414. The erstwhile slugger came through in the clutch, with a pacesetting 7 RBIs. The 1968 postseason was not as successful for the man or the team, as the Cardinals lost in seven games to the Tigers. After the season, Roger Maris retired at 34 years of age, having safely made his place in baseball history, not with the Kansas City A's, but with the New York Yankees.

The Roger Maris trade was the worst and the last trade of the Arnold Johnson era. With Johnson's untimely death in March of 1960, the Yankees access to the A's roster ended. While it is impossible to prove collusion, the pattern was made abundantly clear, and the case is strong. From January 1952, when Arnold Johnson, Dan Topping, and Del Webb joined forces to buy into Automatic Canteen, their business partnership grew. As Yankee owners, Topping and Webb were able to forestall the sincere and legitimate efforts of Kansas City to acquire Blues Stadium and pursue an independent course to Major League status. Instead, they worked behind the scenes to arrange a sale of Yankee Stadium to their business partner and include the minor league park as a throw in. This bonus property would give Johnson a leg up in 1954 in his pursuit to purchase Connie Mack's Philadelphia A's. While other offers for the club were as good, if not better, than Arnold Johnson's, his ownership of Blues Stadium, as well as his alliance with New York, paved his way toward ultimate victory. The Yankees' clout in league circles resulted in other bidders being held to a different standard than Johnson. Despite the objection of other American League owners who saw the trouble of having Johnson, Topping, and Webb so intimately connected, the Yankees, with the seeming help of League president Will Harridge, made things easy for the Johnson group.

The Yankees' ability to select whoever they wanted from the A's roster began almost immediately, and for five years the Yankees had the pick of the A's franchise, so much so, that Arnold Johnson appeared before the House of Representatives, who were skeptical of his independence from the Yankees and incredulous at his unprofessional disposal of his Yankee

Stadium property, which, as seen through legal memos, was not properly sold off. This sorry period, which saw the Yankees control the players of two of the eight teams in the American League only came to a close with the death of Arnold Johnson.

1. Povich, Shirley. "This Morning," *Washington Post and Times Herald*, August 7, 1957, p. C1.
2. James, Bill and Neyer, Rob. *The Neyer/James Guide to Pitchers*. New York: Fireside, 2004, p. 168.
3. Associate Press. "A's Trade of Dickson Angers Fans," *Washington Post and Times Herald*, August 25, 1958, p. A12.
4. *New York Times*. "Carroll and Snyder of Bombers Go to Kansas City in 4-Man Deal," April 13, 1959, p.7.
5. Povich, Shirley. "This Morning," *Washington Post and Times Herald*, May 27, 1959, p. D1.
6. Golenbock, Peter. *Dynasty*. Englewood Cliffs, NJ: Prentice-Hall, 1975, p. 209.
7. Povich, Shirley. "This Morning," *Washington Post and Times Herald*, May 27, 1959, p. D1
8. Drebinger, John. "Yanks Get Lopez, Terry from A's," *New York Times*, May 27, 1959, p. 40.
9. United Press International. "Veeck Calls Trade Disservice to Baseball," *Washington Post and Times Herald*, May 27, 1959, p. D5.
10. Povich, Shirley. "This Morning," *Washington Post and Times Herald*, May 27, 1959, p. D1.
11. Conversation with author.
12. Gallagher, Mark. *The Yankee Encyclopedia*. New York: Leisure Press, 1982, p. 41.
13. Ibid.
14. Drebinger, John. "Yanks Trade Bauer, Larsen and Get Maris in 7-Player Deal," *New York Times*, December 12, 1959, p. 27.
15. United Press International. "Bauer Will Retire After This Season," *Washington Post and Times Herald*, April 1, 1961, p. A16.
16. Shecter, Leonard. *Roger Maris: Home Run Record*. New York: Bartholomew House, 1961, p. 62.
17. Daley, Arthur. "The Newest Yankee," *New York Times*, December 15, 1959, p. 54.
18. Shecter, p. 83.
19. Gray, Sid. "A Man Named Maris," *New York Post*, August 1, 1961, p. 58.
20. Mehl, Ernest. *The Kansas City Athletics*. New York: Holt, 1956, p. 123.
22. Allen, Maury. *Roger Maris: A Man for All Seasons*. New York: D.I. Fine, 1986, p. 86.
22. Schwarz, Alan. "The Man Behind the Myth," *Sport*, October 1998, p. 80.
23. Allen, p. 98.
24. Conversation with author.

25. Shecter, p. 80.
26. Drebinger, John. "Yanks Trade Bauer, Larsen and Get Maris in 7-Player Deal," *New York Times,* December 12, 1959, p. 27.
27. Shecter, p. 84.
28. Dozer, Richard. "Veeck Lashes Out at Yanks, A's 'Alliance,'" *Chicago Daily Tribune,* December 12, 1959, p. A3.
29. Ibid.
30. Shecter, p. 82.
31. Allen, p. 87.
32. Povich, Shirley. "This Morning," *Washington Post and Times Herald,* September 7, 1991.
33. Letter to author.

EPILOGUE

The death of Arnold Johnson left Carmen Johnson and family an estate worth nearly $3.9 million and a ball club she was willing to part with. By 1960, Arnold Johnson, once a hero in Kansas City for delivering the A's, had the fans against him because of his constant trading with the Yankees, trades that saw the A's always getting the short end of the stick. It was time for a change.

A contentious few months ensued, with bidders from Houston and Dallas entering the fray. Kansas City expressed an interest in finding a local buyer. Elliott Stein of St. Louis was willing to purchase all the stock in the club and was approved in mid-November. He withdrew when, after having an agreement in place for the 52 percent of the team held by the Johnson estate, was unable to gain the other 48 percent. That chunk was held by the old group that had bought the Philadelphia A's in 1954—Nathanial Leverone, J. Patrick Lannan, Earl Johnson, and the Roy Mack family. Enter Charles O. Finley. Unsuccessful in 1954 in his quest for the A's, the Gary, Indiana, insurance titan was back in the picture. Finley had also in recent years attempted to purchase the Tigers, White Sox, and the American League expansion team in Los Angeles.

While Mrs. Johnson, now Mrs. Humes after a June wedding, was willing to fight to keep her stock at first, she ultimately approved a sale to Finley in order to pay taxes on the multimillion dollar estate. By December 19, Finley was the only bidder left, and when the Leverone syndicate would not mach his $1,975,000 bid for the Johnson 52 percent, he was in. Probate judge Robert Dunne approved Finley's offer, and all that was left was league approval, which was granted the following day. Although there was fear that Finley's ultimate goal was to relocate the team, he assuaged that concern and went further. "I'll say this—the Athletics will not be a farm for any team in this league," the brash new baseball mogul announced.[1]

The fiery rhetoric got hotter, literally, in early 1961. In a grand publicity stunt, Finley and new general manager Frank Lane stood beaming before a burning bus labeled "Shuttle Bus To Yankee Stadium." As the flames leapt to the sky, the two men held their hats aloft, pointing to the vehicle with pride as they symbolically said goodbye to the A's thrall to the Yankees. It was more than a mere sign. Another sad indication of the changing of the guard came the following day. On February 4 Parke Carroll, who had been replaced by Lane in January, died of a heart attack at the age of 52.

In the next five years the A's would make only two deals with the Yankees. Still, the Yankees, with Roger Maris, Clete Boyer, Ralph Terry, and Hector Lopez, all ex-A's, playing major roles, continued to win American League pennants through 1964. Interestingly, the Automatic Canteen connection would arise again, for on January 1, 1964, the company formerly headed by Arnold Johnson and John Cox, was given the contract for all concessions sold at Yankee Stadium, replacing Harry M. Stevens after a four-decade relationship. It was one of the last major business moves Dan Topping and Del Webb made as Yankee owners, as they announced in August that CBS would be purchasing the team in an $11.2 million deal.

Talk of an A's move started immediately. At first, Finley denied all rumors, but by 1964, Oakland, California, expressed a strong interest in the team, ultimately winning out. The 1968 Oakland A's finished over .500 (82–80), a hurdle the Kansas City A's could never leap. They would rise to second place in the newly created Western Division in 1969 and repeat that performance in 1970. Their first of five consecutive division titles came in 1971, and, from 1972 to 1974, the Oakland A's were the kings of baseball, winning three World Series.

The "Swingin' A's" of the early 1970s were led by a core group that had all signed with the Kansas City A's. From 1960 to 1967, Sal Bando, Bert Campaneris, Reggie Jackson, Joe Rudi, Jim "Catfish" Hunter, John "Blue Moon" Odom, Vida Blue, Dick Green, Dave Duncan, and Rollie Fingers were scouted and acquired by the A's organization. Their rise through the minor leagues would benefit Oakland, not Kansas City. Having witnessed the outflow of talent from Kansas City to New York from 1955 to 1959, it may be that the history of baseball would look very different had Arnold Johnson, Dan Topping, and Del Webb worked together through the 1960's. It might be that the powerful A's dynasty would have been a new incarnation of the Bronx Bombers.

---

1. Prell, Edward. "Court Oks Finkley as A's Owner," *Chicago Daily Tribune*, December 20, 1960, p. C1.

APPENDIX:
AMERICAN LEAGUE STANDINGS

1955 American League

Team	Wins	Losses	Won/Loss%	Games Back
New York Yankees	96	58	.623	—
Cleveland Indians	93	61	.604	3.0
Chicago White Sox	91	63	.591	5.0
Boston Red Sox	84	70	.545	12.0
Detroit Tigers	79	75	.513	17.0
Kansas City A's	63	91	.409	33.0
Baltimore Orioles	57	97	.370	39.0
Washington Senators	53	101	.344	43.0

1956 American League

Team	Wins	Losses	Won/Loss%	Games Back
New York Yankees	97	57	.630	—
Cleveland Indians	88	66	.571	9.0
Chicago White Sox	85	69	.552	12.0
Boston Red Sox	84	70	.545	13.0
Detroit Tigers	82	72	.532	15.0
Baltimore Orioles	69	85	.448	28.0
Washington Senators	59	95	.383	38.0
Kansas City A's	52	102	.338	45.0

1957 American League

Team	Wins	Losses	Won/ Loss%	Games Back
New York Yankees	98	56	.636	—
Chicago White Sox	90	64	.584	8.0
Boston Red Sox	82	72	.532	16.0
Detroit Tigers	78	76	.506	20.0
Baltimore Orioles	76	76	.500	21.0
Cleveland Indians	76	77	.497	21.5
Kansas City A's	59	94	.386	38.5
Washington Senators	55	99	.357	43.0

1958 American League

Team	Wins	Losses	Won/Loss%	Games Back
New York Yankees	92	62	.597	—
Chicago White Sox	82	72	.532	10.0
Boston Red Sox	79	75	.513	13.0
Cleveland Indians	77	76	.503	14.5
Detroit Tigers	77	77	.500	15.0
Baltimore Orioles	74	79	.484	17.5
Kansas City A's	73	81	.474	19.0
Washington Senators	61	93	.396	31.0

1959 American League

Team	Wins	Losses	Won/Loss%	Games Back
Chicago White Sox	94	60	.610	—
Cleveland Indians	89	65	.578	5.0
New York Yankees	79	75	.513	15.0
Detroit Tigers	76	78	.494	18.0
Boston Red Sox	75	79	.487	19.0
Baltimore Orioles	74	80	.481	20.0
Kansas City A's	66	88	.429	28.0
Washington Senators	63	91	.409	31.0

1960 American League

Team	Wins	Losses	Won/Loss%	Games Back
New York Yankees	97	57	.630	—
Baltimore Orioles	89	65	.578	8.0
Chicago White Sox	87	67	.565	10.0
Cleveland Indians	76	78	.494	21.0
Washington Senators	73	81	.474	24.0
Detroit Tigers	71	83	.461	26.0
Boston Red Sox	65	89	.422	32.0
Kansas City A's	58	96	.377	39.0

BIBLIOGRAPHY

Addie, Bob. "DeOrsey, Joe Tucci Enter Bid to Buy A's," *Washington Post and Times Herald*, October 12, 1954.

Addie, Bob. "Sports Addition," *Washington Post and Times Herald*, October 21, 1954.

Addie, Bob. "Sports Addition," *Washington Post and Times Herald*, October 24, 1954.

Addie, Bob. "Griffith Still Hopes for Yanks Trade," *Washington Post and Times Herald*, February 20, 1957.

Addie, Bob. "Dressen Calls Shantz Key in Yanks' Deal," *Washington Post and Times Herald*, February 21, 1957.

Addie, Bob. "Martin Hits Two-Run Homer off Kemmerer," *Washington Post and Times Herald*, June 20, 1957.

Allen, Maury. *Roger Maris: A Man for All Seasons.* New York: D.I. Fine, 1986.

Associated Press. "Macks to Keep Athletics; Sons to Buy Stock," *Chicago Daily Tribune*, August 1, 1950.

Associated Press. "A's Send Robinson, Byrd to Yanks," *New York Times*, December 17, 1953.

Associated Press. "Community Drive Urged by Mayor Clark to Help Save Athletics for Philadelphia," *New York Times*, July 9, 1954.

Associated Press. "'Don't Have a Dime, 'Son Earle Says," *Washington Post and Times Herald*, August 5, 1954.

Associated Press. "16 Civic Leaders Will Try Again Today to Keep the Athletics in Philadelphia," *New York Times*, August 10, 1954, p. 22.

Associated Press. "Macks Meet; See Trouble for Johnson," *Chicago Daily Tribune*, September 23, 1954, p. D2.

Associated Press. "Athletics' Sale to Be Discussed by League Owners Tuesday," *New York Times*, September 24, 1954, p. 24.

Associated Press. "Griffith Opposes Shift of A's to Kansas City," *Los Angeles Times*, September 25, 1954, p. B1.

Associated Press. "Roy Mack Dims A's Transfer; Guards Stock," *Chicago Daily Tribune*, October 15, 1954.

Associated Press. "Expect Verdict Today on A's Syndicate Deal," *Chicago Daily Tribune*, October 17, 1954.

Associated Press. "Philadelphia Keeps A's; $4,000,000 Deal," *Chicago Daily Tribune*, October 18, 1954.

Associated Press. "Johnson Says His Deal Better One for Macks," *Chicago Daily Tribune*, October 18, 1954.

Associated Press. "A's Group Ready to Seek Meeting," *New York Times*, October 22, 1954.

Associated Press. "A's Sale Details Still Unsettled," *New York Times*, October 23, 1954.

Associated Press. "Mack Gives Extension to A's Syndicate," *Los Angeles Times,* October 26, 1954.

Associated Press. "Syndicate to Pay off After League Approval," *Washington Post and Times Herald*, October 26, 1954.

Associated Press. "American League Meets Here Tomorrow on Sale of Athletics," *New York Times*, October 27, 1954.

Associated Press. "Report Hints Indians Hold Key to League Approval of A's Deal," *New York Times*, November 6, 1954.

Associated Press. "Kansas City Is Certain Athletics Will Attract 1,000,000 Yearly," *New York Times*, November 7, 1954.

Associated Press. "Majors Veto Radio-TV Curb; Minors Gain Financial Aid," *Chicago Daily Tribune*, December 8, 1954.

Associated Press. "A's Purchase Blackwell, Two Others," *Los Angeles Times,* March 31, 1955.

Associated Press. "News 'Sickens' Slaughter," *New York Times,* August 26, 1956.

Associated Press. "McDermott, Noren Go to K.C. Club in 13-Man Deal," *Washington Post and Times Herald*, February 20, 1957.

Associated Press. "A's Trade of Dickson Angers Fans," *Washington Post and Times Herald*, August 25, 1958

Baker & Botts Letter, H. Lovett to L. S. Shamblin, January 17, 1973.

Baumgartner, Stan. "'Let Webb Move,' Carpenter Retorts," *The Sporting News*, July 29, 1953, p. 6.

Briordy, William J. "Noren, Coleman Go to Kansas City," *New York Times*, February 20, 1957.

Chicago Daily Tribune. "Halas Spurns Brooklyn Bid for Luckman," October 14, 1939.

Chicago Daily Tribune. "Yankees Net $2,700,00 in Park Deals: Sale Dissolves Corporation," December 18, 1953.

Chicago Daily Tribune. "Earle Gives Views," August 5, 1954.

Chicago Daily Tribune. "Macks Find Angel to Keep Athletics in Philadelphia," August 20, 1954, p. B2.

Chicago Daily Tribune. "Senator Official Challenges A's Shift," October 14, 1954.

Chicago Daily Tribune. "Phils' Owner Not Happy Over Buying A's Park," October 14, 1954.

Chicago Daily Tribune. "Johnson Set to Sue A's Group," October 21, 1954.

Chicago Daily Tribune. "A's Group Presses for League Approval," October 22, 1954.

Chicago Daily Tribune. "League Rejects Syndicate Bid for A's," October 29, 1954.

Chicago Daily Tribune. "Johnson Presses Offer to Buy A's," November 4, 1954.

Chicago Daily Tribune. "Griffith Holds Fast Against Shift of A's," November 5, 1954.

Chicago Daily Tribune. "Griffith Holds Fast Against Shift of A's," November 5, 1954.

Chicago Daily Tribune. "It's Official! A's Move to Kansas City," November 9, 1954.

Chicago Daily Tribune. "A's Sad Secret—Foreclosure," November 9, 1954.

Chicago Daily Tribune. "John Cox of Chicago Buys Yank Stadium," May 23, 1955.

Chicago Daily Tribune. "Negotiations on Sale of A's to Open Today," August 10, 1954, p. B2.

Chicago Daily Tribune. "Trade Helps Yanks, View of Comiskey," February 20, 1957.

Daley, Arthur. "Sports of the Times—Grand Larceny," *New York Times*, December 18, 1953.

Daley, Arthur. "Sport of the Times—Philadelphia Story," *New York Times*, October 19, 1954.

Daley, Arthur. "The Newest Yankee," *New York Times,* December 15, 1959.

Daniel, Dan. "Cries of 'Hate Yankees' Stir Case to Yelps About Rivals," *The Sporting News,* December 8, 1953.

Daniel, Dan. "Weiss Thunders Answer to Critics of Yankee Swaps." The Sporting News, January 13, 1960.

Daniel, Dan. "Daniel's Dope," *The Sporting News*, March 11, 1960.

Dozer, Richard. "Veeck Lashes Out at Yanks, A's 'Alliance,'" *Chicago Daily Tribune*, December 12, 1959.

Drebinger, John. "Athletics Transfer to Kansas City Wins Final American League Approval," *New York Times*, November 9, 1954.

Drebinger, John. "Yanks Get Lopez, Terry from A's," *New York Times,* May 27, 1959.

Drebinger, John. "Yanks Trade Bauer, Larsen and Get Maris in 7-Player Deal," *New York Times,* December 12, 1959.

Ford, Whitey, Mantle, Mickey, and Durso, Joseph. *Whitey and Mickey*. New York: The Viking Press, 1977.

Gallagher, Mark. *The Yankee Encyclopedia*. New York: Leisure Press, 1982.

Golenbock, Peter. *Dynasty*. Englewood Cliffs, NJ: Prentice-Hall, 1975.

Gray, Sid. "A Man Named Maris," *New York Post*, August 1, 1961.

Hand, Jack and Reichler, Joe. "Braves' Milwaukee Move Okayed," *Los Angeles Times*, March 19, 1953.

Hearings Before the Subcommittee (Subcommittee No. 5) of the Committee on the Judiciary House of Representatives. 85th Congress, First Session, Part 2.

Holland, Gerald. "The A's Find Friends in Cowtown," *Sports Illustrated*, April 25, 1955 (Vol. Issue 15).

James, Bill and Neyer, Rob. *The Neyer/James Guide to Pitchers*. New York: Fireside, 2004.

Kansas City Star. "As a Major Site," July 17, 1953.

Kansas City Star. "Major League Opportunity," July 20, 1953.

Kansas City Star. "Push for Majors," August 13, 1953.

Kansas City Star. "Stadium and the Big Chance," August 14, 1953.

Kansas City Star. "Would Sell Stadium," August 17, 1953.

Kansas City Star. "Team, Then a Stadium," August 18, 1953.

Kansas City Star. "How to Lose a Big League Team," August 19, 1953.

Kansas City Star. "Warned by Frick," August 22, 1953.

Kansas City Star. Katz ad, August 23, 1953.

Kansas City Star. "Big League Uprising," August 25, 1953.

Kansas City Star. "Wait in Stadium Talks," September 14, 1953.

Kansas City Star. "For a Stadium Option," September 20, 1953.

Kansas City Star. "May Get Browns Here," September 24, 1953.

Kansas City Star. "To a Big League Decision," September 29, 1953.

Kansas City Star. "Big League Chances Ahead," October 1, 1953.

Kansas City Star. "For Stadium at River," October 14, 1953.

Kansas City Star. "Quick Action Got Team," October 16, 1953.

Kansas City Star. "To Get a Big League Team," November 16, 1953.

Kansas City Star. "Yank, Blues Parks Sold," December 17, 1953.

Kelly, Ray. "A's Fans Skip Ship, but Roy Mack Sticks to 'Burning Deck' to Finish," *The Sporting News*, August 11, 1954.

Letter from Edward Vollers to City National Bank, March 17, 1955.

Los Angeles Times. "Yankees Sell Baseball Park," December 18, 1953.

Los Angeles Times. "Johnson Willing to Pay New York Yankees," October 8, 1954.

Los Angeles Times. "AL Owners Meet, Decide A's Plight," October 12, 1954.

Mann, Arthur. "How to Buy a Ball Club for Peanuts," *The Saturday Evening Post*, April 9, 1955.

McBride, C. E. "Sporting Comment," *Kansas City Star*, October 27, 1953.

McGowan, Roscoe. "Fate of Athletics Is Awaited Today," *New York Times*, October 28, 1954.

McGuff, Joe. "Blues Fans Unhappy over Two Recent Articles by Sports Writer," *Kansas City Star*, June 21, 1953.

McGuff, Joe. "Sports & Culture: An Essay by Joe McGuff," September 18, 2005. Kansas City.com. *http://www.kansascity.com/mld/kansascity/news/special_packages/star_history/culture_sports/12581449.htm.*

Mehl, Ernest. "Sporting Comment," *Kansas City Star*, June 16, 1953.

Mehl, Ernest. "Sporting Comment," *Kansas City Star*, July 14, 1953.

Mehl, Ernest. "Sporting Comment," *Kansas City Star*, August 3, 1953.

Mehl, Ernest. "Sporting Comment," *Kansas City Star*, August 20, 1953.

Mehl, Ernest. "Sporting Comment," *Kansas City Star*, September 1, 1953.

Mehl, Ernest. "Sporting Comment," *Kansas City Star*. September 7, 1953.

Mehl, Ernest. "Sporting Comment," *Kansas City Star*, September 9, 1953.

Mehl, Ernest. "Sporting Comment," *Kansas City Star*, September 22, 1953.

Mehl, Ernest. "Sporting Comment," *Kansas City Star*, September 27, 1953.

Mehl, Ernest. "Sporting Comment," *Kansas City Star*, September 28, 1953.

Mehl, Ernest. "Go to Baltimore," *Kansas City Star*, September 30, 1953.

Mehl, Ernest. "Sporting Comment," *Kansas City Star*, September 30, 1953.

Mehl, Ernest. "Sporting Comment," *Kansas City Star*, October 25, 1953.

Mehl, Ernest. "Sporting Comment," *Kansas City Star*, October 29, 1953.

Mehl, Ernest. "Sporting Comment," *Kansas City Star*, November 27, 1953.

Mehl, Ernest. "Sporting Comment," *Kansas City Star*, December 13, 1953.

Mehl, Ernest. "Sporting Comment," *Kansas City Star*, December 21, 1953.

Mehl, Ernest. "Kansas City Backs Offer for A's with Park Bond Issue," *The Sporting News*, August 11, 1954.

Mehl, Ernest. "Persistence Won Obstacle Race for Kaycee," *The Sporting News*, November 17, 1954.

Mehl, Ernest. "Hammers Ring in Rebuilding of K.C. Park," *The Sporting News*, November 27, 1954.

Mehl, Ernest. *The Kansas City Athletics*. New York: Holt, 1956.

Mehl, Ernest. "A's Rap Rep That They Will 'Trade Only with Yanks,'" *The Sporting News*, December 4, 1957.

Memo from the Office of the Commissioner, Notice No. 25, June 1, 1953.

Morrow, Art. "Philadelphia Frets over A's Future as Macks Deny 'Bids,'" *The Sporting News*, June 16, 1954.

Morrow, Art. "Roy and Earle Mack Feud as 'Save the A's' Drive Fizzles," *The Sporting News*, August 4, 1954, p. 15.

Morrow, Art. "Local Capital Seen Rallying Behind A's," *The Sporting News*, August 24, 1954.

Morrow, Art. "Richardson Group 'to Be Ready to Act,'" *The Sporting News*, October 6, 1954.

Morrow, Art. "Inside Story of the Race for Possession of Athletics," *The Sporting News*, November 10, 1954.

Munzel, Edgar. "Lane Predicts Two Majors of Ten Clubs," *The Sporting News*, May 5, 1954.

Newsday. Obituary, June 1, 1974. Topping, Dan, biographical file, National Baseball Hall of Fame Library.

New York Times. "$4,500,000 Kansas City Offer for A's Matched in Philadelphia," August 7, 1954.

New York Times. "League to Discuss A's Plight," October 12, 1954.

New York Times. "New Owners of Athletics Mark Time Until League Approves Stock Purchase," October 19, 1954.

New York Times. "Carroll and Snyder of Bombers Go to Kansas City in 4-Man Deal," April 13, 1959.

Paxton, Harry T. "The Philadelphia A's Last Stand," *The Saturday Evening Post*, June 12, 1954.

Phillips, McCandlish. "Yankee Stadium Given to Rice U," *New York Times*, July 20, 1962.

Povich, Shirley. "This Morning," *Washington Post*, October 10, 1954, p. 25.

Povich, Shirley. "This Morning with Shirley Povich," *Washington Post and Times Herald*, October 12, 1954.

Povich, Shirley. "Pressure on Move to California Is Resisted," *Washington Post and Times Herald*, October 13, 1954.

Povich, Shirley. "This Morning," *Washington Post and Times Herald*, October 14, 1954.

Povich, Shirley. "Detroit Head Joins Griffith in Dispute," *Washington Post and Times Herald*, October 15, 1954.

Povich, Shirley. "This Morning with Shirley Povich," *Washington Post and Times Herald*, October 28, 1954.

Povich, Shirley. "This Morning," *Washington Post and Times Herald*, August 7, 1957.

Povich, Shirley. "This Morning," *Washington Post and Times Herald*, May 27, 1959.

Povich, Shirley. "This Morning," *Washington Post and Times Herald*, September 7, 1991.

Prell, Edward. "Harridge Urges Decision Today on Athletics' Future," *Chicago Daily Tribune*, October 12, 1954.

Prell, Edward. "League Votes A's Shift to Kansas City," *Chicago Daily Tribune*, October 13, 1954.

Prell, Edward. "Delay in Athletics' Sale Cools Johnson," *Chicago Daily Tribune*, October 17, 1954.

Prell, Edward. "Harridge Asks Facts on Sale," *Chicago Daily Tribune*, October 18, 1954.

Prell, Edward. "Yanks Acquire Athletics' Ditmar in 13 Man Deal," *Chicago Daily Tribune*, February 20, 1957.

President's papers, Norman Hackerman 1970–1985. Courtesy of Woodson Research Center, Fondren Library, Rice University.

Reichler, Joseph L. *The Baseball Trade Register*. New York: Macmillan, 1984.

Robinson, Ray and Jennison, Christopher. *Yankee Stadium: Drama, Glamour and Glory.* New York: Viking Studio, 1998.

Rucker, Leland. "Inept A's Showed Kansas City a Good Time," *USA Today Baseball Weekly*, June 17, 1992 (Vol. 2, Issue 12).

Schwarz, Alan. "The Man Behind the Myth," *Sport*, October 1998.

Shecter, Leonard. *Roger Maris: Home Run Record*. New York: Bartholomew House, 1961.

Smith, William. "Chicago's New Millionaires," *Chicago Daily Tribune*, December 12, 1954.

Spink, J. G. Taylor. "All's Well That Ends Well for K.C." Editorial, *The Sporting News*, November 17, 1954.

Spink, J.G. Taylor. "Yanks—A's Deals Leave Bad Taste With Fans—Editorial." *The Sporting News*, December 23, 1959.

Sports Illustrated. "Philadelphia Album," November 15, 1954 (Vol. 1, Issue 14).

Sullivan, Neil J. *The Diamond in the Bronx: Yankee Stadium and the Politics of New York*. New York: Oxford University Press, 2001.

The Sporting News. "Johnson Offers Reasonable Payment for Kansas City Invasion," October 13, 1954.

The Sporting News. "American League Clears Way, But A's Shift to Kansas City Hangs Fire," October 20, 1954.

The Sporting News. "Frick Denies More Time Sought to Sell Yankee Park," December 22, 1954.

United Press International. "Ten-Man Syndicate Pledges $3,750,000 to Keep Athletics in Philadelphia," *New York Times*, October 16, 1954.

United Press International. "7 Put Up $1,500,000 to Buy Out Connie, Earle Mack of Athletics," *New York Times*, October 17, 1954.

United Press International. "League May Veto A's Sale," *Los Angeles Times*, October 28, 1954.

United Press International. "Veeck Calls Trade Disservice to Baseball," *Washington Post and Times Herald*, May 27, 1959.

United Press International. "Arnold Johnson Dies in Florida; Head of Kansas City Athletics, 53," *New York Times*, March 10, 1960.

United Press International. "Bauer Will Retire After This Season," *Washington Post and Times Herald*, April 1, 1961.

U.S. Senate on Antitrust and Monopoly Subcommittee of the Committee on the Judiciary. 86th Congress, First Session, Part 2.

Vaughan, Irving. "Johnson Re-enters Battle to Buy A's," *Chicago Daily Tribune*, October 27, 1954.

Vaughan, Irving. "Athletics' Status 'Still in the Air,'" *Chicago Daily Tribune*, November 2, 1954.

Vecsey, George. "He's the Man Who Discovered Mick," *Newsday*, July 26, 1966.

Vecsey, George. "Roger Maris: No Asterisk," *New York Times*, December 16, 1985.

Washington Post and Times Herald. "$4 Million Bid for A's To Go to Kansas City," August 4, 1954.

Washington Post and Times Herald. "Griffith Against A's Shift to Kansas City," August 6, 1954.

Washington Post and Times Herald. "Newest Plan to Keep A's in Philly," September 1, 1954, p. 27.

Washington Post and Times Herald. "League Can't Force Shift, Says Harridge," October 15, 1954.

Washington Post and Times Herald. "Connie Mack Plans to Attend Meeting," October 28, 1954.

Washington Post and Times Herald. "The Big Switch," February 23, 1957.

INDEX